ANALYZING AND TREATING READING PROBLEMS

Analyzing and Treating Reading Problems

Dorothy J. McGinnis   Western Michigan University
Kalamazoo, Michigan

Dorothy E. Smith   Western Michigan University
Kalamazoo, Michigan

Macmillan Publishing Co., Inc.   New York
Collier Macmillan Publishers   London

Macmillan Publishing Co., Inc.
866 Third Avenue, New York, New York 10022

Collier Macmillan Canada, Inc.

ISBN: 0-02-379130-6

Printing: 1 2 3 4 5 6 7 8   Year: 2 3 4 5 6 7 8 9

Preface

Analyzing and Treating Reading Problems has been written for teachers who wish to become proficient in helping disabled readers. It is intended for use as a textbook in courses offered by colleges and universities and as a handbook for teachers. It is designed to help teachers meet the needs of individuals who have reading and learning problems and to help them cope with the challenge of mainstreaming—meeting the needs of handicapped individuals in the regular classroom. The text incorporates recent research in language acquisition, psycholinguistics, psychology, and sociology and relates significant findings to the diagnosis and treatment of reading and learning problems. It makes a major contribution in its efforts to correct misguided and oft-quoted errors of phonics instruction. The book differs from others on the market in that it provides an opportunity for the reader to learn about diagnostic procedures and the myriad of factors affecting reading performance by engaging in the process of diagnosis. The student learns by doing, not by merely reading about the subject. Throughout the text students are asked to complete exercises whereby they apply the knowledge they are gaining to the solution of problems.

The Gestalt principle is basic to this book in two ways. We consider the whole person when diagnosing and recommending treatment. An individual's reading capabilities cannot be separated from all of the other attributes that make that person unique. He or she is all of a piece, not a group of single elements that can be examined and mediated without reference to all of the other aspects of that person.

The second direction to our holistic approach is that diagnosis and therapy cannot be separated, at least not in the real world. Each depends on the other, and they occur simultaneously.

Diagnosis for its own sake is worthless. Thus, recommendations for therapy are an integral part of diagnosis and must be considered to be the diagnostician's responsibility.

In this book the reader participates in the diagnosis of individuals with a variety of reading and related problems. Each of the individuals selected for study are real people for whom the authors have provided reading diagnosis and therapy in the Reading Center and Clinic at Western Michigan University. Only the identities of the people have been changed. All pertinent data, including inconsistencies so prevalent in the lives of people, have been retained. Consequently, the task of diagnosis has not been made easy by "pat" examples. Each of the reading problems presents the reader with a challenge as well as with a unique learning opportunity.

The ultimate purpose of this book is to provide the teacher and the reading diagnostician with the theory and practical techniques needed to help children and adults in our society who cannot read. We are convinced that the best way to achieve this goal is through participation in the diagnostic process. This book is our way of providing the reader with experience in better understanding individuals who have reading problems.

D.J.M.
D.E.S.

Contents

Contents

Contents

Tables

Illustrations

1

Principles of Diagnosis and Treatment

OBJECTIVES

This chapter should help you to

1. Understand the serious consequences of reading disability and the personal, social, vocational, and academic penalties that disabled readers experience.
2. Identify seven basic principles underlying the diagnosis and treatment of reading problems.
3. Apply the principles of diagnosis and treatment to the study of disabled readers.

One of the chief concerns of most teachers and school administrators is what to do with the disabled reader. In our opinion, this is a healthy concern because reading disability can have serious consequences for the individual and for society. The individual who cannot read effectively is penalized in many ways. One can be penalized personally so that one is left with a shattered self-concept and feelings of frustration, inadequacy, and failure. One can be penalized vocationally so that one is forever prevented from achieving a vocational goal that is satisfying to oneself. One can be penalized socially so that one becomes a misfit and a noncontributing member of society. One can be penalized academically so that one fails to profit from instruction in the content areas. Reading failure usually results in serious consequences for the individual. This point can be illustrated by briefly describing three disabled readers with whom we, as reading clinicians, have worked.

The first case is a nine-year-old boy. Our first contact with John was through his mother who telephoned us in August a few years ago. We remember the telephone call vividly because during the first few minutes the mother was incoherent and weeping so loudly that we could not understand her. After what seemed to be an interminable length of time, the mother finally became calm enough to indicate that her son could not read and that he needed help. The mother reported that at the end of the school year she was informed that John was being required to repeat the fourth grade. The mother, the wife of a prominent physician in a small town, apparently saw this announcement as a threat to the family's social position and as an acknowledgment of failure on the part of her son. She pleaded with the teacher to change her mind. Finally it was decided that the boy could be promoted if he improved his reading during the summer. The mother accepted this challenge. She bought a fifth-grade basal reader and tried to teach John to read. Every morning for one hour the boy and his mother worked together. Each session ended with both of them in tears. Finally, on the day the mother telephoned, the boy had become thoroughly discouraged and had run away from home. Now, John was a highly intelligent boy who mentally was capable of reading at fifth-grade level but who actually could barely read first-grade material. He was convinced that he was stupid, that no one could help him, and that he would never learn to read. He was a boy with a shattered self-concept, a boy with marked feelings of frustration and inadequacy.

Another person with whom we worked last year was a twenty-eight-year-old man who had dropped out of school when he was in the tenth grade. He too was intelligent, but could not read. He was married, had two children, and had recently lost his job. He told us that he had learned from bitter experience that potential employers would not hire him if they knew that he could not read; so early in life he learned to conceal his reading problem. He had become quite clever in hiding his reading disability. For example, when given a job application form to be filled in, he would feign a sore arm and hand and request to take the papers home with him. This request was usually granted, and his wife would complete the application for him. In fact, his last job was secured in this manner. He told no one that he could not read and apparently was doing well on the job until the day the foreman brought in a new and expensive machine for him to operate. He was given written directions to follow, which, of course, he could not read. He walked off the job.

A third client was in high school at the time we first saw him. Joe was also retarded in reading. In addition, he was unruly in class and disrespectful to his teachers—a real troublemaker. He could not earn recognition by being a good student nor by being an outstanding athlete, but he was able to gain attention by being the school clown and chief mischief-maker. By the time we saw him he had graduated to committing acts of delinquency in the community.

Approximately 15 per cent of schoolchildren in the United States have reading disabilities (3, pp. 1, 5-6). According to the U.S. Office of Education more than 20 million adults are functionally illiterate (1, 2). We believe that many of these people can be taught to read with accurate analysis and proper instruction and therapy. It is the purpose of this chapter to set forth seven general principles of remediation, which will be developed in greater detail throughout the book.

PRINCIPLE 1: FOCUS ATTENTION UPON THE INDIVIDUAL

Each disabled reader is a unique person with different abilities, attitudes, goals, interests, needs, and problems. Consequently, in both diagnosis and treatment, attention must be focused on the individual. It is essential that the reading teacher have a thorough knowledge of the child, his abilities, interests, and attitudes as well as his reading skills, or lack of them. Physical, cognitive, environmental, and emotional factors must be given careful consideration. Treatment must be based on the child's needs and disabilities and on full consideration of his interests and goals. Treatment must be designed to fit the individual and must be changed as the individual's needs change.

PRINCIPLE 2: EMPHASIZE INTERPRETATION

Interpretation of the child's performance should be emphasized rather than evaluation of his achievement or judgment of his worth. The purpose of diagnosis is to determine *why* the individual is having difficulty and *what* can be done to help him. The process involves more than an assessment of reading skills. It requires exploration of the factors that may be causing the problem and interpretation of how these factors are affecting the child's reading performance. The process requires flexibility in planning how to eliminate or mitigate adverse conditions and in determining effective methods of instruction.

PRINCIPLE 3: PROVIDE WELL-PLANNED THERAPY

Instructional procedures should be selected to accomplish specific objectives. The emphasis should be on the skills and abilities that the student does not have but that are essential for immediate success in reading. Instruction must be directed toward helping the student overcome specific weaknesses while keeping the total reading program in balance. All remedial instruction should be meaningful. Students should know the purpose of each lesson and how mastery of the skills acquired will help in becoming a better reader. Time is of the essence to the disabled reader. It is not sufficient to make a year's growth in reading in one year, because such a student will never catch up at this rate. Therefore, skills that have already been learned should not be emphasized. The known can and should be used as a basis for teaching the unknown, but all stress should be placed upon mastering abilities that will help the student to move forward quickly.

Much meaningful practice is essential if the newly learned reading skills are to be developed and maintained. It is not sufficient that students learn *about* reading or be proficient in stating rules. They must be able to use reading skills automatically. Practice must minimize isolated drill and emphasize the use of these skills and abilities in meaningful situations. To be effective, instruction must fulfill a purpose for students. They should know their weaknesses, the goals of the instruction, and how these goals are to be achieved. In addition, they should know the purpose of each lesson and how mastery of the abilities will help them to become better readers. Students soon become bored with practice and drill for which they do not see a real purpose. A variety of activities should be included in each instructional period.

Well-planned therapy for the severely disabled reader consists of more than proper reading instruction. It also includes elimination or mitigation of the physical, cognitive, environmental, and emotional factors that are inhibiting an individual's progress.

PRINCIPLE 4: SELECT APPROPRIATE INSTRUCTIONAL MATERIALS

Materials for remediation should always be selected and used because they accomplish a specific purpose. They must be appropriate to the needs, reading level, interest, and goals of the student. Valid treatment necessitates providing the child with interesting material that he or she can actually read. The needs, abilities, and interests of disabled readers differ greatly. Consequently, no one book is adequate for all.

At the beginning of the therapy program, materials should be sufficiently easy to permit students to have immediate success. As instruction continues, increasingly difficult materials can be used as the student demonstrates that he or she can handle these materials. As progress is made, it is essential to maintain a balance of easy materials to ensure success and more difficult ones to provide stimulation and growth. Materials should be interesting to the reader. Any materials that students associate with failure in reading should be avoided. One of the best ways for teachers to create a reading problem is to use materials that are frustrating to the student.

PRINCIPLE 5: BUILD SELF CONFIDENCE

Most individuals who are failing to learn to read manifest signs of emotional stress. Success must be an integral part of remediation, and the disabled reader must experience success easily and continuously. Frustration can be reduced by selecting materials at the child's interest and reading levels and by relating reading activities to the child's goals. The reading teacher must understand that the individual is seeking satisfaction, security, and recognition and must aid in the realization of these goals. The teacher must demonstrate progress and help the disabled reader to develop confidence in his or her ability to succeed. Disabled readers need to be accepted as persons and at their own level of development. They need to be understood, respected, and liked.

PRINCIPLE 6: MOTIVATE

The most important principle of successful remedial teaching is motivation. The main task is to arouse within the child the drive necessary to improve in reading. Frequently, disabled readers' previous failures have convinced them that the task is hopeless. These feelings about reading and about themselves must be changed. They must be helped to realize that improvement is possible and desirable. This can be accomplished by securing their cooperation in the diagnosis of their individual problems, the planning of therapy, and the evaluation of their own progress. Active effort can be stimulated by using interesting materials, relating reading instruction to each child's goals, and dramatizing his or her progress. Treatment involves guidance from difficulty to success. It builds the child's self-concept and causes him to believe that he can overcome his problems. The teacher must create an enthusiastic environment in which the child can succeed.

PRINCIPLE 7: COORDINATE THE EFFORTS OF SCHOOL AND HOME

The wholeness and continuity of the instructional process in reading should be emphasized. Learning to read is a continuous process. If remediation is to bring lasting improvement, students must continue to improve. In most instances this implies that the school's reading specialist will work closely with classroom teachers. Together a reading program can be planned that will continue to meet students' needs and provide them with material they can use successfully. It also involves securing the cooperation of parents. Parents can produce a favorable environment for learning, develop responsibility, foster emotional stability, and ensure both the physical and mental health of their children. Remediation of most disabled readers requires the cooperation of both home and school.

APPLICATION OF PRINCIPLES UNDERLYING DIAGNOSIS AND TREATMENT

Cynthia is an intelligent eight-year-old third-grade student who can barely read first-grade-level material. Her parents and her teacher, Mrs. Arnold, are concerned and have had many conferences concerning Cynthia's reading problems and her expressed dislike for reading activities. From interviews with the parents, Mrs. Arnold has learned that Cynthia is sixteen months younger than her sister, Linda, who is an excellent reader and that the parents often compare the two children by contrasting Linda's excellence in reading with Cynthia's poor achievement.

Mrs. Arnold has read Cynthia's school records, which indicate that she attended kindergarten and first grade in a school located in another city. The report states that Cynthia made a good adjustment in kindergarten. In the first-grade i/t/a, an initial teaching alphabet consisting of forty-four characters, was used as the medium of instruction, and progress in reading was slow. The family moved during the summer, and Cynthia entered the second grade in Mrs. Arnold's school. A basal reader approach using traditional orthography, our conventional alphabet, was employed, and Cynthia experienced considerable difficulty in reading. Her second-grade teacher attempted to help her by providing additional instruction in phonics. In spite of her reading disability, she was permitted to advance to the third grade at the end of the school year.

During the early part of the year Mrs. Arnold was impressed with Cynthia's obvious intelligence and her artistic ability but was perplexed by her reading difficulty and her statements that she hated to read. Mrs. Arnold decided that she must do more to help Cynthia. She began by observing Cynthia's oral reading. She noted that Cynthia pondered over each word and sounded out each letter. Once she pronounced a word, she seemed content to go on to the next word, paying little attention to the meaning of the sentences. Comprehension of material read was very poor. To substantiate her observations, Mrs. Arnold administered an informal reading inventory. An informal reading inventory provides the teacher with an opportunity to observe an individual as he or she attempts to read increasingly difficult material silently and orally. It provides information regarding the individual's independent, instructional, and frustration levels in reading and his or her listening level. The independent level is the level at which an individual can read materials without any assistance. The instructional level is the teaching level, and the frustration level is the level at which the individual is frustrated in the attempt to understand what is read. The listening level is the highest level at which an individual is able to understand material that is read aloud to him. Cynthia's performance on the informal reading inventory is shown in Table 1-1.

TABLE 1-1. Quantitative Analysis of Cynthia's Informal Reading Inventory

Level	Oral Reading		Silent Reading
	Word Recognition	Comprehension	Comprehension
Independent	Grade 1	Primer	Primer
Instructional	Grade 2	Grade 1	Grade 1
Frustration	Grade 3	Grade 2	Grade 2
Listening		Grade 4	

The results of the Informal Reading Inventory suggest that word recognition is better than comprehension and that Cynthia can read primer materials independently. First-grade materials should be used for instructional purposes. Second-grade materials are too difficult for Cynthia and would be frustrating to her. She has a listening level or potential for reading at fourth-grade level.

During the administration of the informal reading inventory both oral reading and silent reading were characterized by an extremely slow rate. She made more errors or miscues, deviations from the original text while reading orally, on one-syllable high-frequency words than on polysyllabic words. High-frequency words are words that continually reoccur in printed material. The teacher concluded that Cynthia had an inadequate sight vocabulary, a tendency to overanalyze each word by relying too heavily on phonics, and an attitude that reading was not a meaningful activity but merely the calling out of words.

Mrs. Arnold talked with the parents and explained that in her opinion Cynthia was having difficulty in reading because of an inadequate sight vocabulary and overuse of phonics as a word attack technique. She explained that Cynthia was too concerned with word analysis and paid little attention to meaning. In addition, she stated that Cynthia's dislike for reading probably grew out of confusion between i/t/a and traditional orthography and that her dislike for reading interfered with her willingness to put forth effort to improve. This problem was exacerbated by comparisons that were made with the sister. She suggested that the parents help Cynthia by refraining from making comparisons between the two girls and then outlined her objectives and instructional procedures for helping Cynthia. The objectives were (1) to help her understand that the purpose of reading is to gain meaning, (2) to change her attitude toward reading from one of distaste to enjoyment, and (3) to develop a functional sight vocabulary. Mrs. Arnold chose a language experience approach as the vehicle by which she would accomplish these objectives. In a language experience approach children's transcribed dictation or their own writing are the major reading materials. It is an approach that views listening, speaking, writing, and reading skills as interdependent and mutually reinforcing.

Each day Mrs. Arnold's aide worked with Cynthia for approximately one-half hour. Cynthia dictated stories to the aide. These stories were based on her experiences and consequently were meaningful to her. The aide typed the stories, and Cynthia illustrated them. A list of words learned through this approach was kept. In addition, the aide prepared games that Cynthia played with other children in the classroom. The games afforded an opportunity for the words on Cynthia's list to be used in constructing sentences, completing unfinished sentences, and classifying them into categories. As instruction proceeded, Cynthia was encouraged to select and read easy library books that were interesting to her (high-interest, low-vocabulary books). She shared her reactions to these stories with other students in small discussion groups.

From this short account, it is obvious that the following basic principles were applied.

Principle 1: Focus Attention Upon the Individual. Even though Mrs. Arnold had twenty-seven students in her classroom, she focused attention upon Cynthia. She was aware of her as an individual, of her intelligence, and artistic ability. She was aware of her dislike for reading and her many reading problems. She was sensitive to her feelings of inadequacy.

Principle 2: Emphasize Interpretation. Mrs. Arnold was concerned with determining *why* Cynthia was having difficulty in learning to read and in determining *what* could be done to help her. She learned about her previous school experiences. She assessed her reading strengths and weaknesses, and she looked for factors that might be causing or aggravating the problem. She arrived at a diagnosis that led to her selection of treatment.

Principle 3: Provide Well-Planned Therapy. Mrs. Arnold's instructional procedures were selected to accomplish specific objectives and emphasized the skills that were essential for Cynthia to experience success in reading. She chose an approach that would help Cynthia overcome her specific weaknesses without resorting to isolated drills. The language experience approach was chosen because it would be meaningful to Cynthia, and a variety of activities were used to avoid boredom.

Principle 4: Select Appropriate Instructional Materials. Instructional materials at the beginning were developed by Cynthia from her own experiences. As progress was made, the teacher encouraged games that were appropriate to the girl's needs. Later library books of interest to Cynthia were introduced to provide stimulation and growth.

Principle 5: Build Self-Concept. Comparisons with her sister were eliminated, thus reducing some of the frustration experienced by Cynthia. In addition, the language experience approach and games proved satisfying to her and provided considerable recognition for her to combine an area in which she was adept (art) with reading. The list of learned words kept by Cynthia and the number of easy-to-read library books that she enjoyed were tangible and concrete proof of her success in learning to read.

Principle 6: Motivate. An approach was used that Cynthia found interesting and successful. The shift from an excess of phonics instruction to more meaningful reading activities encouraged active effort on Cynthia's part. Furthermore, the teacher's and aide's enthusiasm and confidence proved contagious, and Cynthia caught their spirit and began to put forth concerted effort to improve.

Principle 7: Coordinate the Efforts of School and Home. Mrs. Arnold enlisted the cooperation of the parents. She shared her diagnostic findings and plans for remediation with the parents and encouraged them to assist in a way they were able to do. The parents were asked to cooperate by avoiding all comparisons between their daughters.

A FINAL WORD

In this chapter attention has been directed to the disabled reader and the effect that his or her reading problems may have. General principles underlying the diagnosis and treatment of the disabled reader have been set forth. The authors' philosophy concerning diagnosis and treatment is briefly summarized as follows.

- The diagnostician is aware of the uniqueness of the individual and studies the whole person in his or her environment.
- Reading disability is usually the result of many factors. Consequently, there is need for cooperation with parents, classroom teachers, and others trained in such fields as pediatrics, ophthalmology, otology, neurology, psychology, and sociology.
- The diagnostician is flexible and uses a variety of approaches, numerous techniques, and wisely chosen procedures. He or she does not assign a ready-made diagnosis and the same remediation procedures to all clients.
- Diagnosis is continuous. The diagnostician is aware of the ever-changing organism and realizes that the diagnosis is not static but an ongoing process. The diagnosis changes as the child changes.
- The diagnostician has confidence in the child's ability to learn and understands that each individual is seeking satisfaction, security, and recognition. The diagnostician accepts the individual as he or she is without disapproval and helps him or her to realize personal potential.
- The remedial reading program is highly individualized. Both the diagnosis and the remedial program must be specific. Stress should be placed on mastery of abilities that will help the student to move forward quickly, so that he or she can make up for lost time.
- Remediation begins at an easy level, where the student can experience immediate success. The learning process must be meaningful to the disabled reader. The student needs to be aware of the objectives and benefits of the remedial program and aware of the progress he or she is making.
- Remediation is the result of growth and is most effective when related to the purposes, interests, and goals of the individual.

REFERENCES

1. Harris, Louis. "Survival Literacy Study." Conducted for the National Reading Council, September 1970; discussed by the Hon. Margaret M. Heckler of Massachusetts in the House of Representatives as reported in the *Congressional Record*, E 9719-#9723, 18 (November 1970).
2. Harris, Louis. *The 1971 National Reading Difficulty Index: A Study of Functional Reading Ability in the U.S. for the National Reading Center.* Washington, D.C.: Louis Harris and Associates, 1971.
3. Kaluger, George, and Clifford J. Kolson. *Reading and Learning Disabilities* (Second Edition). Columbus, OH: Charles E. Merrill, 1978.

SUGGESTED READING

Bond, Guy L., Miles A. Tinker, and Barbara B. Wasson. *Reading Difficulties, Their Diagnosis and Correction* (Fourth Edition). Englewood Cliffs, NJ: Prentice-Hall, 1979, Ch. 8.

Ekwall, Eldon E. *Diagnosis and Remediation of the Disabled Reader.* Boston: Allyn and Bacon, 1976, Ch. 2.

Gilliland, Hap. *A Practical Guide to Remedial Reading* (Second Edition). Columbus, OH: Charles E. Merrill, 1978, Ch. 2.

Harris, Albert J., and Edward R. Sipay. *How to Increase Reading Ability* (Seventh Edition). New York: Longman, 1980, Ch. 13.

2

An Overview of the Reading Process

OBJECTIVES

This chapter should help you to

1. Identify the growth areas which should be investigated in analyzing an individual's reading strengths and weaknesses.
2. Develop a point of view concerning reading that will serve as a basis for diagnosis and treatment.

In the study of individuals with reading problems, assessment of reading performance is paramount, for only with accurate analysis can effective instruction and treatment be provided. It is the purpose of this chapter to set forth a point of view concerning reading that will serve as a broad overview of the skills and attitudes to be analyzed. Several technical terms are used in this chapter. They have been defined in the glossary at the end of this book.

WHAT IS READING?

Reading is a purposeful process of identifying, interpreting, and evaluating ideas in terms of the mental content or total awareness of the reader. It is a complex process that is dependent upon the individual's language development, experiential background, cognitive ability, and attitudes toward reading. Reading ability results from the application of these factors as the individual attempts to identify, interpret, and evaluate ideas from written material.

In our opinion, there are seven major growth areas in reading that are of concern to the teacher and diagnostician: (1) word identification, (2) vocabulary development, (3) literal understanding, (4) interpretive meanings, (5) evaluation, (6) application of the process of reading to study activities, and (7) affective dimensions of reading. A broad overview of the skills or attitudes involved in each of these areas is given below to serve as a basis for diagnosing the individual's reading strengths and weaknesses and the strategies he employs in the reading process. This outline is based in part on taxonomies developed by Barrett (1); Krathwohl, Bloom, and Masia (2); Pearson and Johnson (3, p. 53); and Smith and Barrett (4, pp. 63-66).

Word Identification
1. Recognizing words at *sight*.
2. Identifying and determining the meaning of a word through *contextual analysis* by using syntactic, semantic, pictorial, and typographic clues.
3. Analyzing the *structural* or *morphemic elements* of a printed word.
   a. Inflectional word endings.
      (1) Plurals.
      (2) Tense.
      (3) Comparison.
      (4) Possessive forms.

   b. Compound words.
   c. Roots, prefixes, and suffixes.
   d. Contractions.
 4. Analyzing an unfamiliar word through its *letter-sound corre-spondence*.
   a. Single consonants.
   b. Consonant blends.
   c. Consonant clusters.
   d. Consonant digraphs.
   e. Silent letters.
   f. Short vowel sounds.
   g. Long vowel sounds.
   h. *r*-controlled vowel sounds.
   i. Vowel digraphs.
   j. Vowel diphthongs.

Vocabulary Development
 1. Recognizing word meanings by using context, semantic, and syntactic clues.
 2. Recognizing word meanings through structural or morphemic analysis.
 3. Using a dictionary to ascertain the meaning of an unfamiliar word.
 4. Recognizing that two words can have similar meanings.
 5. Recognizing that two words can have opposite meanings.
 6. Recognizing qualifying words and their effects on meaning.
 7. Recognizing that words are often paired because of an attribute relation.
 8. Recognizing that a class label has examples that belong to that class.
 9. Recognizing and understanding analogies.
10. Understanding the denotative and connotative aspects of words.
11. Recognizing that a word can have many different meanings.
12. Recognizing that words alike in spelling can differ in pronunciation and meaning.
13. Recognizing that words alike in sound can differ in spelling and meaning.
14. Recognizing the relationship between a substitute term and its antecedent.

Literal Understanding
Literal understanding requires the reader to recognize or recall facts and ideas that are explicitly stated in the material.

1. Recognizing or recalling *main ideas.*
2. Recognizing or recalling *details.*
3. Recognizing or recalling *sequence.*
4. Recognizing or recalling *comparisons.*
5. Recognizing or recalling *cause and effect relationships.*
6. Recognizing or recalling *character traits.*

Interpretive Meanings
Interpretation requires the reader to infer meaning from information that is implicitly stated in the material. It requires a synthesis of the literal content of a selection with the student's personal knowledge and experience.

1. Inferring the *main idea.*
2. Inferring significant and supporting *details.*
3. Inferring *sequence.*
4. Inferring *comparisons.*
5. Inferring *cause and effect relationships.*
6. Inferring or *predicting outcomes.*
7. Inferring the meaning of *figurative language.*

Evaluation
Evaluation requires the student to make judgments about the content of a reading selection by comparing it with internal or external criteria.

1. Making judgments of *fact or opinion.*
2. Making judgments of *reality or fantasy.*
3. Making judgments of *adequacy or validity.*
4. Making judgments of *worth or acceptability.*

Application of the Reading Process in Study Activities
1. Understanding the specialized vocabulary.
2. Following directions.
3. Selecting and evaluating important parts of the text.
4. Organizing information.
5. Summarizing information.
6. Locating information in textbooks, reference books, and periodicals.

7. Interpreting charts, maps, graphs, and diagrams.
8. Skimming and scanning.
9. Outlining and notetaking.
10. Using the thesaurus.
11. Using the dictionary.
    a. Alphabetizing words.
    b. Using guide words.
    c. Interpreting syllables.
    d. Interpreting accent or stress.
    e. Selecting word meaning appropriate to context.
    f. Interpreting pronunciation key.
    g. Determining part of speech.
    h. Investigating word origin.

Affective Dimension of Reading

The affective dimension of reading involves the way interests, attitudes, and values are involved in and related to the reading process. It is an important aspect because the student's interest in, attitudes toward, and the value he or she places on reading play an important role in how and what the student reads as well as the amount of effort the student is willing to put forth in learning to read. Krathwohl, Bloom, and Masia (2, pp. 95-153) have classified the affective dimension of reading into five major levels. We have included only the first three levels because they seem the most appropriate for diagnosis and treatment.

Level 1. Receiving (The student is willing to read.)

a. Shows an awareness that reading exists.
b. Shows an awareness that reading can provide interesting possibilities.
c. Reads willingly on occasion, particularly on a topic of interest.

Level 2. Responding (The student is responsive to the material being read.)

a. Reads primarily at the request or under the direction of the teacher.
b. Responds by trying to work out words and to understand what he or she reads.
c. Seeks out information and is satisfied with the act of reading.

Level 3. Valuing (The student is committed to reading and believes in its worth.)

  a. Works voluntarily to improve skills through wide reading.
  b. Chooses reading when other equally interesting activities are available.
  c. Shows a commitment to reading. Frequently reads when he or she has spare time. Pursues, explores, and refines his or her interests through independent reading.

EXERCISES

2.1. John typically substitutes words that do not fit the meaning of the sentence or paragraph. What type of word identification problem is he exhibiting?

2.2. Bill is a word by word reader who laboriously sounds out each word. He fails to recognize nonphonetic words like *one, who, what.* What type of word identification problem is he showing?

2.3. Frank knows the words *blue, bird, grand, mother* but cannot read *bluebird* and *grandmother.* What type of problem is he showing?

2.4. Paul can read well orally but cannot discuss the material he has read nor answer questions based on material directly stated in the text. What type of problem is he showing?

2.5. David understands the facts which are presented in written material but does not understand why they are important or what the relationship to other ideas may be. What type of problem is he showing?

2.6. Mark is having difficulty in his geography class. He has told his teacher that he reads his textbook but gets lost in the details. What type of problem is he showing?

2.7. Martha has difficulty in understanding what she reads. She can read words correctly but cannot discuss or answer questions about the material. Martha has a meager experiential background and poorly developed oral language skills. Why do you think Martha is experiencing difficulty in reading?

2.8. Sheryl does not like to read and will do so only when the teacher insists. How could this attitude affect her reading performance?

ADDITIONAL COMMENTS ON READING

It should be kept in mind that the overview is not intended to be a complete outline of skills and attitudes involved in reading. Furthermore, it should be remembered that the growth areas are not separate and distinct from one another but are related and must be integrated in the reasoning process called reading. Reading is a complex process that involves constant interaction between the reader and the author, each of whom has his or her own language pattern and experiences. The reader needs to understand that the reading process is a means of transmitting ideas and feelings and that to read effectively one must be actively and selectively involved in using past knowledge about language and past experiences to predict what is coming next in the text. Reading is more than an accumulation of skills. The parts interact and combine with each other. It is how a person functions as he reads that is important, not how well he performs on isolated aspects of the reading process.

Reading involves thinking. It is not merely a word-calling activity. Reading is a purposeful process of identifying, interpreting, and evaluating ideas in terms of the mental content of the reader. It is more than an accumulation of skills. Reading is a function of the total organism. The whole individual reacts in the quest for meaning. The reader must bring to this activity a background of experiences, knowledge of language, thinking skills, attitudes, and feelings. This concept of reading stresses the importance of the individual and implies that the focus of study is the individual in *his* or *her* environment. If this concept of reading is accepted, the teacher and diagnostician will consider the individual's maturation and experiential background. The teacher will be concerned not only with what the individual knows but with what he or she feels. The teacher will investigate the physical, cognitive, environmental, and emotional factors that may be affecting the student's total behavior. The emphasis will be on the individual and not solely on the reading skills the individual may need to acquire. In the application of treatment, the teacher will stress the teaching of fundamental skills in a goal-oriented process, and not as separate entities. The teacher will understand that the reader must utilize what he knows and feels in order to profit from the act of reading. The teacher will understand that the reader must contribute in order to receive, because meaning comes from the reader and not from the printed page. In both diagnosis and treatment, the individual is the focal point of study.

REFERENCES

1. Barrett, Thomas C. "Taxonomy of Reading Comprehension." *Reading 360 Monograph.* Lexington, MA: Ginn and Company—A Xerox Company, 1972.
2. Krathwohl, David R.; Benjamin S. Bloom, and Bertram B. Masia. *Taxonomy of Educational Objectives, Handbook II: Affective Domain.* New York: David McKay Company, 1966.
3. Pearson, P. David, and Dale D. Johnson. *Teaching Reading Comprehension.* New York: Holt, Rinehart and Winston, 1978.
4. Smith, Richard J., and Thomas C. Barrett. *Teaching Reading in the Middle Grades* (Second Edition). Reading, MA: Addison-Wesley, 1979.

SUGGESTED READING

Ekwall, Eldon E. *Diagnosis and Remediation of the Disabled Reader.* Boston: Allyn and Bacon, 1976, Ch. 3.

Lapp, Diane, and James Flood. *Teaching Reading to Every Child.* New York: Macmillan, 1978, Part III.

Smith, Frank, *Psycholinguistics and Reading.* New York: Holt, Rinehart and Winston, 1973.

Van Riper, Charles, and Dorothy E. Smith. *An Introduction to General American Phonetics* (Third Edition). New York: Harper & Row, 1979.

Zintz, Miles V. *The Reading Process, The Teacher and the Learner* (Third Edition). Dubuque, IA: William C. Brown Company, 1980, Part 4.

3

Identifying and Classifying Poor Readers

OBJECTIVES

This chapter will help you to

1. Identify individuals who have reading problems.
2. Determine the seriousness of an individual's reading problem.
3. Differentiate among various types of poor readers.
4. Understand the four levels of diagnosis.

In order to help an individual who is having difficulty in reading, we must understand him or her, and we must attempt to analyze the reasons why he or she is having difficulty. Diagnosis can be made at different levels by teachers, reading specialists, and special reading clinics.

LEVELS OF DIAGNOSIS

There are four levels of diagnosis. The lowest level is identification of the disability. At the second level the problem is described in some detail, measurements are used, and the problem is differentiated or classified as to type. At the third level of diagnosis the reading needs of the individual are analyzed. The fourth and highest level of diagnosis involves the determination of causal factors. The four levels of diagnosis are shown in Figure 3-1 (2, p. 11).

At level 1, in our illustration, the individual's difficulty in the classroom is identified as being due to the fact that he or she cannot read. At the second level, the problem is described, and measurements

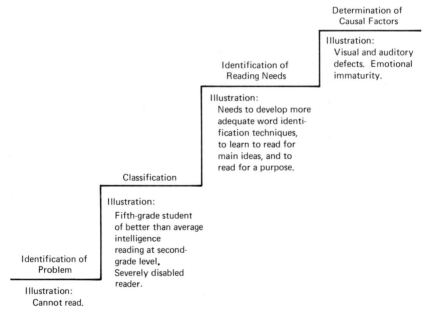

Figure 3-1. Levels of Diagnosis Shown on a Schematic Scale.

are used. In the illustration the child is described as a fifth-grade student of better than average intelligence who is reading at second-grade level. Measurements have been used to determine the student's intelligence and reading level. The student is classified as a severely disabled reader. At the third level of diagnosis, the reading needs of the individual are identified. The student needs to develop more adequate word identification techniques, to learn to read for main ideas, and to read for a purpose. These inferences are based upon the use of standardized tests, observations, informal inventories, and interviewing techniques. The fourth and highest level of diagnosis involves the determination of causal factors. The objective at this level of diagnosis is to determine why the individual has failed to make satisfactory progress in learning to read. Frequently diagnosis at this level involves the need for cooperation with others trained in such fields as ophthalmology, otology, psychology, sociology, and neurology. In the illustration it was determined that the individual was having difficulty in learning to read primarily because of visual and auditory defects. Emotional immaturity was a complicating factor.

The purpose of this chapter is to help you to become skillful in diagnosing at levels 1 and 2. Levels 3 and 4 will be discussed in subsequent chapters.

Diagnosis at Level 1

Diagnosis at level 1 involves identifying the individual's difficulty as being due to a reading disability. This is a fairly easy task and is based primarily on observations by the classroom teacher. Poor readers show many of the following characteristics.

1. Inability to identify printed words.
2. Inability to interpret words in terms of ideas.
3. Inability to understand the literal meaning of written material.
4. Inability to interpret and evaluate ideas presented in written form.
5. Guessing and bluffing in reading situations.
6. Alphabet confusion.
7. Marked reversal tendencies.
8. Slow rate of reading.
9. Excessive lip movement in silent reading.
10. Reading word by word rather than groups of words.
11. Oral reading characterized by
    a. Mispronunciation of words.
    b. Omission of words and letters.

    c. Insertion of words and letters.
    d. Substitution of words.
    e. Repetition of words or groups of words.
    f. Lack of expression.
12. Lack of interest in reading.
13. Failure to enjoy reading activities.
14. Manifestations of emotional reactions in reading situations.
15. Inability to do satisfactory academic work.
16. Infrequent use of the library.

Diagnosis at level 1 is an important step in locating individuals who need additional help in reading. If we are to help poor readers, we must know who they are. Identification of the poor reader should be made as early as possible in his or her school career. The longer the poor reader is allowed to muddle through without proper diagnosis and treatment, the more difficult it is to help him or her because the reading problem becomes overlaid with the student's intense feelings of failure and inadequacy.

Diagnosis at Level 2

Diagnosis at level 2 involves description, measurement, and classification. In no way should this level of diagnosis be confused with labeling. Diagnosis at level 2 is only one step in the total diagnostic process and provides the teacher with information regarding the need for diagnosis at level 3 and/or level 4.

Most poor readers fit into one of the following categories of reading problems (9, p. 144).

    a. Severe reading disability.
    b. Underachievement in reading.
    c. Specific reading deficiencies.
    d. Reading retardation related to limited learning ability.

Severe Reading Disability. The severely disabled reader is an individual who, despite an opportunity to learn to read, has failed to do so. This individual's reading achievement falls significantly below his or her potential for learning. This student is penalized for his or her reading deficiencies—penalized personally, socially, emotionally, or academically because of not achieving in reading. The severely disabled reader is the capable person whose serious deficiencies in basic reading skills are impeding his or her entire reading growth. In spite of opportunities for learning, the individual shows a marked discrepancy between achievement in reading and assumed potential for learning to read. John, who was described in Chapter 1, is an example of a person who has a severe reading disability.

Some of the individuals included in this category have specific learning disabilities. The National Advisory Committee on Handicapped Children set forth the following definition in 1977 (8). "Children with special learning disabilities exhibit a disorder in one or more of the basic psychological processes involved in understanding or in using spoken or written language. These may be manifested in disorders of listening, thinking, talking, reading, writing, spelling, or arithmetic. They include conditions which have been referred to as perceptual handicaps, brain injury, minimal brain dysfunction, dyslexia, and developmental aphasia. They do not include learning problems which are due primarily to visual, hearing, or motor handicaps, to mental retardation, emotional disturbance, or to environmental, cultural, or economic disadvantages." By implication learning disability is caused by dysfunctions of the central nervous system that interfere with perceptual and conceptual processing. The causes may be organic or biochemical in nature. Diagnosis at level 4 is required in order to discriminate learning disabled children from other severely disabled readers whose problems may be caused by physical or environmental factors. Severe reading disability, regardless of cause, requires an assessment of the individual's strengths and weaknesses in reading. This is essentially what we mean by diagnosis at level 3.

Underachievement in Reading. The underachiever in reading is an individual whose reading ability is sufficient for his age and grade placement but whose reading achievement is below his potential for learning to read. Dick is an example of an underachiever in reading. He is a twelve-year-old boy in the sixth grade. He has a mental age of fifteen years and six months and is considered by his teachers, parents, and friends to be highly creative. He reads as well as the average child in the sixth grade and is doing satisfactory work in the classroom. However, Dick is not reading as well as one could expect him to read in terms of his potential for learning to read. The underachiever in reading is frequently not identified as needing reading assistance because he or she may be performing adequately in the classroom. Yet, a tremendous disservice is done to the underachievers in reading by failing to identify them and meet their needs.

Specific Reading Deficiencies. This term applies to individuals who have deficiencies in specific reading skills. If their general reading ability is adequate for their chronological age, mental age, and grade placement, they are not considered disabled in reading.

However, they are classified as reading disabled if their deficiencies are adversely affecting their general reading performance. In either case, their specific areas of weakness should be identified and treated. Kenneth is an example of an individual who has specific reading deficiencies which need correction. When Kenneth entered college, he experienced significant difficulty in reading textbook materials. He did not know how to read for a purpose, his technical vocabulary was inadequate for the courses he was taking, and he was especially weak in organizing material he had read. He needed instruction and correction in these areas but did not require the intensive analysis and treatment which would be necessary in the case of a severely disabled reader.

Another example is Judy, a third-grade student, who is an excellent oral reader. She has a well-developed sight vocabulary and adequate word identification skills. However, she has difficulty in understanding what she reads, often finding it necessary to use the exact words of the text in describing the material she has read. Her basic reading deficiencies are in the area of comprehension. She needs to be taught how to focus on meaning rather than on the sound of words. She needs to learn how to read for ideas and how to relate these ideas to her background of experiences. Her specific reading deficiencies can be identified and treated by her teacher. They do not require the services of a reading specialist.

Reading Retardation Related to Limited Learning Ability. Reading retardation can be caused by limited learning ability. Some poor readers are merely slow learners. For example, a fifth-grade child who is capable of reading only at second-grade level and who is reading at second-grade level is not a disabled reader. He is a slow learner and is reading as well as his level of development can justify. A slow learner can be a disabled reader, however, if his reading ability is below his potential. The classroom teacher has the responsibility of providing instruction in reading for slow learners, and this implies that their needs will be identified and efforts made to teach them.

HOW CAN THE FOUR TYPES OF READING PROBLEMS BE IDENTIFIED?

Determining the type of reading problem exhibited by an individual is important because of its effect on both diagnosis and treatment. The fifth-grade child who is capable of reading only at second-grade level and who is a good reader of second grade material does not require the intensive diagnosis and treatment that is necessary in order to help a severely disabled reader. The fifth-grade child can be helped by giving him more experience in reading and systematic instruction with materials at his level of reading ability. The severely disabled reader, on the other hand, may be experiencing difficulty because of physical, environmental, or emotional problems which need to be identified and treated. Diagnosis at levels 3 and 4 would be necessary.

Differentiating between the four types of reading problems can be made on the basis of information obtained by answering the following questions. This requires a careful consideration of the child's history, general observations of him in the classroom, and his performance on informal reading inventories and on standardized tests. An integration of information from each of these sources is essential if accurate identification and differentiation is to be achieved. "Yes" answers to these questions are significant.

Severe Reading Disability
1. Has the individual failed to make adequate progress in learning to read when taught by regular classroom procedures?
2. Has the individual had sufficient opportunity to learn to read?
3. Does the individual show evidence of adequate oral language competency?
4. Is he or she successful in academic areas which do not require reading ability?
5. Has the child been penalized for reading disability?
6. Can the child adequately solve nonacademic problems?
7. Can he or she successfully solve computational problems in arithmetic?
8. Does the child have an adequate general knowledge of the world in which he lives?
9. Is there a significant discrepancy between listening ability and independent reading level?
10. Is there a significant discrepancy between the student's performance on standardized measures of intelligence and reading ability?

Underachievement in Reading
1. Is the individual's general reading ability at or near grade level?
2. Is there a significant discrepancy between his performance on standardized measures of intelligence and reading ability?

3. Is there a significant discrepancy between listening level and independent reading level?
4. Is the child satisfied with his present level of reading achievement?

Specific Reading Deficiencies

1. Is the individual's general reading ability adequate for his or her grade placement?
2. Is the individual's general reading ability adequate for his or her chronological age?
3. Is the individual's general reading ability adequate for his or her mental age?
4. Is the student deficient in specific reading skills that are adversely affecting his adjustment?

Reading Retardation Related to Limited Learning Ability

1. Is the individual's general learning ability below that of average boys and girls of his chronological age?
2. Is the child experiencing difficulty in making satisfactory progress in most school subjects?
3. Does the child require additional instruction and guidance to understand assignments and directions?
4. Is he or she satisfied to continue doing work of a repetitive nature?
5. Does he need more drill and practice than other children of his chronological age?
6. Does the child have trouble with assignments that are abstract in nature?
7. Is there little discrepancy between the individual's performance on standardized measures of intelligence and reading ability?
8. Is there little discrepancy between listening ability and reading level?

EXERCISE

3.1. Classify, according to type of reading problem, each of the individuals described below and explain why you have placed the individual in this category.

Lee is ten years old and a student in the fifth grade. On measures of intelligence he performs as well as a tenth-grader. He is a youth of wide reading interests and an energetic, hard-working person in the classroom. He reads at fifth-grade level and his academic work is adequate for his grade placement.

Mary is eleven years old and a student in the fifth grade. The school psychologist reports that she has a mental age of nine years. She reads as well as the average seven-year-old.

Stephen is a nine-year-old boy in the fourth grade who is frequently in trouble in the classroom. He is a boy of average intelligence and reads as well as a second-grade child.

Charles is in the seventh grade and reads as well as the average seventh grader. He is doing satisfactory work in the classroom. He reports, however, that he is experiencing considerable difficulty in reading his science and math books. His teacher has observed that his understanding of the technical terms in these areas is weak. He has difficulty with the symbols and specialized abbreviations that are used, and he becomes confused when confronted with an assignment involving the reading and solving of problems.

Karen is ten years old and a student in the fourth grade. She has been examined by the school psychologist who reports that she has a mental age of eight years. She reads as well as the average eight-year-old.

DETERMINING READING POTENTIAL

One of the key factors in determining reading disability is the discrepancy between an individual's actual reading ability and his potential for learning to read. How can reading potential be determined? One of the ways to estimate reading potential is to secure a measure of the child's intelligence. The best and most useful intelligence tests for this purpose are the WISC–R (13) and the Stanford-Binet (12). These tests are individual measures of intelligence and do not require reading ability. They must be administered by a psychologist, and consequently results obtained from the administration of these tests may not be readily available to classroom teachers. Other tests such as the Slosson Intelligence Test (10) and such vocabulary measurements as the Peabody Picture Vocabulary Test (5) and the Ammons Full Range Picture Vocabulary Test (1) can be administered by the teacher. These tests are discussed in detail in Chapter 7.

Listening ability can serve as an estimate of reading potential. If a child can understand material that is read to him, he should be able to comprehend the same material if he is taught the skills that would enable him to read it himself. Therefore, a comparison of listening comprehension with reading performance can be made to determine whether or not a student is reading significantly below his expected level. The listening section of the Informal Reading Inventory, which is discussed in Chapter 6, can be used for this purpose. There are standardized measures which can be used to measure listening ability. The Durrell-Sullivan Reading Capacity Test (7) is one example.

It requires the student to associate words and paragraphs that are read by the teacher with matching pictures. Spache's Diagnostic Reading Scales (11) and the Durrell Analysis of Reading Difficulty (6) both contain sections which measure listening comprehension. For more information regarding standardized measures of listening ability, see Chapter 7.

Still another method is recommended by Cleland (3, p. 428). He suggests averaging four factors to obtain a reading potential score. The four factors are the grade equivalents of: chronological age, mental age, arithmetic computation age, and listening age. The seriousness of the child's reading disability is then found by comparing the reading potential score to the child's reading achievement. Grade equivalents for the mental age and chronological age are obtained by subtracting 5 for the five years the child did not attend school. For example, Jean is ten years old. She has a mental age of 9 years and 6 months. The grade equivalents for these ages are found by subtracting 5. Thus for her chronological age the grade equivalent is 5.0 (10 years − 5 = 5.0). The grade equivalent for her mental age is 4.6 (9 years and 6 months − 5 = 4.6). Jean's grade level on an arithmetic test is 1.5, and her listening grade level, as obtained from the Durrell-Sullivan Reading Capacity Test, is 2.5. The following example shows how to compute the reading potential.

	Grade Equivalents
Chronological Age =	5.0
Mental Age =	4.6
Arithmetic Age =	1.5
Listening Age =	2.5
	13.6

The average grade equivalent is 3.4 (13.6 divided by 4). Thus the reading potential is 3.4. Jean's reading performance on a standardized reading test is equivalent to a grade score of 3.3. Comparing her reading performance to her reading potential, it can be inferred that she is reading as well as one could expect.

EXERCISE
3.2. Using Cleland's reading potential formula, determine whether or not Phillip is seriously disabled in reading.

Phillip is fourteen years old. He has a mental age of 15 years and 6 months. His grade equivalency scores on an arithmetic computation test are 7.8, on a measure of listening ability, 7.9, and on a measure of reading ability, 6.8. Remember to change ages to grade equivalents where necessary.

A decidedly different procedure is recommended by Crowley and Ellis (4, pp. 312-319). Their method involves administering a standardized reading test twice. The first time the test is given normally, and the second time the same test is given with the teacher reading the test to the child. The reading passages and answer choices are read aloud by the teacher while the child reads silently. The child's potential for reading improvement is found by comparing his performance on the two tests. If both scores are the same, the child is considered to be achieving at his ability level. If the teacher-read score is substantially higher, the child is considered in need of reading therapy.

EXERCISE
3.3. Select a student in your class whom you suspect has reading problems. Determine whether or not he or she is in need of reading therapy by using the method recommended by Crowley and Ellis.

Child's name _____

Test administered _____

Performance

    on test when normally administered _____

    on teacher-read test administration _____

Inference _____

FORMULAS FOR IDENTIFYING AND CLASSIFYING POOR READERS

A number of formulas have been developed to aid the teacher in identifying poor readers. Even though such formulas are beginning to lose favor, you may find the formulas developed by Harris useful in identifying disabled readers and in differentiating types of poor readers. The first formula to be discussed is the Harris Expectancy Age Formula (9, pp. 154-155).

Harris Expectancy Age Formula

The Reading Expectancy Age (REA) provides an indication of an individual's reading potential. It is the optimum reading level one can expect of a child in terms of his chronological age and level of mental development. It is based upon the individual's mental age and chronological age and is determined by the following formula.

$$\text{Reading Expectancy Age} = \frac{2 \text{ M.A.} + \text{C.A.}}{3}$$

The mental age is determined by the individual's performance on a standardized measure of intelligence. The chronological age, of course, is the individual's calendar age. Both the chronological age and the mental age are stated in terms of years and months. Years should be converted to months in order to make the calculations easier. For example, Randy is 10 years and 6 months old. This is equivalent to a chronological age of 126 months (10 years $\times$ 12 months = 120 months + 6 months = 126 months). She has a mental age of 12 years and 2 months (12 years $\times$ 12 months = 144 months + 2 months = 146 months).

To find her reading expectancy age, we apply the formula:

$$\frac{2 \text{ M.A.} + \text{C.A.}}{3} = \frac{2(146) + 126}{3} = \frac{292 + 126}{3} = \frac{418}{3} = 139 \text{ months}$$

The reading expectancy age should be stated in terms of years and months. Therefore, we need to convert 139 months to years and months by dividing by 12 (139/12). Her reading expectancy age, when stated in years and months, is 11 years and 7 months. We can infer from this information that Randy has the potential of reading as well as a child of 11 years and 7 months.

EXERCISE

3.4. Using the Harris formula, determine the reading expectancy age for each of the following children. Be sure to convert years into months before applying the formula.

Child	M.A.	C.A.	Reading Expectancy Age
Terry	8-0	8-6	
Doris	13-0	10-3	
Judy	12-4	12-3	

Harris Reading Expectancy Quotient (9, p. 155)

The reading expectancy quotient expresses how an individual's reading ability compares with his expectancy age. For example, a reading expectancy quotient between 90 and 110 is considered to be within normal limits. A reading expectancy quotient below 90 suggests a reading disability. The lower the reading expectancy quotient, the more severe the disability.

To find the Reading Expectancy Quotient (REQ) divide the child's reading age by the reading expectancy age and multiply by 100 to remove the decimal point. The formula is

$$\text{Reading Expectancy Quotient} = (RA/REA \times 100)$$

Tom has a chronological age of 8 years and a mental age of 8 years and 6 months. Using the reading expectancy age formula, we find his reading expectancy age (REA) to be 8 years and 4 months (100 months).

Tom has been given two standardized measures of reading. On a silent reading test he performed as well as the average child of 7 years and 6 months. On an oral reading test he performed as well as a child of 6 years and 6 months. When more than one reading test has been given, as in this example, we need to find his average reading age. The two reading ages should be converted to months, added together, and divided by 2 to find the average reading age, which in this case is 84 months. The reading expectancy quotient is found by dividing the reading age (84 months) by the reading expectancy age (100 months) and multiplying by 100 to remove the decimal point (84/100) × 100 = 84. The reading expectancy quotient is 84 which suggests that Tom is disabled in reading.

EXERCISE
3.5. Using the Harris formula, find the expectancy age and reading expectancy quotient for the following children.

Child	M.A.	C.A.	R.A.	REA	REQ
Rachel	13-0	12-6	10-5		
Cameron	9-1	9-2	8-5		
Tracy	10-4	7-1	9-4		

Which children appear to be seriously disabled in reading?

Harris Reading Quotient

Harris and Sipay (9, pp. 156-160) recommend using a *reading quotient* to differentiate among severely disabled readers, underachievers in reading and slow learners whose reading ability is adequate in terms of their limited learning capability but below age level. The reading quotient is found by dividing the reading age by the child's chronological age and multiplying by 100. The formula is:

$$Reading\ Quotient = R.A./C.A. \times 100$$

For example, a 10 year old child whose reading age is 8 years would have a reading quotient of 80.

$$\frac{8 - 0}{10 - 0} = \frac{8\ yrs. \times 12\ mos.}{10\ yrs. \times 12\ mos.} = \frac{96\ mos.}{120\ mos.} \times 100 = 80$$

If an individual's reading expectancy quotient and reading quotient are both below 90, the child is properly classified as having a severe reading disability. If an individual has a reading expectancy quotient below 90 but a reading quotient of 90 or above, he is considered an underachiever in reading. If an individual has a reading expectancy quotient of 90 or above but a reading quotient below 90, he is considered to be reading as well as one could expect. This information is repeated in the following table. The formulas are not useful in identifying specific reading deficiencies.

TABLE 3-1.   Summary of Definitions of Reading Disability

Type of Reading Problem	Reading Expectancy Quotient	Reading Quotient
Severely disabled reader	Below 90	Below 90
Underachiever in reading	Below 90	90 or Above
Reading retardation related to limited learning ability	90 or Above	Below 90

Ms. Kelsh has administered a standardized reading test to her seventh-grade students. Two boys, both 12 years and 10 months old, have the same reading age on the test—10 years and 10 months. Ray has a mental age of 12 years and 4 months, and Gene has a mental age of 10 years and 11 months. Are these boys severely disabled readers? Let's apply the Harris formula and make a decision. Ray's reading expectancy quotient is 87, and his reading quotient is 84. He is a severely disabled reader. Gene's reading expectancy quotient is 93, and his reading quotient is 84. He is not a severely disabled reader. He is reading as well as can be expected in terms of his level of intelligence. In order to help these boys, their instructional needs must be assessed and met. In addition, the teacher will want to discover and mitigate any factors adversely affecting Ray's progress in reading.

SUMMARY

Individuals experiencing difficulty in learning to read should be identified and given help as soon as possible. If poor readers can be identified and provided with adequate treatment during the primary grades, the chances for success are excellent. Success is harder to attain if the child is older when he is identified and treatment begun. In this chapter a number of suggestions have been given that should help you to identify poor readers and to understand the type of reading problem each is exhibiting.

ADDITIONAL EXERCISES

3.6. How would you classify the following individual? Kenneth is 11 years and 6 months old. He has a mental age of 11 years and 10 months and is in the fifth grade. His achievement ages on a standardized measure for silent reading is 10 years and 3 months and for oral reading 8 years and 5 months.

Kenneth's average reading age is _____

His reading expectancy age is _____

His reading expectancy quotient is _____

His reading quotient is _____

Kenneth is classified as _____

3.7. How would you classify Duncan? He is 10 years and 4 months old. He has a mental age of 13 years and 10 months. His achievement age on a standardized measure is 10 years and 1 month for silent reading and 10 years and 3 months for oral reading.

Analyzing and Treating Reading Problems

Duncan's average reading age is _____

His reading expectancy age is _____

His reading expectancy quotient is _____

His reading quotient is _____

Duncan is classified as _____

3.8. How would you classify the following individual? Janet is 10 years and 6 months old. She has a mental age of 7 years and 2 months. Her achievement age on a standardized measure of reading is 7 years and 8 months for silent reading and 7 years and 6 months for oral reading.

Janet's average reading age is _____

Her reading expectancy age is _____

Her reading expectancy quotient is _____

Her reading quotient is _____

Janet is classified as _____

REFERENCES

1. Ammons, R. B., and H. S. Ammons. *Ammons Full Range Picture Vocabulary Test.* Missoula, MO: Psychological Test Specialists, 1950.
2. Carter, Homer L. J., and Dorothy J. McGinnis. *Diagnosis and Treatment of the Disabled Reader.* New York: Macmillan, 1970.
3. Cleland, Donald L. "Clinical Materials for Appraising Disabilities in Reading." *The Reading Teacher* 17 (March 1964): 428-429.
4. Crowley, Harry L., and Bessie Ellis. "Cross Validation of a Method for Selecting Children Requiring Special Services in Reading." *The Reading Teacher* 24 (January 1971): 312-319.
5. Dunn, Lloyd M. *Peabody Picture Vocabulary Test.* Circle Pines, MN: American Guidance Service, 1981.
6. Durrell, Donald D. *Durrell Analysis of Reading Difficulty.* New York: The Psychological Corporation, 1980.
7. Durrell, Donald D., and Helen Blair Sullivan. *Durrell-Sullivan Reading Capacity Test.* New York: Harcourt Brace Jovanovich, 1973.
8. *Federal Register*, Vol. 42, No. 163, August 23, 1977.
9. Harris, Albert J., and Edward R. Sipay. *How to Increase Reading Ability* (Seventh Edition). New York: Longman, 1980.
10. Slosson, Richard L. *Slosson Intelligence Test.* Los Angeles, CA: Western Psychological Services, 1963.

11. Spache, George D. *Diagnostic Reading Scales.* Monterey, CA: CTB/McGraw-Hill, 1972.
12. Terman, Lewis, and Maud A. Merrill. *Stanford-Binet Intelligence Scale.* Boston: Houghton Mifflin, 1960.
13. Wechsler, David. *Wechsler Intelligence Scale for Children, Revised.* New York: The Psychological Corporation, 1974.

SUGGESTED READING

Bond, Guy L., Miles A. Tinker, and Barbara B. Wasson. *Reading Difficulties, Their Diagnosis and Correction* (Fourth Edition). Englewood Cliffs, NJ: Prentice-Hall, 1979, Ch. 3.

Harris, Albert J., and Edward R. Sipay. *How to Increase Reading Ability* (Seventh Edition). New York: Longman, 1980, Ch. 7.

Rupley, William H., and Timothy R. Blair. *Reading Diagnosis and Remediation.* Chicago: Rand McNally College Publishing Company, 1979, Ch. 17.

4

The Teacher's Role

OBJECTIVES

This chapter will help you to

1. Analyze students' reading behaviors.
2. Choose instruments to use in classroom diagnosis.
3. Follow diagnostic procedures.
4. Set instructional goals for the disabled reader.
5. Choose the means to accomplish the goals.

Every student in the classroom needs a reading program that is geared to his specific strengths and weaknesses, but we are concerned here with the disabled reader who must go farther in a shorter time than the more successful student. On the first day of school the teacher is faced with thirty-two or twenty or fifteen children, most of whom are unfamiliar to him or her. The teacher may have voluminous records on some of them, provided by previous teachers, but for others there may be no information at all. The teacher's job is to identify the ones who can benefit by regular classroom instruction, the ones whom the specialist should see, and the ones who are in need of extra classroom help.

The teacher's goal in using diagnostic procedures with students is to identify their reading levels, ascertain their instructional needs, and decide on appropriate methods of alleviating problems. The more difficult cases of reading disability should be left for the reading specialist. This is not to say that the teacher should ignore the ramifications of the total personalities of his or her students. The degree to which the teaching methods and materials coincide with the unique personality and modes of learning of the student is often the measure of success in reading growth.

In order to provide the best corrective program for the students the teacher should

a. Collect and synthesize relevant data.
b. Set instructional goals.
c. Choose materials and approaches to meet those goals.
d. Carry out the plan of instruction.
e. Alter the plan as needed.

COLLECT AND SYNTHESIZE RELEVANT DATA

In the classroom study of an individual, use is made of standardized measures, basal series placement tests, informal inventories and constant diagnostic observation.

Standardized Tests

Standardized tests have been carefully devised, tried out on many subjects, and validated before formal publication. They come in a wide variety of types and forms and may provide measures of many different reading skills. They can be quite helpful, especially when a teacher wants to get some idea of her students' reading skills even before she gets to know the children personally. By using them early in the school year she can select materials for classroom instruction that are approximately relevant to the students' needs. It should be remembered, however, that standardized tests tend to measure the frustration level of a person's reading ability, and not all of them are as accurate as they purport to be.

Placement Tests

Placement tests designed by publishers of basal reading series fall somewhere between formal and informal measures of assessment. Their primary purpose is to indicate which level book in their series a child should be using. Most of these tests assess word attack skills and comprehension, and some are quite diagnostic in character.

Informal Reading Inventories

These inventories are usually less exact in their results and more time-consuming for the teacher, but can often be more revealing in their results. Their advantage over standardized tests and placement tests is that the teacher can choose exactly what it is she wants to measure and what criteria will be used in examining the results. Since a primary rule in diagnosis is to do the minimum amount of testing for the maximum amount of information, this is an important asset.

Attitudes and Interest Inventories

Besides assessing reading behaviors, it is incumbent on the teacher to make judgments about the attitudes and interests of the students. Needs assessments must be accompanied by ideas on the best ways to meet those needs. There are many informal methods of gaining this information. One of these, the Heathington Attitude Scale (1, pp. 27-32), gives the students a series of statements which they respond to by marking that they strongly agree, agree, disagree, or strongly disagree, with each one. A sample page from the Heathington Intermediate Scale (1, pp. 31-32) is given here.

1. You feel uncomfortable when you're asked to read in class.
2. You feel happy when you're reading.
3. Sometimes you forget about library books that you have in your desk.
4. You don't check out many library books.

5. You don't read much in the classroom.
6. When you have free time at school, you usually read a book.
7. You seldom have a book in your room at home.
8. You would rather look at the pictures in a book than read it.
9. You check out books at the library but never have time to read them.
10. You wish you had a library full of books at home.
11. You seldom read in your room at home.
12. You would rather watch TV than read.
13. You would rather play after school than read.
14. You talk to friends about books that you have read.
15. You like for the room to be quiet so you can read in your free time.
16. You read several books each week.
17. Most of the books you choose are not interesting.
18. You don't read very often.
19. You think reading is work.
20. You enjoy reading at home.
21. You enjoy going to the library.
22. Often you start a book, but never finish it.
23. You think that adventures in a book are more exciting than TV.
24. You wish you could answer the questions at the end of the chapter without reading it.

An instrument for assessing the reading interests of students involves providing them with a list of real or fictitious titles of books along with a short description of each story and asking them to select the ones they really would like to read. A more wide-ranging interest inventory might include such incomplete statements as

1. After school I _____
2. My friends and I like to _____
3. My favorite TV program is _____
4. My favorite movie is _____
5. I like to read about _____
6. I like to go to _____
7. My favorite school subject is _____
8. The game I like best is _____
9. I hate to play _____
10. My parents make me _____
11. The most fun I had this week was _____
12. When I grow up I want to be _____

Constant Diagnostic Observation

The final type of "instrument," constant diagnostic observation, is undoubtedly the most important of all. It should be used in conjunction with the administration of standardized and informal tests, and should continue to be used every day, all day, in the classroom. While actual testing procedures are being carried out (and at all other times) the teacher can be learning many things about the student: his approach to a challenge, reaction to success and failure, rate of response, idiosyncratic behaviors, and a wealth of other information that will be useful in helping the student to grow academically.

Synthesize Relevant Data

Synthesizing data on each child appears to be an insurmountable task and, indeed, it is not easy. Most successful teachers find that a summary sheet for each child is the most coherent way to make all the information accessible. Many basal series include summary sheets for teacher use, and all commercially prepared informal reading inventories have them. An example of a teacher-made summary sheet is given below.

TABLE 4-1. Summary Sheet

Name _____ Semester _____

Standardized Test Results

_____

_____

Informal Reading Inventory

Levels	Grade Levels	
	Oral	Silent
Independent	_____	_____
Instructional	_____	_____
Frustration	_____	_____
Listening	_____	

TABLE 4-1. **Summary Sheet** (continued)

Skill	Needs Help	Is Improving	Satisfactory
Word Meaning	_____	_____	_____
Word Identification:	_____	_____	_____
Alphabet	_____	_____	_____
Sight Words	_____	_____	_____
Contextual Analysis	_____	_____	_____
Structural Analysis	_____	_____	_____
Phonics:	_____	_____	_____
Initial Consonant	_____	_____	_____
Final Consonant	_____	_____	_____
Consonant Clusters	_____	_____	_____
Vowel Clusters	_____	_____	_____
Comprehension:	_____	_____	_____
Main Idea	_____	_____	_____
Details	_____	_____	_____
Sequence	_____	_____	_____
Comparisons	_____	_____	_____
Cause and Effect	_____	_____	_____
Character Traits	_____	_____	_____
Predicting Outcomes	_____	_____	_____
Evaluation	_____	_____	_____
Spelling	_____	_____	_____
Handwriting	_____	_____	_____
Semantic & Syntactic Abilities	_____	_____	_____

Personality

Attitudes and Interests

Social Interaction

Notes

EXERCISE

4.1. Lucille B. indicated on the attitudes and interest inventories that she hated to read and she loved television, especially outer space fantasies. How can the teacher use this information to help Lucille?

SET INSTRUCTIONAL GOALS

Test results and teacher observation are combined in order to make an analysis of the disabled student's reading behavior. When specific areas of deficiency are identified, instructional goals can be formulated. In formulating these goals the teacher should remember to keep the program in balance; reading is made up of word attack skills and comprehension of the material, and one should not supercede the other. The teacher must keep in mind, too, that the pace of learning must be accelerated in order for the student to catch up to his or her potential. Finally, the teacher should involve the student in the planning of the goals, since he or she is the one who will have to make the effort to succeed.

CHOOSE MATERIALS AND APPROACHES

The choice of materials and approaches should depend on the student's interests and on his or her mode of learning. If a child loves cats and hates dogs, stories about cats would provide an incentive for greater effort in reading. As for mode of learning, some people need to hear something in order to remember it, and others need to see it. Auditory learners, for instance, can learn phonics better than visual learners can.

The choice of materials also requires that they be geared to the specific needs of the student. Busy work has no place in a corrective reading program (or in any other reading program, for that matter). The teacher must avoid materials and approaches that have already proved to be ineffective for that particular student.

There should be a balance of easy and more difficult material, so the student is assured of success, but is also growing in ability. A key problem in teaching children to read is in locating material that is stimulating, but not too demanding. If it is too easy, they will become bored; if it creates demands beyond their abilities, they become anxious; and if it is very far above their capabilities, they will not even attend to it. If the teacher gets them at their "learning edge"—a difficult task—their own motivation becomes engaged, and they can learn.

CARRY OUT THE PLAN

Carrying out the plan of instruction should be based on the principles of diagnostic teaching. As soon as progress is made, the plan should be altered to reflect that growth. Once a skill is learned it usually requires only distributed practice for it to be maintained. Flexibility of the plan is also desirable because a change of pace usually results in heightened attention.

One final caution: even though the diagnostic procedure identifies specific elements in the reading process, the ultimate purpose is not fragmentation but integration. Skill building is accomplished best when it is incorporated into the reading act itself. Isolated learning does not automatically transfer to reading as a process.

Transfer of learning is the goal of teaching in general. Teaching a rule is not an end in itself. The rule must be applied in all relevant situations or else there is no reason for teaching it in the first place. If a child can recite "*i* before *e*, except after *c*" but spells *receive* as *recieve* he has learned nothing of value.

The experts tell us that transfer of learning is not automatic. In many cases it must be taught. A teacher should always build this final step of application into her teaching process.

EXERCISE
4.2. Barry, a twelve-year-old, was a marvel at conjugating verbs when doing exercises, but he left off verb endings when reading from a book. How might transfer of this skill be accomplished?

ALTER THE PLAN AS NEEDED

Teachers should be continually on the lookout for any changes in a student's repertoire of strengths and weaknesses. Their careful and copious records should be upgraded every time they see the need. They will realize that there are sudden, unexpected spurts in learning, and there are times when regressions can occur. There are also "false positives," to borrow the psychologists' term, wherein test scores indicate a problem where none exists. The program should change as the child changes.

Example

Joan Marble's fifth-grade class had been given a standardized test during the first week of September, as was the custom in that school. The results of the test suggested to her that two of the children should be examined by the reading specialist. Mary, a little wisp of a girl with straight brown hair and a faraway look in her eyes, appeared to be working diligently on the test, but had not answered a single question on it. All during that first week of school Ms. Marble had been frustrated in her attempts to draw Mary into the class activities. Another child, Donny, had all the indications of poor vision. He squinted, he brought his paper up to her several times to ask what the directions said, and he put his answers, such as they were, above or below the lines on the page.

There were five other students whose reading performance did not match her guess as to their potential. Paul, 10 years and 2 months old, was one of them. Records in his cumulative folder indicated that he was above average in intelligence, but had never received high marks in reading.

He was a stocky, gregarious boy who enjoyed talking with adults as well as with the other children. He said that he hated not being able to read better, but Ms. Marble had already noticed a tendency in him to avoid reading tasks whenever he could. She also noticed that he tried to divert the conversation or said he had a headache whenever any kind of arduous task was asked of him.

Paul's grade-level scores on the standardized test were

Word Recognition	3.5
Reading Comprehension	4.5
Spelling	3.6
Computation	5.5

He was one of the first students that Joan Marble scheduled to take an informal reading inventory. While the rest of the class was busy on an art project, she took Paul into the reading corner and gave him the graded word list and reading paragraphs of her own informal inventory. The results were

	Grade Levels	
Levels	Oral	Silent
Independent	3.0	3.5
Instructional	4.0	4.0
Frustration	5.0	6.0
Listening	7.0	

EXERCISE

4.3. What conclusions can you draw from the findings so far?

Paul used some phonic principles but was not consistent with them. He had difficulty with hard and soft *c* and *g* sounds and with vowel diphthongs. He used syntactic and semantic cues when he encountered an unfamiliar word, except when the material became quite difficult for him. Then he abandoned all cues and rushed through the "reading" with no attempt to use the sense of the passage. For instance, with the sentence, "The brilliant sun sank behind the dull gray mountain," he said, "The brickley sun such behind behind the bull gray many."

He seldom recognized contractions, and he omitted or added inflectional endings indiscriminately. Syllabication was not a problem for him. He responded well to literal questions, but usually said, "I don't know," when asked to make judgments or to make inferences.

EXERCISES

4.4. What skills should the teacher plan to work on with Paul?

4.5. What attitudes of Paul's should she attempt to modify?

After Joan Marble had recorded all of the information in the notebook she kept for her students, she began to plan her strategy. Motivation was a key factor in getting him involved so she decided to have two different activities for each learning element, and he could choose the one that seemed to him to be more fun. She also discovered that he was entranced by trail bikes, which solved her problem of what to give him for free reading time. She had several trade books and catalogues on the subject which were written at or below his independent reading level. The fact that he liked competition suggested to her that she find someone else who needed the same lessons to work together with him.

In setting instructional goals she planned to keep his program in balance by having instruction always include comprehension of the material, in spite of his superior ability to gain meaning from minimal clues. For instance, when Paul worked on contractions, they would be found in meaningful stories rather than in isolation.

When she had her conference with him, she showed him the test and inventory results and discussed with him their implications for his future growth in reading. He reluctantly agreed that he would have to put forth greater effort than before, but he wanted to work on his own rather than with someone else in class. He did not want anyone to know that he was "dumb."

Her solution to that problem proved to be quite successful. She suggested to him that as soon as he became familiar with certain phonic rules he could practice them by tutoring a third-grade boy who needed help in the same area.

Reading instruction in Ms. Marble's room was divided into two parts: free reading and skills improvement. Three times a week a half hour was set aside for the children to read whatever they wanted, with no questions asked before or after reading. She encouraged but did not require student-initiated projects, such as dramatizations, the compiling of a "travel book," and the sharing of their enthusiasms for particular books.

Her daily period for skills improvement was the time when all students were working on activities to meet their specific needs insofar as Ms. Marble could ascertain them with the help of her class chart. A typical period might have six children working on syntactic elements of sentences, four or five others using reference books, some children outlining a chapter in a history book, and several children working alone on special needs such as contextual clues or, as in Paul's case, practicing the identification of verb tenses.

During the next few months Paul made significant progress, although there were backsliding times, too. The teacher showed her pride in his growth, and he basked in her praise. He even began to enjoy free reading time.

SUMMARY

The teacher's role is a difficult but rewarding one. She must take her twenty or thirty students where she finds them and, with all their disparities, she must try to imbue them with

- The ability to read—to understand words and ideas, to read with fluency and flexibility.

- The desire to read—so the very smell and feel of a book is enticing.
- The chance to read—to find the joys in literature, to find the knowledge in textbooks and recipes, to know poetry and essays, editorials and comic books, biographies, encyclopedias, magazines.

She must accomplish this by analyzing their strengths and weaknesses, deciding what are the instructional goals for all her students, and choosing materials and approaches that match their needs and unique qualities. As soon as she has accomplished all of this, she must begin to revise these decisions to keep abreast of the changes the students exhibit as they progress and regress and go off on tangents.

REFERENCES

1. Alexander, J. Estill, and Ronald C. Filler. *Attitudes and Reading*. Newark, DE.: The International Reading Association, 1976.

SUGGESTED READING

Bond, Guy L., Miles A. Tinker, and Barbara B. Wasson. *Reading Difficulties, Their Diagnosis and Correction* (Fourth Edition). Englewood Cliffs, NJ.: Prentice-Hall, 1979, Ch. 3.

Cooper, J. David, Edna Warncke, Peggy Ramstad, and Dorothy Shipman. *The What and How of Reading Instruction.* Columbus, OH.: Charles E. Merrill, 1979, Module COM: 335-371.

Ekwall, Eldon. *Diagnosis and Remediation of the Disabled Reader.* Boston, MA.: Allyn and Bacon, 1976, Ch. 2.

Gilliland, Hap. *A Practical Guide to Remedial Reading* (Second Edition). Columbus, OH.: Charles E. Merrill, 1978, Ch. 3.

Harris, Larry, and Carl B. Smith. *Reading Instruction: Diagnostic Teaching in the Classroom* (Second Edition). New York: Holt, Rinehart and Winston, 1976, Ch. 2.

5

The Reading Specialist's Role

OBJECTIVES

This chapter will help you to

1. Identify the various roles of reading specialists.
2. Think about the factors which may cause reading difficulties.
3. Understand the procedure for conducting a clinical study.
4. Gain practice in ascertaining the causal factors of a severe reading disability.

THE READING SPECIALISTS

In the present day, most schools have a reading specialist whose job is to assist the classroom teacher with some aspects of the reading program. "Reading specialist" is a broad category which includes various titles and duties, and there is no strict agreement in the matching of title and duty. Some of the titles are reading coordinator, reading consultant, reading teacher, reading therapist, reading clinician, reading diagnostician, and reading specialist. In spite of the occasional interchangeability of these titles there are certain duties usually ascribed to each.

The Reading Coordinator or Consultant

The reading coordinator or consultant usually is responsible for the entire reading program in a school or school system. She or he guides the work of the classroom teacher, the reading teacher, and the clinician. Depending on the school system she may or may not be responsible for choosing developmental materials, enrichment and remedial kits and programs, providing recommendations to the classroom teacher, and providing inservice help when new equipment or procedures are introduced.

The Reading Teacher or Therapist

The reading teacher or reading therapist most often works with children outside of the classroom but within the school building. This person may spend stipulated amounts of time in more than one school. She or he works with the children who need more assistance than the classroom teacher can give. The reading teacher combines the teacher's report of the child's problem with her own test results and devises a program for alleviating the difficulty. She usually groups her students according to reading level and type of help needed, but she may work individually with some of her children. Her goal is to improve reading skills to the point where the child can succeed in doing the regular classroom work.

The Reading Clinician or Diagnostician

The reading clinician or diagnostician of a school system is an individual who examines children with severe reading difficulties. She or he may combine his or her efforts with those of the school nurse, social worker, psychologist, and classroom teacher.

SELECTION OF INDIVIDUALS REQUIRING CLINICAL SERVICE

A clinical approach is often necessary, especially for the severely disabled reader. The term *clinical* characterizes a method of studying the individual as a whole. In order to understand and aid the person, the student's specific behaviors are observed, and causal factors may be inferred. Stress is placed on the intuitive judgment of the clinicians as well as on measurement and observation. There is an integration of data from several fields of investigation in determining factors requiring remediation. A clinic provides a team of several individuals who, because of their background in various disciplines, are able to study the whole child in his environment. In every clinical study the purpose is to determine why the individual is disabled and what can be done about it.

Teachers are frequently asked to recommend students for clinical study. This responsibility involves the consideration of many factors and is not an easy one to assume. Obviously, not all individuals who have difficulty in learning to read should be referred for clinical services. Several factors should be given careful consideration.

1. Individuals two years or more retarded in reading who are seriously penalized academically, socially, or emotionally and who, in the opinion of the teacher and principal, are mentally capable should be recommended for clinical study.
2. Individuals displaying a reading disability which, in the opinion of the teacher, may be caused by undiscovered physical problems should be referred for clinical study.
3. Clinical service should be considered for disabled readers who appear to be mentally retarded but show marked ability in two or more subject-matter areas other than the language arts.
4. Children in grades two to four reading one or more years below grade level, demonstrating average intelligence or better, and showing evidence of emotional and social maladjustment should be considered for clinical study.
5. Children who appear to be capable mentally, emotionally and socially but are still not learning, and the teacher cannot determine why, should also be considered.

In determining whether or not an individual should be referred to a team of clinical workers, representatives of the school should consider the following questions carefully.

1. Do the parents and teachers want clinical services for the child?
2. Are they willing to be present and cooperate in interviews?
3. If necessary, are they willing to make adjustments in the home and school in order to help?
4. Are the parents "shopping around" to obtain diagnosis and treatment according to their liking?
5. Are the parents or guardians willing to sign an agreement permitting the examinations, interviews, and discussions of clinical data to be observed by teachers within the school system?
6. Does the individual really want to improve his ability to read? (A *yes* or *no* response may be equally significant.)

WHY EXAMINE CAUSAL FACTORS?

Why should we worry about what originally caused an individual to be a disabled reader? Do we need to search his or her background for causal factors? Why not merely start from a baseline of the person's actual reading behavior, and help him learn what he does not know? Often, this is all that is needed, but in some cases there are people who do not know why they are having trouble reading, nor what to do to ameliorate the problem. No matter what the teachers do, or how hard the individual himself tries, little progress is made.

For example, Bill, an intelligent third-grade boy, had marked difficulty in learning to read. He had an inadequate sight vocabulary and poorly developed word identification skills. In spite of his efforts to learn to read and several teachers' efforts to help him, he failed. Finally he was referred to the reading clinician who discovered that he had difficulties in fusion, which resulted in double vision. He was treated by an ophthalmologist. No aid in reading was provided until the visual difficulty had been corrected. Then, instruction in reading was given, and he made significant improvement in a surprisingly short time.

Another boy, Scott, could read at grade level whenever his teacher or parents could get him to sit still long enough to absorb a page or two of print. Everyone suspected that he was the typical hyperactive child, but examination revealed that his parents doted on his baby brother to the exclusion of any real interaction with Scott, except when he was disruptive or noisy. When that happened he got their full attention. In this case, obviously, it was the parents who needed to change, before Scott could alter his own behavior. Counseling with both parents and child succeeded eventually in enough improvement so that Scott could begin to enjoy learning.

The reading behaviors of these children had their roots imbedded deeply in their backgrounds, and the way to their reading improvement had to come from mitigating the causal factors.

THE CAUSAL FACTORS

In general, possible causes of reading disability can be grouped under one or more of the following headings: physical, cognitive, environmental, and emotional.

Learning to read is a complex process which can be affected by such physical conditions as vision, hearing, speech, general health, neurological factors, and, according to some authorities, lateral dominance. Impairment in any of these areas, or a lag in the developmental process can precipitate difficulties in learning to read.

The cognitive factor includes intelligence and mental content, or the sum of the individual's experiential background. Perceptual skills, style of learning, and understanding of what reading is are additional cognitive factors which affect the process of learning to read.

As for environmental factors, the home, the community, and the school contribute in large measure to what the child becomes. Attitudes, points of view, language and learning skills, all are influenced appreciably by the environment, and all affect the process of learning to read.

Emotional factors can have a great impact on a person's ability to read. Emotional maturity and stability, attitudes toward success and failure, methods of coping with anxiety and tension, and the individual's self-concept all may affect reading performance.

These factors, physical, cognitive, environmental and emotional, may work singly or in combinations to impede or enhance reading acquisition. The factors as listed are more for convenience than as truly separate entities. Each may influence the others, and probably does. Self-concept and emotional well-being, for instance, depend on such things as one's physical characteristics, cognitive abilities, and the environment. Each of these factors will be discussed in detail in subsequent chapters.

THE CLINICAL STUDY

In the clinical study of an individual, use is made of standardized tests, informal measures, the person's history which is obtained from interviews and records, and pertinent observations. The diagnostician is concerned with explaining why the individual has had difficulty in learning to read and in planning therapy which is tailor-made to the disabled reader's needs.

In making a clinical study of the disabled reader, the diagnostician

1. Becomes acquainted with the child and helps him to become an active participant in the diagnostic and remedial procedures that are to follow.
2. Gathers information about the individual and his problem by interviewing his teachers, parents, and the individual himself. The diagnostician also reviews the individual's school and medical records.
3. Selects and administers appropriate informal inventories and standardized tests.
4. Observes the child in a variety of situations.
5. Summarizes and interprets all data which have been obtained through interviewing, observing, testing, and informal procedures.
6. Formulates a diagnosis that explains what the child's major difficulties in reading are, what factors caused the reading problem, and what persistent factors are still impeding progress.
7. Plans a remediation program to correct the problem.
8. Periodically evaluates treatment and modifies the diagnosis and remediation procedures to meet the changing individual's needs.

ILLUSTRATION OF A CLINICAL APPROACH

An illustration of the clinical method may help the reader identify the sequential acts and evaluate the importance of each in the study of the disabled reader.

Trudy was 8 years and 5 months old and was in the second grade. By the end of October her teacher, Carl Aston, had been unable to find a way to help her learn to read. After discussing the problem with her parents, he contacted the nearby university reading clinic for help.

On the appointed day, Trudy, her parents, and her teacher arrived at the clinic. The head diagnostician met them and, after some inconsequential chatter, began talking directly with Trudy. In a warm and friendly manner, she asked Trudy how she felt about her school work and her reading. Trudy admitted that she found it difficult and that she would like it if she could read better. The clinician told her that she would be given some tests so that they could find out how to help her; that some of the activities would be boring, some difficult, and some would even be fun, but that they were all necessary in order to find out what Trudy was especially good at and what she needed to improve.

As Trudy began her testing day, other clinicians were interviewing the parents. The background information elicited during the interview, and also supplied by the Case History Data Blank (see Appendix A), which the parents had filled out before the appointment, included the following information.

Trudy was adopted by her present parents when she was one month old. She had been born with wryneck, caused by a breech delivery. (Wryneck, or Torticollis, is a condition of persistent, involuntary contraction of the neck muscles, causing the head to be twisted to an abnormal position.) At that time the method of correcting this condition was to force the lengthening of the contracted muscle by using pressure against the head and neck. Until she was eleven months old Trudy slept with a one-pound salt bag forcing her head to the left. Then, for a month, she was put into a body cast that extended from her head to her hips. The family watched with tearful compassion as she would bump into furniture and walls when she crawled. After the cast was removed on her first birthday, her parents went through the daily exercise program with her and reintroduced the salt bag regime at bedtimes. She began to walk when she was fifteen months old, and as time went on her neck muscles became more and more flexible. Eventually, she was considered cured. When she was four-years-old, she had to wear a patch over one eye for several months to treat a minor case of amblyopia. This is a "dullness of vision not traceable to any intrinsic eye disease." (2, p. 43)

Trudy was a tiny girl and was perceived by herself and others as younger than her chronological years. When the diagnostician asked her how old she was she insisted that she was six. Finally, after prodding, she conceded, "Well, I'm eight now, but last year I was six." She lived in the country with her father, an elementary school principal, her mother, a former fourth-grade teacher, and her seven-year-old brother, Matt, who was also in the second grade. Trudy generally played by herself, and she enjoyed working with her hands on such hobbies as hooking rugs and doing macrame and needlepoint. Because of her earlier physical difficulties the parents tended to shield Trudy from any apparently threatening situation, even to the point of talking for her on many occasions. Their habit of smoothing Trudy's pathway of any extra problems had the effect of building a cocoon around her. Even though they provided many opportunities to enlarge her experiential background, she was a passive observer who made little effort to participate.

EXERCISE
5.1. What factors in her background might be contributory to her academic difficulties? What might be some positive factors that could aid in her future success?

The interview with Mr. Aston, Trudy's teacher, elicited the following information. In school Trudy had problems from the beginning. She started school at age five and was kept in kindergarten for a second year. She was using a basal series that stressed rhyming words and using phonic principles to sound out each word, followed by exhaustive practice. Mr. Aston said, "Trudy reads 'puh . . . i . . . g' for 'pig' and I can't make her say it all as one word." Her attention span was short, and she did not seem to care if she made mistakes or read poorly. She chose the easy and enjoyable games at the Learning Center rather than those activities that were academically oriented. In the classroom she usually seemed oblivious to the presence of others. However, because she was tiny, adults and other children found it easy to hug her and hold her on their laps.

EXERCISE
5.2. What causal factors might be suggested from the above paragraph?

Test Results

Wechsler Intelligence Scale for Children, Revised (3)

Verbal IQ	95
Performance IQ	115
Full Scale IQ	105

The results of this individually administered intelligence test indicate that Trudy has an average IQ, but she is far more adept at manual skills than she is at answering questions. The twenty points difference between her verbal IQ and performance IQ suggests a deficiency in her languaging ability. Her lowest score was in her fund of general information, and her highest score was in arranging blocks in quite complicated patterns.

Informal Reading Inventory

	Oral	Silent	Listening
Independent Level	—	—	—
Instructional Level	Preprimer	—	Primer
Frustration Level	Primer	—	—

In oral reading she used little expression, and she substituted many words, most of which were either syntactically or semantically inappropriate. She used her finger and whispered when reading silently. She answered only detail questions accurately, merely shrugging when main idea or inference questions were asked.

Informal Handwriting Analysis. Her manuscript printing was adequate for her grade level.

Standardized Tests of Reading Comprehension and Word Attack Skills

	Grade		Grade
Letter Identification	Adequate	Word Comprehension	1.2
Word Recognition	1.3	Reading Comprehension	.4
Phonics	2.5	Spelling	1.5
Structural Analysis	—	Math	2.1
Contextual Clues	.5		

Trudy used some phonics rules, but she seldom attached meaning to what she read. She sounded out each word in a laborious sing-song manner.

Learning Disabilities and Learning Modalities Tests. She excelled in using the visual and kinesthetic sense modalities. Her auditory perception and memory were average. There was no evidence of reversals. Although she met one of the criteria for specific learning disability, twenty points difference between her verbal and performance IQ scores on the WISC—R, none of the other symptoms was present. Her electroencephalogram was normal.

Vision and Hearing Tests.   Her visual and auditory acuity were excellent. (Acuity and perception do not necessarily go hand-in-hand, as you will see in a later chapter.)

Personality Tests.   According to the tests, Trudy had a good feeling of being loved. She felt inadequate at school, and her sense of her own personal worth was low. She saw little need for developing social skills.

Observation of Client Behavior

Trudy often needed to have directions repeated. She expected to be helped when problems became difficult, but when help was not forthcoming she usually managed to succeed. Her conversational output was scanty, and she made little effort to be friendly.

EXERCISES
5.3. What were Trudy's major difficulties in reading?

5.4. What factors caused the problem, and were they continuing to impede her progress?

5.5. What recommendations might be given to the school to correct the problems?

5.6. What recommendations would you give the parents?

For Trudy, and for many other people with reading problems, the road to success must be reached by a circuitous route. Her oral language needed to be enhanced before any appreciable gains could be made in her reading ability. Her complacent acceptance of her own immaturity also had to be dealt with, so that she could come to terms with growing up and start enjoying learning.

One of the most pressing problems was her narrow outlook on life. In spite of the fact that her parents had exposed her to many broadening experiences, these had little effect on her since she was an observer rather than a participant. J. McVicker Hunt (1, p. 59), a pioneer in advocating a rich experiential background, said, "Development doesn't come just from exposure to environment. It comes from the child's attempt to cope with his environment—from his *experiences* in acting on the things and people around him and getting a response from them."

The parents were very cooperative and little by little they became aware of how completely they had sheltered her. They began to let her extricate herself from minor difficulties and to hold conversations without their interference. All in all, they complied with most of the recommendations, difficult as it was for them.

The teacher, Mr. Aston, too, was cooperative. He changed her reading program to one which emphasized the meaning of the passages rather than word attack skills. He found the language experience approach so helpful that soon most of his students became involved in its use.

Trudy's real growth was slow. She fought the changes in her life and often at first felt abandoned by her parents. But eventually she became proud of her own independence, and finally, when she was finishing the third grade, she was reading with the best of them in her classroom.

SUMMARY

In this chapter the specialists' roles have been defined and the reasons for using a full-fledged diagnostic procedure with a disabled reader have been explored. The causal factors which can affect reading performance have been identified. After outlining the steps toward diagnosis, an illustrative clinical case has been presented.

REFERENCES

1. Hunt, J. McVicker, quoted in "A Head Start in the Nursery." by Maya Pines, *Psychology Today* 13 (September 1979), 168.
2. *Webster's New World Dictionary* (Second College Edition). New York: William Collins and World Publishing Company, 1978.
3. *Wechsler Intelligence Scale for Children, Revised.* New York: The Psychological Corporation, 1974.

SUGGESTED READING

Alexander, J. Estill, gen. ed. *Teaching Reading.* Boston: Little, Brown, 1978, Ch. 1.

Maslow, Abraham H. "Some Differences between Intrinsic and Extrinsic Learning." in Don E. Hamachek, ed. *Human Dynamics in Psychology and Education* (Third Edition). Boston: Allyn and Bacon, 1977, 10-12.

Otto, Wayne, Charles W. Peters, and Nathanial Peters. *Reading Problems: A Multidisciplinary Perspective.* Reading, MA: Addison-Wesley, 1977, Ch. 9.

Wilson, Robert M. *Diagnostic and Remedial Reading for Classroom and Clinic* (Third Edition). Columbus, OH: Merrill, 1977, Ch. 2.

Zintz, Miles V. *Corrective Reading* (Third Edition). Dubuque, IA: William C. Brown Company, 1977, Ch. 2.

6

Informal Assessment of Reading Performance

OBJECTIVES

This chapter will help you to

1. Determine an individual's independent, instructional, and frustration levels in reading.
2. Determine an individual's listening level.
3. Analyze a student's reading strengths and weaknesses.
4. Develop skill in administering, scoring, and interpreting an Informal Reading Inventory.
5. Develop skill in miscue analysis.

Both the teacher and the reading specialist in assessing reading performance are searching for answers to the following questions.

- What is the individual's reading level?
- What are his reading strengths and weaknesses?
- What reading strategies does he use?

Answers to these questions can be obtained through the use of an informal reading inventory, miscue analysis, the cloze procedure, and the maze technique.

THE INFORMAL READING INVENTORY

One of the most popular diagnostic tools is the Informal Reading Inventory (IRI). The IRI is an individual measure that provides the examiner with an opportunity to observe an individual as he attempts to read increasingly difficult material silently and orally. It serves four purposes: (1) to determine the individual's independent, instructional, and frustration levels in reading, (2) to obtain an indication of his or her listening level, (3) to analyze his or her reading strengths and weaknesses, and (4) to help the reader become aware of those strengths and weaknesses.

The typical IRI is made up of a word recognition inventory and a reading inventory. It can be constructed by the teacher or obtained commercially. Several published informal reading inventories are listed in Appendix B.

The Word Recognition Inventory

The purpose of the word recognition inventory is to assess the individual's sight vocabulary and use of word analysis skills when words are presented in isolation. To construct the word recognition inventory, from 20 to 25 words for each grade level are selected. The graded word lists should range from preprimer level to the highest level to be measured. A record sheet similar to the one shown in Table 6-1 should be prepared.

The first requirement in administering an informal reading inventory is to establish rapport and to explain the procedure which is to be followed. During this time, the examiner talks informally with the child and has an excellent opportunity to observe his vocabulary,

TABLE 6-1.   Word Recognition Inventory

Name _____   Age _____ Date _____

Examiner _____

Preprimer Level

	Word	Sight	Untimed
1.	come	_____	_____
2.	big	_____	_____
3.	it	_____	_____
4.	to	_____	_____
5.	in	_____	_____
6.	little	_____	_____
7.	play	_____	_____
8.	for	_____	_____
9.	see	_____	_____
10.	down	_____	_____
11.	look	_____	_____
12.	you	_____	_____
13.	not	_____	_____
14.	is	_____	_____
15.	can	_____	_____
16.	up	_____	_____
17.	go	_____	_____
18.	said	_____	_____
19.	fun	_____	_____
20.	make	_____	_____
Percentage Correct		_____	

sentence structure, and ability to respond to questions. The examiner can also observe the student's interests and attitudes toward self and toward reading. As soon as the examiner believes that he or she has the child's full cooperation, the examiner should prepare the child for the word recognition inventory by explaining that the student will be asked to read words that will be exposed to him or her at a rapid rate and that at the beginning the words will be easy and will increase in difficulty as the inventory progresses.

In administering the word recognition inventory, the examiner usually begins with the list of words that are two years below the individual's grade placement. If the child makes an error at this level, the examiner drops back to easier levels until a level is reached where the child has 100 per cent recognition of the words. The percentage is based on both the sight and untimed responses of the child. Each word is presented separately for approximately one second. The examiner indicates on the record sheet whether the word was recognized at sight. If the word is not recognized immediately, the child is given time to analyze the word. His response is recorded in the untimed column of the record sheet. The word recognition inventory usually is continued until the child reaches a level where he fails to read accurately five or more words on a particular list. The number of word errors that determines when to discontinue the word recognition inventory may vary depending on the instrument used.

The individual's performance can be analyzed to determine the adequacy of his sight vocabulary and the effectiveness of his word analysis skills. The major purpose of the word recognition inventory, however, is to secure information that will suggest the level at which the reading inventory should be initiated. This is usually two levels lower than that at which the child had a percentage of 75 on the word recognition inventory.

The Reading Inventory

To construct this part of the IRI, the teacher selects passages representing succeeding grade levels, usually from preprimer to the highest level to be measured. Two selections for each level are chosen. One of these is to be used for oral reading and the other for silent reading. The length of each selection is important. Preprimer and primer passages should contain from thirty to sixty words. First and second grade levels should be longer, approximately one hundred and twenty-five words in length, and for the higher grades two hundred to three hundred words. The selections should be interesting and should contain enough information so that questions about the facts and ideas in the selection can be asked. At least five questions should be developed for each selection. The questions should tap a number of reading skills. For example, one question might deal with vocabulary meaning, one with the main idea, two with detail, and one with the drawing of an inference. The student's copy contains only the paragraphs. The examiner's record sheet includes a copy of the reading material, the motivational statement, and the comprehension questions. Each question on the record sheet is labeled as to type of comprehension as an aid to the examiner in assessing reading skills. A sample of the examiner's record sheet is in Table 6-2.

Administering the Reading Inventory. The examiner begins administering the reading inventory at a level two years lower than that at which the word recognition inventory was discontinued. He

TABLE 6-2.   An Example of a Record Sheet for an Informal Reading Inventory

Fourth Level

Motivational Statement: This is a story about schools during the pioneer days. Read the story to find out what these schools were like.

Pioneer Schools

Sally was a little girl who lived in pioneer days. At first there was no school in the settlement where she lived. Then all the parents met together and decided to build a schoolhouse. The school was built of logs and had windows made of oiled skins. School was held for the three months between harvest in the fall and planting in the spring. Since they had no teacher, one of the fathers acted as schoolmaster. The children learned to read, write and do arithmetic. They had to learn to read from Bibles brought from home. They had no pencils and wrote with pens made from goose feathers. Their ink was made from bark and berries.

Total Words: 118

Word Errors:

	0	1	2	3	4	5	6	8	10
Percentages:	100	99	98	97	96	95	94	93	91

Comprehension Questions:

Main Idea	1. Why did the parents build the school?
Detail	2. How long did school last?
Detail	3. Who was the schoolmaster?
Vocabulary	4. What does the word, harvest, mean?
Inference	5. Why do you think school was held only between the fall harvest and the spring planting?

Comprehension Errors:

	0	1	2	3	4	5
Percentages:	100	80	60	40	20	0

or she prepares the child for the paragraph by reading the motivational statement and by reminding the child that after the passage is read, questions about it will be asked. The child is then given the first passage to be read orally. When he or she has finished, the paragraph is removed and the questions are asked. A record is kept of the student's reading errors and responses to the questions. When the child's performance on the first selection is ended, readiness for the second selection is developed by reading the motivational statement. The second selection is at the same level as the first but this time the child reads silently. The reading material is removed following the silent reading, and questions are asked. This procedure is followed at each level until the child has answered only sixty per cent of the comprehension questions on both the oral and silent reading selections. This is called the frustration level. Then the child is asked to listen to the examiner read a selection and to be prepared to answer questions about it. Usually the examiner begins at the next level following the one at which the frustration level was reached and continues at successively higher levels until the child fails to maintain a level of eighty per cent accuracy in answering questions.

The oral portion of the IRI should be recorded on audio tape. The examiner can then replay the tape as often as necessary to hear and make note of all the miscues and nuances of oral reading behavior made by the child.

Recording. The examiner should record every miscue or error which the child makes while reading orally. Table 6-3 explains the typical errors readers make and provides a marking system for easy recording.

It is also suggested that a record be made of word by word reading, incorrect phrasing, finger pointing, and head movement. In observing silent reading, the examiner should record evidence of lip movement, finger pointing, and vocalization. Evidence of insecurity, nervous tension, frustration, or visual difficulties should also be recorded.

EXERCISE

6.1. Master the marking system suggested in this chapter and without referring to the text, identify the types of miscues recorded below.

Sally was a (little) girl who lived in pioneer days. At first there was
no school in the ~~settlement~~ *place* where she lived. Then all the ~~parents~~ *people* met
together and ˄*they* decided to build a schoolhouse. The school was ~~built~~ *made* of
logs and had windows made of ~~oiled~~ *old* skins. School was held for (the)
three months between harvest in the fall and planting in the spring.
Since they had no teacher, one of the fathers acted as school ~~master~~ *teacher*.
The children learned to read, write and do arithmetic. They had to
learn to read from Bibles brought from home. They had no pencils
and wrote with pens made from (goose) feathers. Their ink was made
from ~~bark~~ *black* and berries.

TABLE 6-3. Marking System for the Informal Reading Inventory

Type of Error	Explanation	Marking	Example
Repetition	A word, part of a word, or part of a sentence is repeated.	Underline the repetition.	Jane and her father <u>went</u> for a walk.
Substitution	Another word is put in the place of the printed word.	Draw a line through the printed word and write the substituted word above it.	Jane and her ~~father~~ went for a walk. *brother*
Omission	A word, part of a word, or part of a sentence is omitted.	Encircle the omission.	They stopped at the (big) red farm house for a drink of water.
Insertion	Any word that is read by the child which does not appear in the printed material.	Place a caret (∧) and write the added word.	They stopped at the big red farm house for a drink of ∧water. *cold*
Mispronunciation	A child mispronounces the word by incorrect accent or wrong pronunciation of vowels or consonants.	Draw a wavy line through the word and write the mispronounced word phonetically.	The ~~raven~~ is flying low in the sky. *rắven*
Transposition	The reader reverses the order of the words in the printed text.	Use the printer's mark (⌐⎵) around the transposed words.	"Look out!" ⌐Judy cried.⎫
Words Aided	If a student hesitates for approximately five seconds on a word, the examiner pronounces it for him.	Double check the word. (✓✓)	He thought he saw a mouse in the kitchen. ✓✓
Self-correction	Child corrects an error on his own.	Place a c beside the error.	He thought he ~~saw~~ a mouse in the kitchen. *was* c

Scoring. In scoring the oral reading section of the Informal Reading Inventory, count the number of miscues or deviations from the text in each passage. Do not count proper names, dialect miscues, repetitions, or self corrections as errors. If a child omits or inserts a phrase of two or three words, count only as one miscue. If a miscue is made more than once on the same word, count only as one miscue. Determine the percentage of words read correctly for each selection by dividing the number of correct words read by the number of words in the passage. For example, if there are 300 words in the passage and the child reads 270 of them correctly, his word recognition score is 90 (270/300 = .90). Determine the percentage of correct responses to the comprehension questions for each passage. For example, if there are five questions, each one is given a value of 20 points. If the child answers three of them correctly, his accuracy percentage is 60 (3 X 20 = 60). Record the scores on the Summary Sheet, Table 6-4.

In scoring the silent reading section of the Informal Reading Inventory, count the number of correct responses to the comprehension questions for each passage and determine the accuracy percentage. The accuracy percentages for each passage should then be entered on the Summary Sheet.

Using the responses to the comprehension questions on both the oral and silent reading sections of the Informal Reading Inventory, determine the percentage of accuracy for each type of question. Record this information on the Summary Sheet.

Interpreting. One of the most useful purposes of the Informal Reading Inventory is to determine the individual's independent, instructional, and frustration levels in reading as well as his listening level. The independent level is the highest level at which the individual can read easily with no help from others. It is the level at which the child can read with full understanding and freedom from mechanical difficulties, the level at which he can function on his own. Homework assignments and recreational reading should be at this level. The material should be read with approximately ninety-nine per cent accuracy in word recognition and an average comprehension score based on oral and silent reading of at least ninety per cent.

The instructional level is the highest reading level at which systematic instruction can be initiated. At this level the child can read with a degree of fluency but with enough difficulty to make instruction essential. This is the level of material that should be used by the child in the classroom when he or she is working under the guidance

TABLE 6-4. Summary Sheet for Informal Reading Inventory

Name _____ Age _____ Date _____

Examiner _____

Passage Level	Oral Reading		Comprehension Following		
	Word Recognition Inventory	Reading Inventory	Oral Reading	Silent Reading	Listening
PP					
P					
1					
2					
3					
4					
5					
6					
7					
8					

Comprehension (Record percentage of accuracy)
Vocabulary
Main Idea
Detail
Inference

Levels
Independent
Instructional
Frustration
Listening

of the teacher. The criteria are approximately ninety-five per cent word recognition and an average comprehension score of eighty per cent. In addition, there should be no observable symptoms of difficulty.

The frustration level is the level at which the individual becomes confused by the material. The vocabulary, sentence structure, and ideas are too difficult for him. Word recognition is usually ninety per cent or less and comprehension is sixty per cent or less. At this level tension and anxiety are evident.

The listening level is the highest level at which the student can understand material that is read to him. The child should be able to understand at least eighty per cent of the material. The listening level provides an index to the severity of the child's reading problem. A difference of two or more years between the child's listening level and his instructional level is significant. The listening level also suggests the child's potential for improving his reading performance.

In actual practice, a reader's accuracy percentages for word recognition and comprehension often do not meet the suggested standards perfectly. When this occurs, the examiner will want to base his decision regarding the appropriate levels on additional information, such as the amount of interest the student seems to have in the subject and his knowledge of the subject matter discussed in the passages.

Various writers set forth different criteria for determining these levels. We have found the percentages given in Table 6-5 to be the most useful. We have also found that where there is a discrepancy between the comprehension scores for oral and silent reading that the silent reading scores are more reliable for determining levels.

TABLE 6-5. Minimum Percentage Correct for Independent, Instructional, Frustration, and Listening Levels

| | Oral Reading | Comprehension Following | | |
| | Word Recognition | Oral | Silent | |
Level	in Passages	Reading	Reading	Listening
Independent	99	90	90	
Instructional	95	80	80	
Frustration	90	60	60	
Listening				80

Example. In the example provided in Table 6-6, the data suggest that this student has an independent reading level of third grade. Materials for recreational reading should be at this level. His instructional level is fourth grade. This is the level at which he should be working under the guidance of the teacher. Materials at fifth-grade level and above are too difficult for him and should be avoided. The data also suggest that with the right kind of instruction, the child has the ability to make significant progress in reading. This inference is based on his listening level which is at the seventh grade level. His performance on the comprehension sections of the Informal Reading Inventory suggests that reading instruction should focus on vocabulary development and drawing inferences.

TABLE 6-6. Summary Sheet for Informal Reading Inventory

Name _____ Age _____ Date _____

Examiner _____

| | Oral Reading | | Comprehension Following | | |
Passage Level	Word Recognition Inventory	Reading Inventory	Oral Reading	Silent Reading	Listening
PP					
P					
1					
2		100	100	100	
3	100	99	100	100	
4	95	95	80	80	
5		85	60	60	
6					100
7					80
8					60

Comprehension (Record percentage of accuracy)
Vocabulary   75%
Main Idea   100%
Detail   100%
Inference   50%

Levels
Independent   3
Instructional   4
Frustration   5
Listening   7

EXERCISE

6.2. Joe has been given an Informal Reading Inventory by his teacher. Some of the data resulting from his performance on the IRI are summarized here. In the opinion of the teacher Joe appeared totally uninterested in Passage 4 of the oral part of the IRI, and he was able to answer the comprehension questions accompanying Passage 7 of the silent part from previous knowledge about the subject. The teacher also observed that Joe squirmed in his chair and tapped his fingers on the desk while reading Passages 7 and 8. What are his independent, instructional, frustration, and listening levels?

| Passage Level | Oral Reading | | Comprehension Following | | |
	Word Recognition Inventory	Reading Inventory	Oral Reading	Silent Reading	Listening
3	100%	100%	100%	100%	
4	100%	100%	80%	100%	
5	94%	100%	100%	100%	
6		90%	80%	80%	
7		85%	60%	80%	
8		85%	60%	40%	
9					80%
10					60%

Qualitative Analysis of Reading Inventory. A qualitative analysis and interpretation of a reader's oral reading performance can also be made. Each miscue can be analyzed in terms of whether or not it preserves the meaning of the text, is syntactically correct, or is similar to the sound/symbol relationship of the text word.

In making a qualitative analysis, the first step is to record the miscues on a Summary Sheet for Classifying Oral Reading Miscues. A sample Summary Sheet is shown in Table 6-7. The example is taken from the same paragraph in exercise 6.1.

TABLE 6-7. Summary of Oral Reading Miscues

Name _____ Age ____ Date _____

Examiner _____

Text	Child's Response	Was It Similar in Meaning to the Text Word?	Was It the Same Part of Speech?	Was It Similar in Sound or Written Form?	Did It Change the Meaning of the Text?
pioneer	olden	Yes	Yes	No	No
windows	widows	No	Yes	Yes	Yes
spring	winter	No	Yes	No	Yes
pencils	pens	Yes	Yes	Yes	No

After all of the miscues have been entered on the Summary Sheet, the following questions based on those developed by Kenneth Goodman (1), Yetta Goodman (2, pp. 49-64; 3, pp. 94-102; and 4) and Carolyn Burke (4) can be used as a guide to analyzing the individual's reading strengths and weaknesses.

1. Did the miscue change the meaning of the text?
2. Is there a pattern to the type of miscue, such as adjectives, adverbs, nouns, multisyllabic words, or word parts?
3. Were the miscues similar in shape to the text words?
4. Did the error indicate an attempt to sound out the word?
5. Did the miscue begin with the same letter or letters as the text word?
6. Was the miscue the same part of speech as the text word?
7. Did the miscue interfere with responding correctly to the comprehension questions?
8. Did the miscue make sense when earlier miscues are taken into account?
9. Were portions of a word pronounced correctly and was there a pattern such as initial, medial, or ending parts of words?
10. Were any of the miscues the result of dialect differences?
11. Does the reader rely on the sound-letter similarity to the exclusion of concern with gaining meaning?
12. Does the student indicate through his miscues that he does not understand certain concepts or ideas that are presented in the text?
13. Is the reader able to understand certain concepts and ideas even if he mispronounces words or phrases related to them?
14. To what extent does the reader succeed in interrelating the graphic-phonic with the semantic and syntactic cueing system in his reading? For example if the reader relies heavily on phonics to sound out each word that is unknown to him, he probably has not interrelated the graphic-phonic with other cueing systems.
15. To what extent is the reader aware of his miscues?

EXERCISE
6.3. Make a qualitative analysis of the miscues recorded in exercise 6.1.

READING MISCUE INVENTORY

The Reading Miscue Inventory (RMI) developed by Goodman and Burke (4) is a systematic and thorough procedure for observing and interpreting strategies employed by readers as they linguistically process written material. The RMI provides the examiner with insight into readers' comparative ability to gain meaning as they read. This insight is based on the analysis of miscues and on readers' abilities to retell what they have read. A miscue is a response in oral reading that does not match the printed material. In assessing oral reading performance the quality, not the number, of miscues is important. By analyzing miscues, it is possible to learn how readers reconstruct written messages. By analyzing the retelling of the story, it is possible to assess readers' abilities to remember what they have read.

Miscue analysis is done on the oral reading of a story that is unfamiliar to the reader. The selection should be long enough so that the student reads for approximately twenty minutes. For upper-grade students the selection will be from four to eight pages in length. The material should be of interest to the student and difficult enough so that he or she makes at least twenty-five miscues. An audio recording of the student's oral reading of the material is made so that later the teacher can replay it for analysis. No assistance is given to the student during the reading of the selection. All miscues are written by the examiner on a copy of the story being read. After the story has been read orally, the student is asked to retell it. This information is recorded on a prepared sheet which contains an outline of the story. When the student has completed his or her retelling, the teacher asks general questions in order to elicit additional information about the story. The questions that the teacher asks should not make use of specific information not already introduced by the reader nor should they lead the reader to conclusions which did not result from his or her own reading. Furthermore, any mispronunciations made by the reader should be retained in the teacher's questions.

The first twenty-five miscues are recorded, and the following questions are asked about each miscue.

1. Is a *dialect* variation involved in the miscue?
2. Is a shift in *intonation* involved in the miscue?
3. How much does the miscue *look* like what was expected?
4. How much does the miscue *sound* like what was expected?

5. Is the *grammatical function* of the *miscue* the same as the grammatical function of the word in the text?
6. Is the miscue *corrected*?
7. Does the miscue occur in a *structure* which is *grammatically acceptable*?
8. Does the miscue occur in a structure which is *semantically acceptable*?
9. Does the miscue result in a *change of meaning*?

When the nine questions have been answered, the interrelationship of various patterns are examined to gain insight into the reading strategies used by the student as well as the degree of proficiency in using the strategies.

The student's retelling of the story is assessed primarily in terms of character analysis, theme, plot, and events. From this information the examiner evaluates the reader's strengths and weaknesses and plans treatment which uses the reader's strengths as the basis for overcoming weaknesses.

The Reading Miscue Inventory is particularly helpful when a thorough analysis is required. For many classroom teachers, however, it is too complicated and too involved to be of practical use. Easier versions of miscue analysis can be used such as the qualitative analysis of the Informal Reading Inventory described earlier in this chapter. You may also find the shorter version developed by Laura Smith (8) or the one described by Constance Weaver (9, Chapter 7) easier to use.

THE CLOZE TECHNIQUE

The cloze procedure is another useful diagnostic technique for determining the student's reading levels and his or her ability to understand the structure of written English. Although it does not provide an analysis of word attack skills, it has the advantage of being a group measure. Thus an entire class of students can be given the cloze technique at one sitting. It is an efficient way for the teacher to determine whether a particular book is at the student's independent, instructional, or frustration level. The cloze procedure consists of a written passage of approximately three hundred words in length with every fifth or tenth word omitted. A straight line of uniform length is substituted for each missing word. The first and last sentences of the passage are left intact. The student is given the passage and instructed to fill in the blanks with appropriate words to fit the context of the sentences from which they were omitted. The inventory is untimed and is scored in terms of the percentage of correct responses. To be correct, the exact word must be written by the student. A synonym is incorrect. To determine the percentage of correct responses, divide the number of correct cloze items by the total number of cloze items in the passage. If the student has 57 per cent or more correct, the material is at his or her independent reading level. A score between 44 and 56 per cent is the instructional level, and a score of less than 43 per cent is the frustration level.

The following is an abbreviated example of the cloze procedure.

Emotional maturity, as the term suggests, means growing up emotionally; that is, one learns to do the thing that needs to be done when it needs to be done whether or not one wants to do it. The emotionally mature child (1) _____ readily make the adjustment (2) _____ home to school. He (3) _____ accept change in routine (4) _____ and calmly. He can (5) _____ opposition and defeat without (6) _____ unduly upset. He assumes (7) _____ in the home and (8) _____ school. He plans and (9) _____ things on time. He (10) _____ able to meet and (11) _____ to strangers without shyness (12) _____ undue boldness. Studies have (13) _____ that the emotionally immature (14) _____ is dependent upon the (15) _____ or other adults and (16) _____ unaccustomed to responsibility for (17) _____ task. Frequently such a (18) _____ is infantile in manner, (19) _____ and interest. Because he is completely satisfied in this dependency upon others, he may refuse to learn to read.

The student records his responses on a separate answer sheet which is numbered from 1 to 50 as shown in the example below.

1. can
2. from

   3. can
   4. easily
   5. meet
   6. becoming
   7. responsibilities
   8. at
   9. does
  10. is
  11. talk
  12. and
  13. shown
  14. child
  15. parents
  16. is
  17. any
  18. child
  19. behavior

In scoring the above example, the student's answers are compared with the answer key.

ANSWER KEY
   1. can
   2. from
   3. can
   4. quickly
   5. accept
   6. being
   7. responsibilities
   8. at
   9. does
  10. is
  11. talk
  12. or
  13. shown
  14. child
  15. parents
  16. is
  17. any
  18. child
  19. behavior

Answers 4, 5, 6, and 12 are considered incorrect. Only exact reproductions of the missing word are scored as correct. Synonyms are not acceptable. Therefore, the student scored 79 per cent and the material is at his independent level.

THE MAZE TECHNIQUE

The maze technique is constructed directly from the material to be used in instruction. It is a modification of the cloze procedure. The first and last sentences of the 250-300 word passage are left intact. Every fifth word is deleted and a three-word choice is provided. The choices include the correct word, a word that is the same part of speech as the correct word, and a word that is a different part of speech. For example,

stamps

David likes to save walk

dogs

The material is at the student's instructional level if he accurately completes at least 70 per cent of the test. This multiple-choice adaptation of the cloze procedure was suggested by Ransom (7, pp. 477-482) for young children who could not write the responses to complete cloze procedures. Guthrie and others (5) called this procedure the maze technique and suggested its use as a clinical technique. A study by Pikulski and Pikulski (6) suggests that the maze technique is not discriminating enough for use with regular classroom students.

SUMMARY

Analyzing an individual's reading performance is an ongoing process. It begins with careful observation of the reader in the classroom and continues day by day as instruction and guidance are provided. The careful use of informal techniques, such as those described in this chapter, can enhance the accuracy of the diagnosis. Information gained from using informal reading inventories, miscue analysis, the cloze procedure, and the maze technique can be used to provide more effective instruction in reading.

REFERENCES

1. Goodman, Kenneth S. *Study of Children's Behavior While Reading Orally.* USOE Final Report, Project No. 5425. Washington, D.C.: U.S. Department of Health, Education, and Welfare, March 1968.

2. Goodman, Yetta M. "Miscue Analysis for In-Service Reading Teachers." in Kenneth S. Goodman, ed. *Miscue Analysis: Application to Reading Instruction.* Urbana, IL: National Council of Teachers of English, 1973, 49-64.
3. Goodman, Yetta M. "Strategies for Comprehension." in P. Allen and D. Watson, eds. *Findings of Research in Miscue Analysis: Classroom Implication.* Urbana, IL: National Council of Teachers of English, 1976, 94-102.
4. Goodman, Yetta M., and Carolyn L. Burke. *Reading Miscue Inventory.* New York: Macmillan, 1972.
5. Guthrie, J. T., M. Seifert, N. Burnham, and R. Kaplan. "The Maze Technique to Assess, Monitor Reading Comprehension." *The Reading Teacher* 28 (November 1974): 161-169.
6. Pikulski, John J., and E. J. Pikulski. "Cloze, Maze, and Teacher Judgment." *The Reading Teacher* 30 (April 1977): 766-770.
7. Ransom, Peggy. "Determining Reading Levels of Elementary School Children by Cloze Testing." in J. A. Figurel, ed. *Forging Ahead in Reading.* Newark, DE: International Reading Association, 1968: 477-482.
8. Smith, Laura, and Constance Weaver. "A Psycholinguistic Look at the Informal Reading Inventory, Part I: Looking at the Quality of Readers' Miscues: A Rationale and An Easy Method." *Reading Horizons* 19 (Fall 1978): 12-22.
9. Weaver, Constance. *Psycholinguistics and Reading: From Process to Practice.* Cambridge, MA: Winthrop Publishers, 1980, Ch. 7.

SUGGESTED READING

Goodman, Kenneth S. "A Linguistic Study of Cues and Miscues in Reading." *Elementary English* 42 (October 1965): 639-643.
Goodman, Kenneth S., ed. *Miscue Analysis: Application to Reading Instruction.* Urbana, IL: ERIC Clearinghouse on Reading and Communication Skills, National Council of Teachers of English, 1973.
Johnson, Marjorie S., and Roy A. Kress. *Informal Reading Inventories.* Newark, DE: International Reading Association, 1965.
May, Frank B., and Susan B. Eliot. *To Help Children Read.* Columbus, OH: Merrill, 1978, Ch. 5.
Pikulski, John J. "A Critical Review: Informal Reading Inventories." *The Reading Teacher* 28 (November 1974): 141-151.
Stauffer, Russell G., Jules C. Abrams, and John J. Pikulski. *Diagnosis, Correction, and Prevention of Reading Disabilities.* New York: Harper & Row, 1978, Ch. 4.

7

Standardized Tests

OBJECTIVES

This chapter will help you to

1. Understand what a standardized test is.
2. Become familiar with the specialized vocabulary of standardized tests.
3. Differentiate among the various kinds of standardized reading and achievement tests.
4. Establish criteria for selecting appropriate tests.
5. Understand their administration, scoring, and interpretation.
6. Be aware of their limitations.

Anyone associated with education today needs to understand standardized tests and to be able to make use of the results. Whether a teacher administers a test or a clinician does it, the teacher must be able to interpret the scores to the best academic advantage of the person taking the test. In order to do this the teacher must have a working knowledge of what constitutes a standardized test, what the scores mean, and how much trust to put in those results.

THE ADVANTAGE OF STANDARDIZED TESTS

Although informal measures often can glean more information than standardized tests, or at least they can be directed more exactly to the things the examiner wants to know, there still is an important place for standardized tests in the classroom and clinic. Standardized tests by their very nature are more objective and therefore can be used to substantiate or negate the more subjective results of informal measures. They also measure an individual's functioning against a wider population than is usually the case with informal procedures. Another advantage of standardized tests is that they can provide the classroom teacher with immediate information on the comparative functioning of all of his or her students. In this way, reading instruction can be geared to the students' approximate reading levels even before the teacher has identified each of their specific strengths and weaknesses.

A DESCRIPTION OF STANDARDIZED TESTS

A definition of "standardize" is to cause to be without variations or irregularities, and this is the basic principle underlying standardized tests. Authors of these tests choose the skills or qualities they want to measure, decide on the means by which they can measure them, try out those items on many people, assess the adequacy of the items, change them where needed, and then establish a hierarchy for the results. They use various methods to "prove" that their instruments measure what they are supposed to measure and that they do it consistently.

A standardized test has a fixed set of test items, specific directions for administering and scoring, and has been given to representative groups of individuals for the purpose of establishing norms. These "norms" are typical or average scores made by the groups of individuals at various age and/or grade levels. An individual's score is compared to the normative group most nearly like him in age or grade or some other quality. This is called a "norm-referenced" scale. Some standardized tests provide "criterion-referenced" data; the degree of mastery an individual portrays on a skill. A third method of interpreting test scores combines these two: joint norm-referenced, criterion-referenced interpretations which are said to predict relative mastery at different levels of difficulty. An example for this last method can be found in the Woodcock Reading Mastery Tests. (17) Thus, norm-reference compares a person to others, criterion-reference shows a person's performance relative to mastery of the skill, and the joint interpretation describes the person's achievement level compared to others on that same skill.

Some Useful Definitions

There is no need, in this book, to provide a treatise on test construction and the statistical procedures required for producing test scores, but there are some terms that you should be able to recognize in order to understand the test results of your students.

Raw Score. The number of points an examinee accumulates on a test is his raw score. This number must be converted into a score that can be used for comparison. A number such as 72 or 53,823 has no meaning until you can answer the question, compared to what?

Derived Score. Converted from the raw score, a derived score indicates a person's relative position compared to the normative group or the standards of mastery decided on by the testmaker. Derived scores may be expressed in several ways.

1. Standard scores are arbitrary numbers chosen to represent the location of an examinee's raw score in relation to the mean or average of the norm group scores.
2. Percentiles indicate an examinee's relative position in a group in terms of the percentage of people who score below him or her. For instance, if a person's score is at the 74th percentile this means that the examinee did as well as, or better than, 74 per cent of the people in the normative group.
3. Stanine is a portmanteau word meaning <u>sta</u>ndard score of <u>nine</u>. It is a simple, nine point scale of standard scores, with values

from 1 up to 9, with a midpoint of 5, which represents the mean.

4. Sten is a normalized <u>st</u>andard score with <u>ten</u> units. It is similar to stanine except that the mean appears between the fifth and sixth units.

5. There are also z-scores, T-scores, and many others, which you can read about in any number of books on testing. (Also, see Figure 7-1.)

Standard Deviation. This indicates the variability of test scores. If, on a 200-item test, the normative group's scores range between 90 and 110, the standard deviation is much smaller than if their scores range between 15 and 185. The use of standard deviation provides the means for attaching scores to the normal curve and thereby making it possible to understand the results. A rough, inexact description of standard deviation might be to call it the average amount of deviation from the mean. Standard deviation is usually represented by the symbol σ (sigma) and, as you can see in Figure 7-1, it ranges from -4 σ at the low extreme, through zero at the mean, and on up to $+4$ σ at the other end.

Standard Error. This is the range of probable error that would occur during repeated testing. For instance, if a piece of typewriter paper is measured repeatedly, the results will show some minor variations. The average of these results is taken as the true measurement, but with a statistically computed band of probable error surrounding it. This is done because the repeated measurements were only a *sample* of the infinite number of times the paper could be measured. If the standard error is calculated at 3 for a particular test, then it is assumed that the true score of an individual will be within 3 points above and 3 points below the obtained score. For example, Grace receives a score of 80 on a test whose standard error is 5. Thus it is assumed that her true score would fall somewhere between 75 and 85.

Normal Curve. This is the picture of the expected (idealized) distribution of scores when a large number of people are tested. The greatest number of people will have scores at the mean, and there will be an equal number of scores above and below the mean. 68.26 per cent of the group will be in the average range of scores, from 1 standard deviation below the mean to 1 standard deviation above the mean. The percentage of scores drops sharply beyond each of these points.

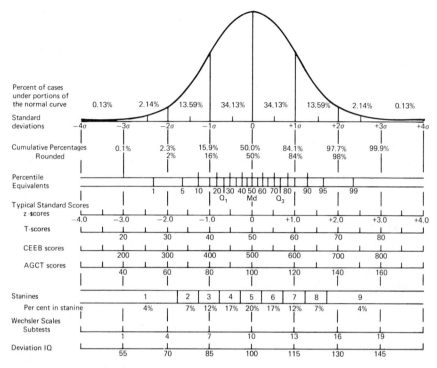

Figure 7-1. Normal curve.

EXERCISES

7.1. Billy Dee's height was measured at 4 feet, 8 inches, which compared to the average child his age gave him a T-score of 60. Using Figure 7-1 as an aid, answer these questions.

  a. What is his raw score in inches?
  b. What is his z-score?
  c. What is his percentile?
  d. What is his standard deviation?
  e. What is his stanine?

7.2. Is Billy Dee taller or shorter than the average child his age?

7.3. By what percentage is Billy Dee taller or shorter than the average?

Reliability. This is a measure of the consistency of scores obtained by the same individual on different days, or on different forms of the same test, or on different parts of the same test. It is necessary that a test be reliable so that the examiner can have confidence in the results. A reliability of 1.00 would be perfect consistency, and so coefficients in the .70s, .80s and .90s are considered adequate.

Validity. This is the extent to which the test measures what it says it measures. There are different types of validity. Content validity measures whether the test items are similar to the behaviors found in the student's classroom. Construct validity determines the adequacy of the administration, scoring, and interpretation of the results. Concurrent validity addresses itself to how closely the test results agree with other tests which purport to measure the same skills. The degree of validity of a test is expressed in per cents, as is reliability. What is a good validity coefficient? Cronbach (5, p. 116) says, "The only sensible answer is 'the best you can get,' since any positive number means it is that much better than chance." However, a coefficient of .80 or better is necessary in order to have confidence that we are measuring what we want to measure.

TYPES OF STANDARDIZED TESTS

By now there are standardized tests to measure the variations in behavior of almost anything under the sun, in spite of the fact that many people object to their use on moral or ethical grounds. It is not our prerogative to editorialize on the matter but merely to report on the types of tests that are most often used in assessing reading performance.

The standardized tests we are concerned with in this book include assessments of physical, cognitive, environmental and emotional factors affecting a person's reading performance. In this chapter achievement tests are discussed, and Chapters 9, 10, and 11 will deal with the instruments for assessing other aspects than reading itself.

CRITERIA FOR SELECTING TESTS

Although many school systems have a particular battery of tests available to teachers and specialists, there are times when they can make their own choices. In order to make a decision on what test to buy the teacher or clinician should consider such questions as the following.

1. Does the test measure the skills which the examiner considers important?

2. Does it have enough age and/or grade levels or a broad enough scope so that all the students in a particular classroom will be measured?
3. Does it have more than one form so that student growth can be measured?
4. Are the directions for administering clear, easy, and definite?
5. Can it be scored with a minimum of error?
6. Is it reliable?
7. Is it valid?
8. Are norms based on a population comparable to the group being measured?
9. Is it up-to-date in its items and in concert with any new developments in the field?

CRITERIA FOR SELECTING READING TESTS

In addition to all of the above questions, reading people are faced with many more considerations when choosing reading tests.

1. What type of reading tests should be used? There are *survey* tests which give a single score or just a few scores such as sight words, reading comprehension, and reading rate. There also are *analytical* tests which categorize reading ability into five or six or even forty separate skills. These are often called diagnostic tests although it is the examiner who makes the diagnosis from the assessments provided by the test results.
2. What is the method of administration? Is the test given individually or to groups? Must it be read to the students or do they read it to themselves?
3. What is the test population, i.e., what age or grade levels does it include? Reading tests are generally constructed for certain segments of school populations, such as primary grades, elementary, middle school, and so on. Some tests, such as the SRA Achievement Series (16), or the Woodcock Reading Mastery Scales (17), or the California Tests (4) include levels all the way from kindergarten through high school.
4. What means of reference are provided? Does the test measure students' scores against a normative population or against a standard of performance on a reading skill?
5. What kind of answers must the student provide? Does he merely

point to his response, must he choose among several alternatives, or does he generate an answer in his own words?

These are only some of the questions that must be answered by a person choosing a standardized reading test. A valuable source of information about all of these considerations and many more is Oscar Buros' *Reading Tests and Reviews II* (3).

STANDARDIZED READING TESTS

Each year new reading tests are devised, and it is difficult to remain current on the subject. Any discussion of specific tests or lists of test names must be viewed with this limitation in mind. However, describing certain tests can be helpful since many of their aspects can be generalized to form opinions on the type of test a person might choose. The tests that are described in this chapter were chosen as examples only and do not necessarily imply endorsement by the authors.

Survey Tests

Survey tests, which yield only a few scores, are intended primarily for placing students in the appropriate grade level books. Some survey tests must be administered individually, while others may be given to groups of students. We will describe briefly two quite different survey reading tests; the Wide Range Achievement Test (11) and the Gates-MacGinitie Reading Tests (9). Both of these tests include levels from preschool through 12th grade.

Wide Range Achievement Test, Fourth Edition (11). This test battery has three subtests: Reading, Spelling, and Arithmetic. We are concerned here with the Reading subtest. It must be administered individually, and it has two levels. Level I is used for children from 5 years to 11 years, 11 months old. Level II is for ages 12 to adult. There is only one form for each level. The reading subtest consists of the following.

1. Naming the thirteen letters of the alphabet printed on the record booklet.
2. Matching ten letters of the alphabet with another row of letters immediately below it.
3. Correctly writing at least two letters of the student's name.

4. Reading aloud lines of words which progress from very simple to very difficult. For example, the first word on Level I is "cat" and the last word in Level II is "synecdoche." The student receives credit for each correct pronunciation.

For either level, tasks one, two, and three are administered only if there was a mistake in pronouncing any of the words in the first line. If only task four is given the individual receives credit for the first three tasks.

Scoring is simply a matter of counting correct responses and assumed credit. The grade norms for each total score are printed right on the record book page. Standard scores and percentiles may be found in the manual.

This test, familiarly called the "Wrat" is quite popular with school psychologists and diagnosticians from fields other than reading. The authors of the test contend that word naming is a legitimate test of reading since there is a high correlation between comprehension and word recognition.

The *Gates-MacGinitie Reading Tests, Second Edition* (9). There are seven levels of this test, covering students from grade one through grade twelve, and there are at least two forms for each level. It is group administered and provides scores for vocabulary, comprehension and total reading.

The reading comprehension section of the test consists of paragraphs of ascending difficulty which the student reads, one at a time, and then answers questions concerning each.

The Gates MacGinitie test has many advantages. Its up-to-date material, the comparative lack of cultural bias, and the ease of administration and scoring, all make for a valuable screening device for teachers.

Some survey tests offer a wider variety of scores than the foregoing without becoming as detailed as the analytical tests. These are used when a teacher wants to assess a student's reading grade placement and also wants a rating of just a few of his reading skills.

Some tests which belong to this category are the American School Achievement Tests: Reading (1), the Durrell-Sullivan Reading Capacity and Achievement Tests (8), and the McGrath Test of Reading Skills, Second Edition (12).

The *American School Achievement Tests: Reading* (1) provides scores for sentence meaning, word meaning, paragraph meaning, and a total reading score. Reading levels include grades one to nine.

The *Durrell-Sullivan Reading Capacity and Achievement Tests* (8), for grades one to nine, measures comprehension of both isolated words and paragraphs. The Capacity portion of the test measures comprehension of spoken language and the Achievement portion measures the student's understanding of what he reads.

The *McGrath Test of Reading Skills* (12) evaluates oral word recognition, oral reading, silent reading vocabulary, and rate of oral reading.

Analytical Tests

These tests offer evaluation of a great variety of skills and sub-skills in the area of reading. The problem for the teacher or clinician here is to match a test with his or her own philosophy of what constitutes the reading skills, or at least what aspects of the reading process he or she plans to incorporate into the student's reading program. Analytical tests can be individually or group administered, and they yield five or more separate scores. The Gates-McKillop Reading Tests (10), for instance, provide twenty-eight scores for each student, and the Analysis of Learning Potential (2) has thirty-nine subtests.

One widely used group test is the Stanford Achievement Test which yields six scores: Vocabulary, Reading Comprehension, Word Study Skills, Spelling, Listening Comprehension, and Total Reading.

Analytical tests also can be quite different in their manner of assessment. We will describe two individually administered tests which illustrate this: the Durrell Analysis of Reading Difficulty (7) and the Woodcock Reading Mastery Tests (17).

Durrell Analysis of Reading Difficulty, New Edition, 1980 (7). Grades: nonreader to sixth grade. This venerable test which was published originally in 1937 has been updated and enlarged, but it has kept the many features which have made it so popular for all these years. There are thirteen subtests, but not all are given to any one student. There are eight graded paragraphs for oral reading and the student must read at least three of them. The examiner times the reading of each one and marks any errors he or she makes. The examiner then asks the student questions about its content. Graded silent reading paragraphs come next, which also must be timed. The student then is asked to recall everything he or she can about the story, and is prompted with questions about any items he or she neglected to mention. The third set of paragraphs is for the teacher to read to the student and then ask questions about their content. The teacher reads until the student has missed more than one question in a selection. All three sets of paragraphs plus a supplementary set are in a separate notebook.

Test 4 is a word recognition and word analysis test that requires the use of a handheld, cardboard tachistoscope. Following this are tests on visual memory of words and hearing sounds in words. Test 8 is for assessing the nonreading student's ability to remember words that are taught to him. The next three tests are Phonic Spelling of Words, a spelling test, and a handwriting test.

The final two tests are new with the 1980 edition. The first enables the teacher to compare a student's listening vocabulary with his reading vocabulary. The last test is a prereading phonics inventory.

There are grade norms and checklists for most of the subtests. The checklists are considered to be one of the most helpful aspects of this test battery. Used appropriately they can provide a comprehensive analysis of the student's reading behaviors.

Woodcock Reading Mastery Tests (17). Kindergarten through twelfth grade. There are two forms of the test and five subtests, plus total test scores. One of the best features of this test is the ease of administration. Rather than the examiner having to juggle manual, record form, booklets of test items, tachistoscopes, and so on, the Woodcock requires only the record form and an easel-type test notebook. This sturdy notebook is propped up in tent form with the test items on the student's side, and on the examiner's side are exact directions for starting points, what to say to the subject, and the answers to all test items. This easel-type notebook also has the advantage of screening the response form from the student. Of course, after the test is administered, the clinician also uses the manual to convert raw scores into grade, age, percentile and standard scores. A Mastery Scale that predicts relative success of the student at different levels of difficulty, separate norms for boys and girls, and adjusted norms for socioeconomic status are also provided.

For three of the subtests it is only necessary to administer those items which are across the critical range for the subject. The first subtest, Letter Identification, is given only to students whose estimated reading level is below sixth grade. They are asked to identify letters of the alphabet that are in upper or lower case, and in various printed forms. The Word Identification subtest has one hundred and fifty words of graduated level of difficulty which the subject is to pronounce. The Word Attack test has fifty real or artificial "words" for the subject to pronounce. Its purpose is to ascertain which phonic and syllabication rules the subject employs.

Word Comprehension contains seventy analogies, with one of the four elements left blank. For instance, Item fifty-nine on Form B is "Electricity (is to) generator, (as) petroleum (is to) _____." This manner of testing vocabulary is more far reaching than usual since the definition of the missing word must fit a narrow framework, and all three of the words given must be identified in order to evoke the fourth. All four sample items must be given because it is vital that the student understand the mechanics of the test. Tense and plurality variations are acceptable, but not different parts of speech.

Paragraph Comprehension has eighty-five sentences or short passages, each of which contains a blank in place of a significant word. This variation of the Cloze Procedure is considered to be a highly effective and efficient means of ascertaining a person's ability to comprehend what he reads. He must understand the whole passage before he can produce the missing word.

Raw scores on these subtests produce grade levels that are somewhat analogous to the informal reading inventory's Independent, Instructional, and Frustration levels. For this test they are called Easy Reading Level, Reading Grade Score, and Failure Reading Level.

Another popular individually administered test is the Diagnostic Reading Scales (14). The test battery comprises three word recognition lists, twenty-two reading passages, and six supplementary phonics tests.

TEST ADMINISTRATION

When administering any standardized test, procedures must be followed exactly in order to make the results meet the standards set up in the normative process. Test scores are not to be relied on absolutely, even under the best of circumstances; the standard error of measurement must always be taken into account. Also, any degree of deviation from the instructions given with the test will compound the expected error and, in fact, will totally invalidate the results.

There are some rules of administration which are common to almost all standardized tests.

1. The examination room should be quiet, comfortable, and un-adorned with extraneous appurtenances.
2. Chairs and desk or table should be adequate to the tasks, and they should be comfortable.
3. All materials should be at hand but out of sight until needed.
4. The examinee should be in optimal condition; not overly tired, hungry, or ill. Also, the test should not be scheduled at a time when a favorite activity of his or hers is going on.
5. The tester should

a. Wear unobtrusive clothing with no distracting items such as jangling jewelry or hairpieces that slide down one's forehead.
b. Speak clearly.
c. Be encouraging, but objective.
d. Follow the manual exactly in its instruction of what to say.
e. Eliminate habitual body language and stock phrases which can be interpreted as approval or disapproval of an answer. Over the many years of observing clinicians, it has become obvious that we all fall into patterns of behavior. Such things as saying "good" when the answer is correct and "hmm" when it is not are habits that are difficult to recognize in ourselves but are easily deduced by the examinee.

TEST SCORING

Some tests are machine scored, others have plastic overlays so they may be scored easily, and still others must be hand scored by the examiner. In any case, accuracy is obviously a vital requirement. The scorer must follow instructions exactly and must do all in his or her power to verify the results. The scorer must also fight any inclination to "read into" answers any more or less than is actually written or stated. If, for example, on the question, "Where does the sun set?" a child persists in saying "over there, behind the barn," when you are sure the child knows it sets in the west, you must score him wrong without any prompting for the correct answer.

PRACTICE IN ADMINISTERING AND SCORING A STANDARDIZED TEST

As a model for the appropriate procedure to use in administering and scoring a standardized test, we will describe in detail the use of the old form of the Peabody Picture Vocabulary Test (6). This test has been revised in 1981 and now is made up of two forms, L and M (6). Since disclosing test items could make norms meaningless in future testing we present here, with the publisher's permission, the outdated version. Using it as a model for standardized testing procedures, we will go into greater detail on its description than we have with other tests. The PPVT, as it was commonly called, was chosen because it investigates only one aspect of communication skills and is therefore less complicated than many other tests. Another reason for choosing it is because it is used extensively by teachers and clinicians and should therefore be part of the repertoire of most diagnosticians.

Despite the importance of vocabulary growth to learning to read there are very few standardized tests for vocabulary alone. In order to assess vocabulary one generally must use subtests from diagnostic reading tests or intelligence tests.

PEABODY PICTURE VOCABULARY TEST (6)

The test consists of an easel-type test booklet with one hundred and fifty plates containing four pictures on each plate, a record booklet, and an examiner's manual.

Purpose

To provide an estimate of a subject's verbal intelligence by sampling his receptive (listening) vocabulary.

General Rules of Administration

1. May be used with subjects from 2 years, 6 months to 18 years.
2. May be administered by anyone who has familiarized himself with the instrument.
3. Testing atmosphere should be quiet, comfortable, and free from interruption. Examiner should be pleasant, business-like, and ready with praise for effort, never for accuracy.
4. Either or both of the two forms, A or B, may be used.
5. Administration is untimed, and takes 10 or 15 minutes for each subject.
6. The stimulus word must be stated verbatim.
7. Articles ("a" "an" "the") are not to be used.
8. Since there is no penalty for guessing, the subject should be urged to try to respond to each word.
9. Subject's final response is the one to be scored.
10. Subject may point to the picture of his choice or he may give the number of the picture.

Specific Rules of Administration and Scoring

1. *Figuring Age.* There is a place on the front of the individual test record booklet for figuring age. The procedure is to subtract the date of birth from the testing date. Begin by subtracting the days. If you must borrow, take thirty days from the month total. Next, subtract the months and, if necessary, borrow twelve months from the year. For this test, drop the number of days if there are fifteen or fewer and add a month for more than fifteen days.

   Example: Louise was born October 25, 1984, and was tested on March 11, 1992.

	1	214	41	
Date of Testing	1992	3	11	
Date of Birth	1984	10	25	
	year	mo.	day	
Age of Client	7	4	16 = 7 yrs., 5 mos.	

EXERCISE

7.4. Four of Mrs. Hogan's children were brought to the reading specialist, on May 10, 1994, so that an assessment of their vocabulary growth could be made. Figure the chronological age of each child.

Amy was born on January 3, 1982.

   Date of Testing   _____

   Date of Birth   _____

   Chronological Age   _____

   C.A. to use for PPVT _____

Brent was born on February 27, 1984.

   Date of Testing   _____

   Date of Birth   _____

   Chronological Age   _____

   C.A. to use for PPVT _____

George was born on July 14, 1987.

Date of Testing   _____

Date of Birth   _____

Chronological Age   _____

C.A. to use for PPVT   _____

Jennifer was born on February 19, 1991.

Date of Testing   _____

Date of Birth   _____

Chronological Age   _____

C.A. to use for PPVT   _____

2. *Suggested Starting Points.* Since it is time-consuming to administer any more of a test than necessary, there are suggested starting points for the different age categories which can be found on the record booklet and in the teacher's manual.

3. *Basal and Ceiling.* It is necessary for the subject to attain eight consecutive correct responses in order for the examiner to assume that he will know the meaning of all of the easier words preceding that point. From the starting point, work forward until the subject makes his first error. If he has not made 8 consecutive correct responses prior to his first error, drop back to the starting point and work backward until a basal is reached. If no actual basal is possible (if the subject makes an error in the first eight words of the test), the basal is considered to be #1. An important fact to remember is that the highest point at which the subject gets eight correct responses is considered the basal. It is conceivable that a person could have three or four possible basals. He could have 8 correct responses, miss one or two, get 8 more right in a row, miss another, and finally respond correctly on the next eight items. This highest point is his basal and any errors he made below this point are ignored.

Continue testing until the subject makes six errors in eight consecutive responses. The last item in this series of eight is his ceiling. The very first time he makes six errors in eight consecutive responses is his ceiling, and any correct responses beyond that point are ignored. If no ceiling can be established because the subject always made more than two correct responses in any series of eight, the final item, #150, is considered to be his ceiling.

4. *Recording Responses*. Always write in the test booklet the <u>number</u> of the picture chosen by the subject. If his choice is incorrect, also draw a diagonal line through the geometric figure to the right of that number. Every eighth geometric figure is identical, so that the examiner can tell at a glance when a basal or ceiling is reached.

5. *Scoring*. On the top of page three of the record booklet write the number of the final ceiling item. Count all the errors made between the basal and ceiling. Subtract this number from the ceiling item, and you will have the raw score.

EXERCISE

7.5. Jennifer, age 3 years, 3 months (see Exercise 7.4) gave the following responses to the PPVT test items. First, score these responses by drawing a diagonal line through the geometric figure of any incorrect item. Next, fill in the blanks below.

Jennifer's basal is item number   _____

Her ceiling is item number   _____

Her raw score is   _____

Plate No.	Word	Key	Resp.	Errors*	Plate No.	Word	Key	Resp.	Errors*
1	car	(4)	4	●	18	tying. . . .	(4)	1	✚
2	cow	(3)	3	■	19	fence. . . .	(1)	1	♥
3	baby	(1)	1	▲	20	bat	(2)	2	★
4	girl	(2)	2	✚	21	bee.	(4)	4	◆
5	ball.	(1)	1	♥	22	bush	(3)	3	●
6	block . . .	(3)	3	★	23	pouring . .	(1)	1	■
7	clown . . .	(2)	2	◆	24	sewing. . .	(1)	1	▲
8	key.	(1)	1	●	25	wiener. . .	(4)	4	✚
9	can.	(4)	4	■	26	teacher . .	(2)	2	♥
10	chicken . .	(2)	2	▲	27	building. .	(3)	3	★
11	blowing. .	(4)	4	✚	28	arrow . . .	(3)	3	◆
12	fan	(2)	2	♥	29	kangaroo .	(2)	2	●
13	digging . .	(1)	1	★	30	accident. .	(3)	3	■
14	skirt	(1)	1	◆	31	nest	(3)	3	▲
15	catching. .	(4)	4	●	32	caboose. .	(4)	4	✚
16	drum. . . .	(1)	1	■	33	envelope .	(1)	1	♥
17	leaf.	(3)	3	▲	34	picking . .	(2)	1	★

Plate No.	Word	Key Resp.	Errors*	Plate No.	Word	Key Resp.	Errors*
35	badge . . . (1)	2	◆	56	transportation . . (1)	4	◆
36	goggles . . (3)	3	●	57	counter . . . . . . (1)	1	●
37	peacock . . (2)	2	■	58	ceremony . . . . . (2)	3	■
38	queen . . . (3)	3	▲	59	pod . . . . (3)	3	▲
39	coach . . . (4)	3	✚	60	bronco . . . . . . (4)	4	✚
40	whip . . . . (1)	1	♥	61	directing . . . . . (3)	3	♥
41	net . . . . . (4)	4	★	62	funnel . . . . (4)	2	★
42	freckle . . (4)	4	◆	63	delight . . . . (2)	2	◆
43	eagle . . . . (3)	3	●	64	lecturer . . . . . . (3)	1	●
44	twist . . . . (2)	2	■	65	communication . (2)	2	■
45	shining . . (4)	4	▲	66	archer . . . . (4)	2	▲
46	dial . . . . . (2)	2	✚	67	stadium . . . . . . (1)	2	✚
47	yawning . . (2)	2	♥	68	excavate . . . . . . (1)	1	♥
48	tumble . . (2)	3	★	69	assaulting . . . . . (4)	3	★
49	signal . . . (1)	4	◆	70	stunt . . . . (1)	4	◆
50	capsule . . (1)	2	●	71	meringue . . . . . (1)	4	●
51	submarine (4)	1	■	72	appliance . . . . . (3)	___	■
52	thermos . . (4)	4	▲	73	chemist . . . . . . (4)	___	▲
53	projector . (3)	3	✚	74	arctic . . . . (3)	___	✚
54	group . . . (4)	2	♥	75	destruction . . . . (4)	___	♥
55	tackling . . (3)	3	★				

6. *Conversion of Raw Scores.* There are three types of derived scores which can be converted from the raw score: mental age, intelligence quotient, and percentile equivalent. The conversion tables are in the manual. A fourth type of derived score, grade equivalent, can be obtained by subtracting five years from the mental age.

7. *Other Information.* The value of test results is enhanced appreciably by any relevant information about the subject and his behavior. On page four of the record booklet is a section on Test Behavior and Physical Characteristics and on page one is a section on Language Background. The information gleaned from an analysis of these sections can help the examiner make more comprehensive recommendations for the client.

EXERCISE

7.6. George, age 6 years, 10 months (see Exercise 7.1) had the following test scores on the PPVT.

Raw Score	55
Intelligence Quotient	89
Percentile Score	25
Mental Age	5-11

Additional information included:

Language Background:
   Quality of language: poor for age
   Quantity of speech: taciturn
   Intelligibility of speech: fair

Test Behavior:
   Type of response: subject pointed
   Rapport: sporadic
   Guessing: prone to guess
   Speed of response: fast
   Attention span: distractible
   Need for praise: much needed
   Effort: perfunctory

Physical Characteristics:
   Apparent hearing acuity: good
   Apparent visual acuity: good
   Motor activity: hyperactive
   Sedation: none

Write as many recommendations as you think are appropriate from the above data.

TEST INTERPRETATION

Once the test scores and addendum information are gathered the real work begins. The integration and interpretation of the results are vital steps in the process of helping the individual. For instance, a sixth-grader receives the following scores on a reading test:

	Grade Score
Word Recognition	2.6
Word Meaning	6.5
Paragraph Comprehension	5.2

These scores tend to suggest that the child has an adequate meaning vocabulary but his poor word recognition skills are impeding his reading comprehension. He does have the ability to predict meaning in spite of this handicap. Perhaps also he is skilled in contextual analysis and in using semantic and syntactic clues. The teacher might decide that intensive diagnostic effort in word attack skills is indicated.

EXERCISE
7.7. Jack's scores on the Durrell Analysis of Reading Difficulty (7) are shown here.

	Grade Equivalents
Oral Reading	3.0
Silent Reading	2.7
Flashed Words	2.8
Visual Memory of Words	2.5
Hearing Sounds in Words	3.5 (above norms)
Phonic Spelling	4.0
Spelling	2.3

Assuming that these score differences are significant, what are his special strengths?
What might this tell you about his mode of learning?
What areas need the most improvement?

It is well to remember that standardized tests are not infallible. Children sometimes fail items on tests when they actually possess the ability to perform the task. They also may pass an item through sheer guessing. Tests can have dubious diagnostic value since most subtests are too short for high reliability. Another possible shortcoming occurs when errors are made in administering and scoring them. Standardized tests can be very helpful in assessing an individual's attributes and abilities so long as more is not expected of them than they can deliver. And they should always be interpreted in terms of the child's history and the observations you have made of him or her.

SUMMARY

The use of standardized tests in assessing and analyzing an individual's reading performance has been discussed in this chapter. The description of standardized tests included definitions of terms that are used in their construction and scoring. Practice was given in a detailed examination of a vocabulary test. Some suggestions to aid in choosing appropriate instruments and reminders of their limitations were set forth.

REFERENCES

1. *American School Achievement Tests.* Indianapolis: Bobbs-Merrill, 1955.
2. *Analysis of Learning Potential.* New York: Harcourt Brace Jovanovich, 1970.
3. Buros, Oscar, ed. *Reading Tests and Reviews II.* Highland Park, NJ: The Gryphon Press, 1975.
4. *California Achievement Tests.* Monterey, CA: CTB/McGraw-Hill, 1977.
5. Cronbach, Lee J. *Essentials of Psychological Testing* (Second Edition). New York: Harper & Row, 1968.
6. Dunn, Lloyd M. *Peabody Picture Vocabulary Test.* Circle Pines, MN: American Guidance Service, 1965 & 1981.
7. Durrell, Donald D. *Durrell Analysis of Reading Difficulty, New Edition.* New York: The Psychological Corporation, 1980.
8. Durrell, Donald D., and Helen Blair Sullivan. *Durrell-Sullivan Reading Capacity and Achievement Tests.* New York: Harcourt Brace Jovanovich, 1973.
9. Gates, Arthur I., and Walter H. MacGinitie. *Gates-MacGinitie Reading Tests* (Second Edition). Boston: Houghton Mifflin, 1978.
10. Gates, Arthur I., and Ann S. McKillop. *Gates McKillop Reading Tests.* New York: Teachers College Press, 1962.
11. Jastak, J. S., and S. R. Jastak. *Wide Range Achievement Test* (Fourth Edition). Wilmington, DE: Guidance Associates, 1976.
12. McGrath, Joseph E. *McGrath Test of Reading Skills* (Second Edition). Detroit: McGrath Reading Clinic, 1967.
13. "The Normal Curve." Test Service Bulletin #54, January 1956. New York: The Psychological Corporation.
14. Spache, George D. *Diagnostic Reading Scales.* Monterey, CA: CTB/McGraw-Hill, 1963.
15. *Stanford Achievement Test.* New York: Harcourt Brace Jovanovich, 1972.
16. *SRA Achievement Series*, 1978 Edition. Chicago: Science Research Associates.
17. Woodcock, Richard W. *Woodcock Reading Mastery Tests.* Circle Pines, MN: American Guidance Service, 1973.

SUGGESTED READING

Della-Piana, Gabriel M. *Reading Diagnosis and Prescription: An Introduction.* New York: Holt, Rinehart and Winston, 1968, Appendix A.

Ekwall, Eldon E. *Diagnosis and Remediation of the Disabled Reader.* Boston: Allyn and Bacon, 1976, Ch. 16.

Harris, Larry A., and Carl B. Smith, *Reading Instruction Through Diagnostic Teaching.* New York: Holt, Rinehart and Winston, 1972, Ch. 6.

Otto, Wayne, Charles W. Peters, and Nathanial Peters. *Reading Problems: A Multidisciplinary Perspective.* Reading, PA: Addison-Wesley, 1977, Ch. 9.

Zintz, Miles V. *Corrective Reading* (Third Edition). Dubuque, IA: Wm. C. Brown Company, 1977, Ch. 5.

8

Observation and Interview

OBJECTIVES

This chapter will help you to

1. Develop skill in analytical observation.
2. Develop skill in interviewing.

Observation and interviews are two means of gathering information about a student that appear on the surface to be about as fruitful as fortune telling and, indeed, are only as reliable as the individual who is using them. The teacher and reading specialist, however, can discover much about students by becoming proficient in the use of these techniques. To observe analytically and to interview objectively, one must know what to look for and must possess the experiential background and knowledge to understand the implications of the results. This chapter has been written to serve as a guide to these two techniques. First, it is a guide to observing the individuals in a variety of situations for the purpose of learning more about them and their reading behavior. The second half of the chapter outlines the purposes of the interview and the guidelines for making it successful. The steps to follow and the questions to ask are also included.

The information to be gleaned by observation and interviewing are more important now than ever before, as it has become apparent that sociocultural factors and adaptive behavior influence learning as much as a person's level of intelligence does. Public Law 94-142 (2) includes the statement that placement procedures are to "draw upon information from a variety of sources, including aptitude and achievement tests, teacher recommendations, physical condition, social or cultural background, and adaptive behavior." Observation and interviews are the most available means of getting at these last two factors.

OBSERVATION: A MEANS OF STUDYING THE INDIVIDUAL

Teachers and clinicians have an opportunity to learn more about a student by using their powers of observation than any formal test can reveal. Noting the student's reading behaviors and becoming aware of his or her interests and attitudes will make subsequent teaching much more relevant for that individual.

Some Basic Suggestions

The accuracy of observations can be increased if the observer follows certain precautions.

1. Make a written notation immediately of what has been seen and heard.

2. Differentiate carefully between the facts observed and inferences that can logically be drawn from these facts. For example, if a teacher notices that Abigail is holding her book very close to her face, she may suspect that Abigail is nearsighted. The position of Abigail's book is a fact. Any conclusion drawn from that fact is an inference until such time as it is proved or disproved. Also, everything that is unprovable is an inference. "Mary is pretty" is an inference, even if she wins a beauty contest.

3. Be aware of sampling errors. Conditions and situations change from day to day, and consequently the observer must be certain that he has an adequate sampling of the individual's total behavior. This can be accomplished by observing specific behavior on many occasions. In the example of Abigail, above, she might be holding her book very close to her face because she is surreptitiously eating a piece of candy. In order to avoid sampling errors the teacher should pay attention to all of the child's reading behaviors and should observe his or her reading on many occasions.

4. Minimize observer errors. Keep in mind that the reliability and validity of observed facts are to a considerable degree dependent on the observer's awareness of his or her own prejudices, preconceptions, and emotional bias. A typical example of this is when a teacher labels a rowdy child as hyperactive.

5. Be explicit and do not infer too much. Adhere to the facts. Make judgments only when you have enough information to be sure of your opinions.

EXERCISE

8.1. Read each sentence given below. If the sentence is a statement of fact, write the word *fact* on the line preceding the sentence number. If it is an inference, write the word *inference*. Remember that an inference may or may not be true; only subsequent proof can establish it as fact.

_____ 1. Terry is emotionally immature.

_____ 2. Judy says she likes ice cream.

_____ 3. Judy's score on a standardized reading test is 49.

_____ 4. Judy likes to read.

_____ 5. Judy is an intelligent child.

_____ 6. Terry is experiencing difficulty in learning to read because of immaturity.

_____ 7. Judy mispronounced three words while reading aloud today.

_____ 8. Mary has a large, meaningful vocabulary.

_____ 9. Mary's parents are happily married.

_____ 10. Judy's parents are divorced.

_____ 11. Jim has a short attention span.

_____ 12. Jim says he cannot see the writing on the chalk-board.

_____ 13. John missed twenty days of school last year.

_____ 14. John is self-confident.

_____ 15. Mary displays excessive anxiety.

Observation of Reading Performance

The classroom teacher and the reading diagnostician have an opportunity to observe an individual's reading behavior during the administration of informal inventories, standardized reading tests, and during group or individual instruction in the classroom. The following questions suggest factors to investigate through observation.

General Reading Behavior

1. Does the individual show evidence of insecurity in reading situations?
2. Does the pitch of his voice during oral reading suggest tension?
3. Does the student lose his place easily?
4. Does he use a finger or pointer to keep his place?
5. Does he move his lips or vocalize when reading silently?
6. Does the student appear easily distracted?
7. Does the student become discouraged when the material is hard?
8. Does poor attention necessitate rereading?

Oral and Silent Reading

1. Does the student try to make sense of written material?
2. Does the student respond to grammatical clues?
3. What word attack skills is he or she able to use effectively?
4. Does she mispronounce words when she reads orally?
5. Does the student read word by word?
6. Is he able to read phrases adequately?
7. Does she have an adequate sight vocabulary?

8. Does the student make many repetitions?
9. Does she read to accomplish a purpose?
10. Does he adjust his rate of reading to his purpose and to the nature of the material?
11. Can the student read to answer questions?
12. Can she identify main ideas?
13. Does he read effectively for detail?
14. Can the student follow printed directions?
15. Can she make effective use of the dictionary?
16. Can the student read critically?
17. Can he recall what he has read?

Observation of Reading Interests and Attitudes

Important information concerning an individual's reading interests and attitudes can be gleaned through observation. The following questions are suggestive of factors to observe.

1. What attitudes does the individual display toward reading?
2. To what extent does he become involved in reading activities?
3. Does the student show evidence of reading at home?
4. What are his or her hobbies?
5. What does the student enjoy doing?
6. What does she like to talk about?
7. How does he spend his leisure or free time?
8. Does the student like books?
9. Does he like to read orally?
10. Does she want to learn to read?

Other Observation Possibilities

Accurate observation by a perceptive teacher or clinician can produce information that goes beyond reading behaviors and attitudes and interests. Environmental, emotional, cognitive, and physical factors which might be affecting reading performance can be inferred by careful observation. Suggestions for ways to look for these potential problems will be discussed in the following three chapters.

INTERVIEW: ANOTHER MEANS OF
STUDYING THE INDIVIDUAL

One of the most neglected areas in the subject of assessing the problems of people with reading difficulties is interviewing techniques. There is a feeling that you must be born with the insight and charm of an interviewer rather than being able to acquire the necessary skills. This is not usually true. Most people who have a real desire to help a disabled reader can learn to be an effective gatherer of personal information. The sine qua non of a successful interview is a real interest in the solution to the problem, and the capacity to be tactful, yet probing, in the pursuit of the information.

The use of interviews is more the prerogative of the specialist than the teacher in the classroom although even for the latter there is much to be gained during parent-teacher conferences. The teacher can get, with a few well-placed questions, a feeling for the "life space" of a student. A child is the product of the home environment, so the family structure and its interests and attitudes can be quite revealing in the assessment of that child.

The diagnostic interview is far more extensive than the one a teacher might conduct and is therefore given the greater emphasis in this chapter.

The Diagnostic Interview

Most diagnostic interviews are conducted in an informal way, often following a list of preformed questions, or at least an outline of the general subjects that should be covered. There are, however, a few standardized interview instruments which elicit age levels of maturity and adaptive behavior. One of these, the Vineland Social Maturity Scale (1) is somewhat out of date (1965), but still can be useful as a guide to expected behavior at the various age levels. Another instrument is the Parent Interview segment of the SOMPA, the System of Multicultural Pluralistic Assessment (4), which came out in 1977. It has an exhaustive set of questions which takes up to two hours to administer. Both of these formalized interview tools can be helpful, at least until the interviewer becomes more comfortable in the role. The informal interview, on the other hand, has the advantage of being more specifically aimed at the particular client in question.

Purpose

In general, the purpose of the diagnostic interview is to become acquainted with the client's most significant others; to understand as much as possible what their goals are, how they act in ordinary everyday life, and to get a feeling for the milieu in which the client lives.

The interviewer also wants to get background information on possible causes of the difficulty and any typical household routines that might affect the client's learning behavior. Another important area to explore is what the parent and client themselves think is the cause of the difficulty.

Guidelines to Interviewing

There are some general rules to follow when interviewing.

1. The physical setting should be as comfortable as possible and should be completely out of earshot of any unauthorized people.
2. Establish at the outset that the purpose of the interview is solely to help the client.
3. Notetaking should be kept to a minimum.
4. A tape recorder should be used only if the interviewee agrees to its use, and even then it should be as unobtrusive as possible.
5. Always keep the purpose of the interview in mind, no matter how entrancing some byways may appear to be.
6. Follow the cues given by the interviewee.
7. Do not be judgmental under any circumstances. Avoid questions that imply disapproval such as, "Do you punish your child when he misbehaves?" It is better to say, "When your child does something you don't want him to, how do you handle it?"
8. Be tactful.
9. Use appropriate language; neither too erudite nor too informal.
10. Keep control, even with excessive talkers.
11. Encourage taciturn people. Avoid questions that require simply a yes or no answer.
12. Do not be afraid of silences. They often elicit important information.
13. Constantly be aware of nonverbal communication.
14. When in doubt, clarify what was said to insure against talking at cross-purposes.

15. Assuage parental anxiety whenever it manifests itself.
16. Maintain rapport by refraining from hostility or from a supercilious attitude, and never appear impertinent.
17. Assure confidentiality by words, deeds, and implication.

Questioning the Parents

The first questions should be quite nonthreatening, and should establish the rapport necessary for the rest of the interview. Nondirective techniques can often elicit more pertinent information than the direct approach. The interviewer might say, "We need to find out everything we can about your child so that we can help him learn to read better. For instance, what have you observed about your child?" Open-ended questions such as this can lead in many different directions depending on the most immediate concerns of the parents. The general areas to be explored are as follows.

1. The physical history including gestation, birth, rate of growth, traumas, physical dexterity, and so on.
2. Cognitive factors, such as an estimation of the client's rate of intellectual growth, his strengths and weaknesses, and degree of parental stimulation.
3. Environmental considerations, including parents' employment, family size and hierarchy, type of neighborhood or community they live in, language spoken in the home, parental attitude toward schooling in general and reading in particular.
4. Emotional factors, such as maturity, stability, degree of self-confidence, and peer relationships.

Some Specific Questions for Parents. Begin each segment with a generalized, open-ended question. Specific questions might go something like the following. This list is not intended to be comprehensive nor does it indicate the many divergent pathways that a dynamic interview should take.

- Tell me about your family.
  Listen carefully to the response and, only when necessary, fill in the gaps by asking,

  1. How many sisters and brothers does your child have?
  2. Do they all live at home? Who else lives in the house?
  3. Do you live in the city or country?

4. Has your family always lived there, or have you moved frequently?
5. Whom does your child usually play with? What is his favorite entertainment?
6. How well does he get along with other children and with adults?
7. Do you both work? What are your jobs?
8. Tell me about any daily chores he has.
9. There are differences of opinion about allowances for children. Does he get an allowance? If so, how does he spend the money?
10. If I asked him or her which of your children was your favorite, what do you think he or she would say?

- Now tell me something about your child's birth and early development. How was your health during pregnancy? Was delivery easy?

    1. How has his health been? Have there been any physical problems?
    2. When did he or she learn to walk?
    3. When did he or she learn to talk?

- How old was he when he began school?

    1. How did the child react to going to school?
    2. What did the teachers and report cards tell you about his school work? Was he held back in any grade?
    3. What was his or her reaction to learning to read?
    4. What kinds of things do you like to read?
    5. Did you or someone else at home ever read to your child?

- What do you think caused his or her reading problem?

These are merely guideline questions, and they should be asked in as sympathetic a manner as possible. They are the fairly standard questions that need to be answered, but the successful interviewer knows equally well that sometimes she or he should abandon the guidelines and follow wherever the questions and answers lead. This is the time to listen with what Theodor Reik (3) calls the "third ear." This is the time when a routine question can produce an answer that veers sharply from the expected. When an interviewer asks, "When did Jill begin to talk?" and the answer is, "When she was four years old," this is no time to go on to the next question on the list, but rather to find out why speech was delayed so long. Or, if the mother hesitates a long, long time before answering the question that asks if Steve likes school, there might be a wealth of information behind that hesitation.

EXERCISE
8.2. Below are some inappropriate questions. Why are they inappropriate and how can the questions be restated so that they are more acceptable?

1. Are you on welfare?

2. Was Frankie sickly as a baby?

3. Do you let your children stay up late at night?

Questioning the Teacher

An interview with the teacher should elicit information on the client's academic history, his degree of social interaction in classroom and playground, motivational factors, and his interests and attitudes.

Usually it is easier to conduct an objective interview with the teacher than the parents since there is less emotional involvement. However, interviewers should beware of implying that the teacher's methods or behavior may have contributed to the child's problem.

Some Specific Questions for Teacher

1. Tell me about your reading program. Do you use a basal series? Which one?
2. How is your room set up? Do you have three reading groups? Do you use learning centers?
3. What happens during the reading period? How long is it each day?
4. How long have you known this child?
5. What is he or she like in school? How would you characterize him or her?
6. Does he have friends? How well do the other children like him?
7. How well is she reading?
8. What reading group is this child in?
9. In your judgment what are his reading strengths and weaknesses?
10. What do you think caused the child's difficulty?

11. Does this child see a reading teacher? When? For how long? What does the teacher work on with him?
12. How well is he or she doing in other subjects?
13. Do his parents attend conferences? What do you think is their attitude toward school?
14. In your opinion what effect does the home environment have on the child?

EXERCISES

8.3. Why should you ask what reading program is used in the classroom?

8.4. What other questions do you think should be asked?

Questioning the Client

The person most intimately involved in the diagnostic process is the client himself, and it is interesting to note how often his perceptions are at variance with those of his teacher and even of his parents. We had a client once who blurted out during an interview that he was a "retard" and couldn't learn. He explained that one day when he was in first grade he had been sent to his room without supper for some infraction of the family rules. When he crept downstairs to forage for something to eat, he heard his father say, "Matt takes after your family—they're all retarded." The parents had had no idea why he had changed from a curious, excited learner into a behavior problem.

Some Specific Questions for the Client. Obviously the age of the client dictates the language and even the content of the questions, but some of the essential topics to cover are contained in the following.

1. What is your favorite thing to do after school?
2. Who is your best friend? Why do you like him or her?
3. Which of your brothers and sisters do you like best? Why?
4. If you had a problem, would you ask your mother or your father to help you solve it?
5. What chores do you have to do at home? How do you feel about them?
6. What happens when you do something your parents don't like?
7. Who was your favorite teacher? Why?
8. What do you think of school?
9. What is your favorite subject? Your least favorite?
10. What happens during the reading period in your room?

11. Are there any parts of the reading lessons that you like? What are the hardest parts?
12. Why do you think you are having trouble with reading?

These questions, and those for parents and teachers, are incomplete and sometimes irrelevant. To dredge up an old cliche, circumstances alter cases and the circumstances of each case should dictate the pattern of the questions as well as the questions themselves.

SUMMARY

The world is made up of unique individuals who can not be forced completely into formal, preset molds. Tests are necessarily limited by their need to be applicable to a wide portion of humanity, and their use leaves many, if not most, aspects of a person unidentified. This chapter has presented two ways that a teacher or clinician can capture more of the real essence of a person; observation and interviewing. Basic suggestions for accurate observation were given. The particulars to look for in observing reading performance and the student's interests and attitudes were listed. The second half of the chapter offered interviewing techniques and questions to ask parents, teachers, and clients.

REFERENCES

1. Doll, Edgar A. *Vineland Social Maturity Scale.* Circle Pines, MN: American Guidance Service, 1965.
2. Public Law 94-142. *Education for All Handicapped Children Act.* November 29, 1975.
3. Reik, Theodor. *Listening with the Third Ear.* New York: Grove Press, 1948.
4. *System of Multicultural Pluralistic Assessment.* New York: The Psychological Corporation, 1977.

SUGGESTED READING

Benjamin, Alfred. *The Helping Interview* (Second Edition). Boston: Houghton Mifflin, 1974.

Beveridge, W. E. *Problem Solving Interviews* (Second Edition). London: George Allen and Unwin, 1973.

Carter, Homer L. J., and Dorothy J. McGinnis. *Diagnosis and Treatment of the Disabled Reader.* New York: Macmillan, 1970, Ch. 5.

Counseling Interaction Profile Training Tape. Minneapolis: Paul S. Amidon & Associates, 1979.

Ekwall, Eldon E. *Diagnosis and Remediation of the Disabled Reader.* Boston: Allyn and Bacon, 1976, Chs. 7 and 8.

Gilliland, Hap. *A Practical Guide to Remedial Reading.* Columbus, OH: Charles E. Merrill, 1978, Chs. 3 and 5.

Maggs, Margaret Martin. *The Classroom Survival Book.* New York: New Viewpoints, 1980.

Wilson, Robert M. *Diagnostic and Remedial Reading for Classroom and Clinic.* (Third Edition). Columbus, OH: Charles E. Merrill, 1977, p. 225.

9

Physical Factors

OBJECTIVES

This chapter will help you to

1. Understand how vision, hearing, speech, general health, and neurological factors can affect the process of learning to read.
2. Assess formally and informally various physical factors that may interfere with reading achievement.
3. Discover what the teacher can do to mitigate physical factors that may be affecting progress in reading.

Many theories have been set forth to explain why children fail in reading. No single factor has ever been identified which accounts for all reading disorders. Causation is multiple, and maladjustment in reading is usually the result of a sequence of several contributing factors. As early as 1939 Witty and Kopel stated, "Poor reading may well be considered in most instances a retarded or inhibited developmental condition, which reflects the reciprocal interaction, over a period of time, of physical, mental, emotional, social, and educational factors. Hence the problem of diagnosing reading disability necessitates identifying not specific minutiae but rather patterns of growth and development" (37, p. 205). Learning to read is a long and complicated process. There are many opportunities for various factors to inhibit progress in reading. In this chapter attention will be focused on such physical conditions as vision, hearing, speech, general health, and neurological factors.

VISION

There are a number of terms that should be understood by the reading teacher or diagnostician who wishes to identify and evaluate visual disorders.

Accommodation. The act of adjusting the lens of the eye to keep a sharply focused image on the retina.

Amblyopia or suppression. Psychological blocking of vision in one eye. Unless corrected, the less effective eye ceases to function.

Aniseikonia. A condition in which there is a difference in the size and/or shape of the image of each eye. An individual with this condition has difficulty fusing.

Astigmatism. The condition of an eye whose refraction is not the same in all parts. It is a defect of vision caused by irregularly shaped refractive media.

Binocular Coordination. The coordinated action of the two eyes. Loss of binocular coordination may be caused by the presence of a gross visual defect.

Color Discrimination. The ability to discriminate red, green, yellow, and blue colors is important for reading diagnosis because primary schools often demand these discriminations in seatwork.

Convergence. The act or power of turning the eyes inward from their normal position of rest so that the image of a near object will fall on corresponding parts of the retina in each eye.

Far Point Acuity. The clearness of the visual image at a distance of twenty feet or farther.

Fusion. The blending of the right and left eye images into one composite image. Without proper fusion, double vision results.

Hyperopia. Farsightedness. Objects at a distance are seen more plainly than those near at hand.

Lateral Imbalance. A tendency of one or both eyes to deviate inward or outward from their normal position.

Myopia. Nearsightedness. Objects are seen clearly only when close to the eye.

Near Point Acuity. The clearness of the visual image usually measured at a distance of fourteen to eighteen inches.

Ophthalmologist. A physician who diagnoses and treats eye disorders and diseases.

Refractive Errors. Nearsightedness, farsightedness, and astigmatism.

Stereopsis. Depth perception. The ability to judge distances in space is determined in part by maturational factors.

Strabismus. Inability of one eye to attain binocular vision with the other eye because of imbalance of the muscles of the eyeball.

Vertical Imbalance. A tendency of one eye to deviate upward.

Visual Acuity. Keenness of vision.

Many research workers have attempted to determine whether or not visual deficiencies cause reading disability. The results, although conflicting, suggest that there is a slightly greater percentage of visual defects among children with reading disability than among children without reading disability. Since it is reasonable to assume that undetected visual problems can create difficulty in seeing print, individuals who are experiencing severe problems in learning to read should be administered a visual test and those who demonstrate visual problems should be referred to an eye specialist for further examination.

It is generally agreed that two major visual defects can contribute to retardation in reading. Refractive dysfunction is one of these and binocular difficulties is the other. Certain types of refractive errors are more closely associated with reading disorders than other types. The hyperopic child who finds it difficult to focus clearly at near point is more likely to experience difficulty than the child with normal vision or even the nearsighted or myopic child.

Binocular difficulties involve problems in focusing the two eyes accurately and simultaneously on a visual stimulus. Lack of binocular coordination can be caused by muscular imbalance of one or both eyes and causes images to be blurred. In extreme cases, it results in the individual seeing two images of a single object. Fusion difficulties appear to be associated with reading disability. Harris and Sipay (11, p. 298) report that partial or incomplete fusion is more apt to interfere with vision than a complete absence of fusion and that slow fusion may interfere with the rapid and precise focusing needed in reading. Aniseikonia, a condition where ocular images are unequal in size or shape in the two eyes, has also been found to be related to reading difficulties.

Symptoms of Visual Problems

Individuals with visual problems often exhibit symptoms which the alert teacher can observe. These are the following.

1. Watering or inflammation of the eyes.
2. Covering one eye to read.
3. Squinting.
4. Frequent rubbing of the eyes.
5. Distorted facial expression.
6. One eye turning in or out at any time.
7. Complaints of headaches.
8. Complaints of burning or itching of eyes after reading.
9. Complaints of blurring after reading a short time.
10. Holding book too close.
11. Loss of place while reading.
12. Needing a finger or marker to keep place.
13. Head turning as the child reads across page.
14. Omitting words too frequently.
15. Rereading or skipping lines unknowingly.

Instruments for Testing Vision

The Snellen Chart is widely used in schools for testing vision. Designed in 1862, it presents several lines of letters of various sizes to correspond to their appearance at different distances from the viewer. Each line contains six or eight capital letters in vertical position and several capital *E*'s tilted in different directions. We do not recommend the use of the Snellen Chart because it measures only far point vision. There is little relationship between acuity at far point and near point. Consequently, it is possible for a child to pass the Snellen test and yet experience difficulty in dealing with printed material at near point. Furthermore, the Snellen test is administered to each eye separately with the other eye covered. It does not measure the effectiveness of vision when both eyes are used, as in reading.

Two instruments that are useful for testing vision are the Keystone Visual Survey Telebinocular (14) and the Bausch and Lomb School Vision Tester (3).

The Keystone Visual Survey Telebinocular measures at far point the following: simultaneous perception, vertical and lateral imbalance, fusion, visual acuity, stereopsis, and color blindness. It also measures lateral posture, fusion, and visual acuity at near point. The Spache Binocular Reading Cards (31) can be used with the Keystone Telebinocular. They measure the relative participation of both eyes in the reading act. Three levels of the Spache Binocular Reading Cards are available—preprimary, primary, and intermediate. There is also a Peek-A-Boo Series of cards (23) for use with the Keystone Telebinocular. This test battery is designed to test the visual abilities of children between the ages of three and six. It can also be used for older children with specific learning disabilities and those with mental retardation.

The Bausch and Lomb School Vision Tester measures visual acuity, depth perception, binocular vision, and color blindness.

There are several informal tests of vision that can be used. One is the Skeffington String Test. This test consists of a two or three foot string with a knot in it. The examiner holds both ends of the string, placing one end on the bridge of the student's nose, and asks him to focus on the knot, about sixteen inches away. The student is to describe what he sees. He should see two strings form a V at the knot. If he sees only one string, he is suppressing vision in one eye. If he sees two strings crossing before the knot, he is overconverging. If he sees two strings crossing after the knot, he is underconverging. If one string is higher than the other, vertical imbalance is indicated (32, pp. 28-29).

Helping Children with Visual Problems in the Classroom

Many individuals with visual difficulties are successful in reading. Nevertheless, all children with visual deficiencies should be identified for treatment. Children who exhibit symptoms of visual problems should be referred to an ophthalmologist for examination. If glasses are prescribed, the teacher should help the child to remember to wear them. The child should be seated in the classroom so that he will be able to see the chalkboard and other visual aids. Lighting should be controlled. The teacher should provide well-lighted areas for reading instruction and should minimize glare on the chalkboard and on all reading materials. Children with visual problems often need adjustable desks in order to get the right angle of light on the work that they are doing. Frequently children with visual problems find it easier to read large-print materials and require oral explanations and directions from the teacher. Attention should also be paid to children who have color perception problems. They may find blue-lined paper and ditto copies with a purplish cast difficult to see. Whenever possible, these materials should be avoided. Some children even find the chalk marks on green chalkboards difficult to see.

Eye Movement

During the act of reading an individual's eyes jump across the line of print from one stop or fixation to the next. A fixation takes only a fraction of a second, and it is during the period of fixation that comprehension occurs. Occasionally the reader makes a regression from right to left. This usually occurs when he encounters a difficult word or thought. After a series of fixations the end of the line is reached, and the reader's eyes make a return sweep to the next line of print. Eye movements during reading can be photographed by an instrument known as an ophthalmograph. Studies based on eye movement photography have shown that poor readers exhibit the following characteristics.

1. An unusual number of fixations.
2. A large number of regressions.
3. Lengthy fixation time.
4. Inaccurate return to the next line of print.

Many training programs and mechanical devices have been developed to eliminate regressions and to reduce the number of fixations by increasing the recognition span. The value of such training programs is dubious. Poor eye movement patterns are the result rather than the cause of poor reading. Therefore, we recommend that the teacher's effort be directed toward treating causes of the reading problem, not symptoms.

EXERCISE
9.1. What are some possible causes of poor eye movements?

HEARING

There are a number of terms that should be understood by the reading teacher or diagnostician who is interested in the measurement of auditory acuity.

Audiogram. A graph showing variations in the hearing acuteness of an individual.

Audiologist. An individual trained in the measurement of auditory acuity.

Audiometer. An instrument to gauge and record acuteness of hearing.

Auditory Acuity. Keenness of hearing.

Decibel. A measure of sound intensity.

Frequency. The number of cycles per second of a sound wave.

Intensity. Loudness or softness of a sound.

Otologist. A physician who diagnoses and treats disorders and diseases of the ear.

Pitch. High and low sounds. Sounds of human speech, for example, vary in pitch from the high sound of a word such as *see* to the low sound of a word such as *go*.

The influence of the learner's ability to hear pitches of different levels and loudness upon his or her reading achievement is well known. The hard-of-hearing and deaf show distinct retardation in reading and other language skills. The average reading level of deaf adults, for example, is about fourth grade (9, p. vii). Temporary hearing losses due to respiratory and throat infection can interfere with learning. If this occurs between the ages of 18 months and 4 years, it can delay the child's speech and interfere with the development of auditory discrimination which is needed to make phoneme-grapheme associations.

Spache (34, p. 90) points out that losses in acuity involving the high tones affect the child's ability to deal with some consonant sounds and blends and that such children are seriously handicapped in responding to the usual phonics sequence that begins with consonants, blends, and digraphs. In low tone losses, vowel sounds are not heard clearly nor are the consonants *r, g, b, h,* and their blends. Individuals whose hearing losses are uncorrected cannot profit from instruction that they do not hear.

Symptoms of Poor Auditory Acuity

The following symptoms suggest the possibility of an auditory problem.

1. Confusing words that sound alike.
2. Indistinct speech.
3. Inattentiveness.
4. Failure to follow simple directions or to respond when called upon.
5. Speaking in a monotone or in a very loud voice.
6. Turning an ear in the direction of the speaker.
7. Cupping a hand behind an ear.
8. Tense facial expression while listening.
9. Complaints of frequent earaches or "runny" ears.

Measurement of Auditory Acuity

Auditory acuity can be measured by an audiometer (1). This instrument tests ability to hear sounds of varying pitch at varying degrees of loudness. Pitch is based on frequency or vibration rate. The slower the rate, the lower the pitch. The audiometer usually ranges from 125 to 8,000 cycles per second. In administering the hearing test, the subject is seated where he cannot see the dials on the audiometer. Headphones are placed on the subject's head, and each ear is tested separately. He signals whenever he can hear the sound. The examiner determines the lowest level of loudness at which the subject can hear each pitch. The examiner records the individual's responses for each pitch or frequency on an audiogram. The amount of loss for each frequency is measured in terms of decibels. A hearing loss above 15 decibels normally causes difficulty. The use of an audiometer requires the services of an audiologist.

Classroom teachers can informally measure hearing ability by the spoken and whispered voice test. In administering the conversational voice test, the student is placed twenty feet from the examiner so that first one ear and then the other is directed toward the examiner. The student plugs the ear not under testing with the index finger. He is instructed to repeat the words he hears the examiner saying. The examiner speaks numbers, simple words, and simple phrases in a "normal" level of voice. If the individual is unable to repeat these, the examiner moves toward the student until he is able to repeat what the examiner is saying. A score of 10/20 means that the examiner had to move to a distance of ten feet from the student before he was able to repeat what the "normal" ear is supposed to hear at twenty feet.

Helping Children With Auditory Problems

Individuals who are suspected of having a hearing problem should be referred to an otologist for a careful examination and medical treatment. In the classroom the teacher can make many helpful adjustments. The teacher can seat the child near the front and center of the room and away from sources of excessive noise. If the loss is in one ear, the child can be seated to one side with the good ear closest to the teacher. She can face the child when speaking so that he can see her lips. She can enunciate clearly and, if necessary, refer the child for training in lip reading. She can use written directions along with oral directions and she can check with the child to be sure that the child has understood them. The teacher can employ a language experience approach to reading and not rely entirely on a code-breaking approach.

SPEECH

Two aspects of speech that are important to reading are speech problems and language productiveness.

Speech Problems

Articulation disorders seem to be closely associated with reading disability. Lyle (16) found that retarded early speech development and articulatory speech defects between the ages of two and a half and four years are highly related to later reading retardation. Both inaccurate articulation and reading difficulties seem to be associated with other factors such as slow intellectual development, neurological problems, or poor auditory acuity and discrimination. Faulty articulation may affect reading by causing confusion between the sounds the child hears others make and the sounds he hears himself make when he associates printed symbols with sounds in reading. Many children with speech defects become upset when asked to read aloud and as a result may develop a mental set against reading.

Students with speech problems show many of the following symptoms.

1. Mispronunciation of words.
2. Peculiar movements of head, tongue, lips, or teeth.
3. Signs of hesitation, stammering, or stuttering.

4. Short gasps of breath which interfere with speech.
5. Inability to produce some speech sounds.
6. Refusal to talk.
7. Slurred sounds.

There are a number of tests that can be used to screen and test students with speech problems, such as the Templin-Darley Screening and Diagnostic Tests of Articulation (35), The Riley Articulation and Language Test, Revised (26), and the Arizona Articulation Proficiency Scale, Revised (8). Because these tests are often not readily available to teachers, we recommend that the teacher identify the speech problems of students through the use of a speech-sound checklist, such as the one developed by Ransom (25, pp. 174-175). The checklist consists of a series of stimulus words which are read aloud by the teacher. After each word is pronounced by the teacher, the child repeats it. The teacher listens carefully to determine whether or not the child has correctly spoken the beginning or ending of the word, and the child's responses are recorded by the teacher on the checklist. An analysis of the completed checklist provides the teacher with specific information regarding the child's speech problems.

The reading teacher should be alert to those students who have speech defects and should seek the assistance and cooperation of a speech therapist. In addition, she can avoid placing the child in a situation which he may view as threatening to his self-concept. Oral reading in an audience situation should be minimized. Such a child needs a warm and accepting environment where he can feel that he is an important and worthwhile person.

Language Productiveness

There is a relationship between language development and reading achievement. Children who are slow in oral language acquisition generally tend to be low in reading achievement. According to a study by deHirsch, Jansky, and Langford (7), measures of language proficiency in kindergarten showed significant correlations with reading failure in first and second grades. Monroe (17, pp. 76-82) points out that quality speech production depends on abilities in expressiveness, meaning, sentence structure, definition, and the child's experience. Inadequate language productiveness often indicates a need for special help in concept building.

Tests that can be used to investigate language productiveness are the Illinois Test of Psycholinguistic Abilities (15), the Northwestern Syntax Screening Test (20), and the Picture Story Language Test (18).

The Illinois Test of Psycholinguistic Abilities is a tool for analyzing the integration of language, conceptual learning, and motor expression. It measures auditory decoding, visual decoding, auditory-vocal association, vocal encoding, automatic sequential ability, visual-motor association, auditory-vocal sequencing ability, and visual-motor sequencing ability. It also measures visual, auditory, and grammatic closure. It is designed for children between the ages of two and nine.

The Northwestern Syntax Screening Test evaluates syntactic development. It provides measures of receptive and expressive syntactic forms and identifies children who need further testing in this area. It is for children between the ages of three and eight.

The Picture Story Language Test is a standardized procedure for appraising normal facility with language. It is comprised of three scales: (1) Productivity, (2) Syntax, and (3) Abstract-Concrete, which measures content or meaning.

The teacher can informally investigate the child's level of language productiveness by showing a child a picture, asking him or her to tell a story about it and to point to and define certain objects in the picture. The child's responses are evaluated in terms of the level of expressiveness, level of meaning, level of sentence structure, and level of defining. Monroe (17, pp. 75-87) provides standards for evaluation.

In helping children whose language productiveness is inadequate, the teacher can do the following.

1. Focus instruction on comprehension of oral language as well as on the production of language. Johnson and Myklebust (13) suggest that children who have problems with listening and reading should receive instruction in comprehension of oral language prior to instruction in expression.
2. Provide opportunities for many experiences.
3. Emphasize concept development.
4. Build meaning vocabulary.
5. Encourage the child to describe fully objects in his environment and experiences he has had.
6. Provide opportunities for children to retell stories that are told or read to them.
7. Use sequential pictures, such as comic strips, and have the student verbalize the sequence of actions.
8. Use the Peabody Language Development Kit (22) for children in grade three and below. The Peabody Language Development Kit stresses the development of overall oral language skills through reception, expression, and the cognitive processes.

9. Integrate reading, writing, listening, and speaking into all aspects of classroom instruction.
10. Use a language experience approach so that reading is meaningful to the children.

GENERAL HEALTH

Any condition that hinders activity can affect reading growth and development. Reading is a process of identifying, interpreting, and evaluating ideas in terms of the mental content of the reader. Mental content is based on the experiential background of the individual. Physical defects, poor health, and inadequate nutrition tend to restrict activities and consequently retard the development of the mental content required for effective reading. Learning to read requires sustained attention and active participation. Poor health interferes with the child's ability to sustain attention and to participate actively in the work of the classroom and causes frequent absences from school.

Some health problems are due to poor living habits rather than disease. Many children, instead of eating balanced meals and drinking milk and fruit juices, eat junk food and sugary drinks. Furthermore, children who are malnourished or extremely obese often find it difficult to concentrate in school. There is some evidence that food preservatives and excessive consumption of sugar are causes of hyperactivity in children (29). Some children are not able to work well in the classroom because they haven't had enough sleep, which may be the result of late-night television viewing or other late-night activities.

The teacher can best detect the possibility of health problems through observation of the child in the classroom and school cafeteria, and on the playground. The following questions can serve as a guide.

1. Does the individual appear to be or complain of being tired?
2. Does he or she sleep during class?
3. Is the student hyperactive?
4. Does he or she often complain of being hungry?
5. When given the opportunity, does he or she select a poorly balanced meal?
6. Does the student refuse to participate in playground activities?
7. Is the student frequently absent from school?

8. Does he or she frequently complain of not feeling well?
9. Does he or she have persistent colds?
10. Is he or she too thin or too fat?
11. Does he or she have any noticeable physical defects?
12. Does the student frequently talk about activities which he or she engages in late at night?

Children who are suspected of having a health problem or poor nutrition should be referred to the school nurse and the cooperation of the parents should be sought.

NEUROLOGICAL FACTORS

The results of research concerning the causal relationship between neurological deficits and reading difficulties is conflicting. During recent years there has been a marked tendency to relate neurological impairment to reading disability. Critchley (6) and Rabinovitch (24) believe that some type of neurological impairment, other than known brain pathology, causes difficulty in learning to read. Rourke (27) also expresses the view that neurological dysfunction, in the absence of known brain damage, is a common correlate of reading disability. However, Bond, Tinker, and Wasson (5, p. 85) report that recent case studies suggest that known brain lesions, unless very severe, often do not retard learning and that many children with verifiable brain damage make good progress in reading. Spache (34), based upon a critical review of current literature in this field, has concluded that brain damage as a basis or frequent cause of reading disability must be rejected.

Lateral Dominance

One of the most controversial issues in reading is the cause-effect relationship between reading disability, cerebral dominance, and laterality. Lateral dominance is the preference for and consistent use of the eye, hand, and muscles of one side of the body. The dominant cerebral hemisphere is the one on the opposite side from the dominant hand, eye, or foot. Cross dominance is a state of control in which the dominant hand and dominant eye are on opposite sides. Incomplete dominance exists when the individual does not show a consistent preference for one eye, hand, or foot. It is hypothesized that laterality is still developing in some children until the age of twelve.

131

Laterality can be investigated with the Harris Tests of Lateral Dominance (10). They measure eye, hand, and foot dominance. Laterality can also be studied informally. Handedness can be determined by observing the child as he picks up small objects, erases the chalkboard, or throws a ball. It can also be measured by asking the child to make crosses with the right hand for three thirty-second periods and then to make crosses with the left hand for three thirty-second periods. The examiner counts the number of crosses made with each hand for each of the three periods. The median score for each hand is selected. Usually more crosses are made with the dominant hand. Eye preference can be measured by asking the child to look through a hole, 1/4 inch in diameter in the center of a sheet of cardboard 8 1/2 by 11 inches. He is asked to hold the sheet in both hands at arm's length from his face, to keep both eyes open, and to look at a pencil held by the examiner about 8 inches from the sheet. As he looks at the pencil, he is to pull the paper closer to his face. He will look through the peephole with his dominant eye. Another informal measure is to have the student look at some object in the room through a cardboard tube. The tube will be brought to his dominant eye.

Orton (21) has theorized that records of letters and words exist in both the left and right hemispheres of the brain and that in one hemisphere the record is a mirror image of the record in the other hemisphere. If cerebral dominance is well developed when the child begins to read, difficulty in reading is not likely. If the child has not developed cerebral dominance by the time he begins to learn to read, the two sides of the brain will be in conflict, according to Orton, and the child will experience difficulty. He contends that reversal tendencies result from cross dominance and is an important factor in learning to read.

Spache (33), however, disagrees very emphatically on the meaning of reversals. He says, "Reversals are not related to handedness or eyedness, or cerebral dominance nor are they indicative of laterality or visual handicaps." Spache (p. 200) criticizes the cerebral dominance theories of reading disability and cites over thirty-five research studies which refute any relationship between laterality and reading development and concludes that it is "amazing that the claims for significant effects of laterality upon reading persist in view of this overwhelming negative evidence . . ."

Central Processing Dysfunctions

Rupley and Blair (28, p. 50) define central processing dysfunctions or learning disabilities as those that inhibit the processing of information obtained by way of auditory, visual, and haptic (touch) stimuli. Sensory stimuli are transmitted to the brain through the visual, auditory, and haptic sense organs. The brain processes this information. When central processing dysfunction occurs, the processing of information is interfered with and resulting behavioral responses are disorganized.

Central processing dysfunction should be suspected if the individual shows a combination of the following symptoms and no other factor can be found to explain the child's behavior.

1. Reads considerably below potential.
2. Shows evidence of poor visual-motor coordination. For example, has difficulty printing, writing, and drawing. Has difficulty copying geometrical figures.
3. Reverses letters and order of letters in words or changes the order of sounds in a word when reading.
4. Poor in organizing work.
5. Often appears clumsy and awkward.
6. Exhibits hyperactivity. Is constantly in motion or restless.
7. Distractible. Has a short attention span.
8. Perseveration. Has difficulty in shifting from one activity to another. Repeats the same behavior over and over.
9. Impulsiveness.
10. Slow in finishing work.
11. Often shows a lag in maturation.

Individuals can exhibit any of the behaviors listed above and not experience learning problems due to central processing dysfunction. The behaviors must be considered in terms of their persistence and in relationship to the typical behavior of the average child of the same chronological age.

Identification of central processing dysfunction requires the services of a multidisciplinary team. Identification is made on the basis of observations and patterns of test scores. Some of the instruments which are often used are The Pupil Rating Scale (19), the Goodenough-Harris Drawing Test (12), The Bender-Gestalt (4), the Wechsler Intelligence Scale for Children (36), the Slingerland Test (30), and the Illinois Test of Psycholinguistic Abilities (15). No one test can identify central processing dysfunction. We emphasize again that identification must be made by a multidisciplinary team and the child must meet the following criteria.

1. The child does not achieve commensurate with his age and ability levels in one or more of the following areas when provided with appropriate learning experiences.

     a. Oral expression.
     b. Listening comprehension.
     c. Written expression.
     d. Basic reading skill.
     e. Reading comprehension.
     f. Mathematics calculation.
     g. Mathematics reasoning.

2. The child has a severe discrepancy between achievement in one or more of the above areas and in intellectual ability.

3. The child's severe discrepancy between ability and achievement is not primarily the result of
     a. A visual, hearing, or motor handicap.
     b. Mental retardation.
     c. Emotional disturbance.
     d. Environmental, cultural, or economic disadvantage.

It is evident that this problem can only be inferred. So far we have no way of knowing whether input, transmission, or output is the culprit. If a child is identified as having a learning disability, the teacher needs to assess his or her strengths and weaknesses and to provide an instructional program planned to meet his specific needs. For example, if the child has good auditory perception but is weak in visual memory, the emphasis when teaching word identification skills should be on phonics, not on whole word recognition. All instruction should be brief and clearly presented. The teacher must be consistent in her treatment of the child. He should know what is expected of him and should not be placed in a position where he will experience frustration. Instruction should be carefully planned for sequential development, and continual reinforcement should be provided. Overlearning of skills is recommended. Additional suggestions for teaching the learning disabled child are provided in a later chapter.

SUMMARY

This chapter has discussed how vision, hearing, speech, general health, and neurological factors affect reading achievement and has shown how the teacher can formally and informally assess these factors. In addition, suggestions have been made for mitigating the various physical factors that may be affecting an individual's progress in learning to read.

REFERENCES

1. Audiometers are manufactured by Maico Hearing Instruments, 7375 Bush Lake Road, Minneapolis, Minnesota; Zenith Radio Corporation, Auditory Instrument Division, 6501 W. Grand Avenue, Chicago, Illinois; and Beltone Electronics Corporation, Hearing Test Instruments Division, 4201 W. Victoria Street, Chicago.
2. Baker, Harry J., and B. Leland. *Detroit Tests of Learning Aptitude.* Indianapolis: Bobbs-Merrill, 1955.
3. Bausch and Lomb School Vision Tester, Bausch and Lomb Optical Company, Rochester, NY.
4. Bender, Lauretta. *Bender Visual-Motor Gestalt Test for Children.* New York: The Psychological Corporation, 1962.
5. Bond, Guy L., Miles A. Tinker, and Barbara Wasson. *Reading Difficulties, Their Diagnosis and Correction* (Fourth Edition). Englewood Cliffs, NJ: Prentice-Hall, 1979.
6. Critchley, M. *The Dyslexic Child.* Springfield, IL: Charles C. Thomas, 1970.
7. deHirsch, Katrina, Jeannette Jansky, and William S. Langford. *Predicting Reading Failure: A Preliminary Study.* New York: Harper & Row, 1966.
8. Fudala, Janet Barker. *Arizona Articulation Proficiency Scale, Revised.* Los Angeles: Western Psychological Services, 1970.
9. Geoffrion, Leo D., and Karen E. Schuster. *Auditory Handicaps and Reading.* Newark, DE: International Reading Association, 1980.
10. Harris, Albert J. *Harris Tests of Lateral Dominance.* New York: The Psychological Corporation, 1958.
11. Harris, Albert J., and Edward R. Sipay. *How to Increase Reading Ability* (Seventh Edition). New York: Longman, 1980.
12. Harris, Dale B. *Goodenough-Harris Drawing Test.* New York: Harcourt Brace Jovanovich, 1963.
13. Johnson, D. J., and Myklebust, H. R. *Learning Disabilities: Educational Principles and Practices.* New York: Grune and Stratton, 1967.
14. Keystone Visual Survey Telebinocular, Keystone View Company, Davenport, IA.
15. Kirk, S. A., J. J. McCarthey, and W. Kirk. *Illinois Test of Psycholinguistic Abilities.* Urbana, IL: University of Illinois Press, 1968.
16. Lyle, J. G. "Certain Antenatal, Perinatal, and Developmental Variables and Reading Retardation in Middle-Class Boys." *Child Development* 41 (1970): 481-491.
17. Monroe, Marion. *Growing Into Reading.* Chicago: Scott, Foresman, 1951.
18. Mykelbust, Helmer R. *Picture Story Language Test.* New York: Grune and Stratton, 1965.

19. Mykelbust, Helmer R. *The Pupil Rating Scale.* New York: Grune and Stratton, 1971.
20. *Northwestern Syntax Screening Test.* Evanston, IL: Northwestern University, Department of Communicative Disorders, 1969.
21. Orton, Samuel T. *Reading, Writing and Speech Problems in Children.* New York: W. W. Norton, 1937.
22. *Peabody Language Development Kits.* Circle Pines, MN: American Guidance Service, 1965, 1966, 1967 and 1968.
23. Peek-A-Boo Series, Keystone View Company, Davenport, IA, 1975.
24. Rabinovitch, Ralph D. "Dyslexia: Psychiatric Considerations." in John Money, ed. *Reading Disability: Progress and Research Needs in Dyslexia.* Baltimore: Johns Hopkins Press, 1962: 73-79.
25. Ransom, Grayce A. *Preparing to Teach Reading.* Boston: Little, Brown and Company, 1978.
26. Riley, Glyndon D. *The Riley Articulation and Language Test, Revised.* Los Angeles: Western Psychological Services, 1971.
27. Rourke, B. P. "Brain-Behavior Relationship in Children with Learning Disabilities." *American Psychologist* 30 (1975): 911-920.
28. Rupley, William H., and Timothy R. Blair. *Reading Diagnosis and Remediation.* Chicago: Rand McNally College Publishing Company, 1979.
29. Safer, D. J., and R. P. Allen. *Hyperactive Children: Diagnosis and Management.* Baltimore: University Park Press, 1976.
30. Slingerland, Beth H. *Slingerland Test.* Cambridge, MA: Educator's Publishing Service, 1970.
31. Spache Binocular Reading Cards, Keystone View Company, Davenport, IA, 1955.
32. Spache, George D. *Diagnosing and Correcting Reading Disabilities.* Boston: Allyn and Bacon, 1976.
33. Spache, George D., "Factors Which Produce Defective Reading," *Corrective Reading in Classroom and Clinic.* Supplementary Educational Monographs 79. Chicago: University of Chicago Press, 1953: 49-57.
34. Spache, George D. *Investigating the Issues of Reading Disabilities.* Boston: Allyn and Bacon, 1976.
35. Templin, M. C., and F. L. Darley. *Templin-Darley Screening and Diagnostic Tests of Articulation.* Iowa City: Bureau of Educational Research and Service, University of Iowa, 1960.
36. Wechsler, David. *Wechsler Intelligence Scale for Children–Revised.* New York: The Psychological Corporation, 1974.
37. Witty, Paul, and David Kopel. *Reading and the Educative Process.* Boston: Ginn and Company, 1939.

SUGGESTED READING

Bond, Guy L., Miles A. Tinker, and Barbara B. Wasson. *Reading Difficulties, Their Diagnosis and Correction* (Fourth Edition). Englewood Cliffs: Prentice-Hall, 1979, Ch. 4.

Harris, Albert J., and Edward R. Sipay. *How to Increase Reading Ability* (Seventh Edition). New York: Longman, 1980, Chs. 7 and 11.

Rupley, William H., and Timothy R. Blair. *Reading Diagnosis and Remediation, A Primer for Classroom and Clinic.* Chicago: Rand McNally College Publishing Company, 1979, Chs. 4 and 16.

Spache, George D. *Investigating the Issues of Reading Disabilities.* Boston: Allyn and Bacon, 1976, Chs. 2, 3, and 7.

10

Cognitive Factors

This chapter will help you to

1. Become aware of the elements that make up cognitive factors.
2. Relate these factors to reading.
3. Know how they can be tested.
4. Know how observation can help in assessment.
5. Become aware of how the teacher can mitigate the problems.

Cognition is the process of knowing in the broadest sense. It is a combination of genetically determined growth patterns and environmental factors. It encompasses intelligence, mental content, perception, and attention, and, when we are relating it to reading, it also includes language development. The cognitive factors we take to the reading act determine the limits of our success in gaining meaning from what we read.

INTELLIGENCE

The question of what intelligence is has not yet been answered to everyone's satisfaction in spite of attempts that have been going on since antiquity. It is agreed that the brain is the primary site of intelligence, and there have been great strides in mapping out the intricate functions of different areas of the brain. All thought, including reading, involves the activation of many neuron systems in the brain. Dr. Carl Sagan tells us

> There is in the neocortex a striking separation of function, which is contrary to such common-sense notions as that reading and writing, or recognizing words and numbers, are very similar activities . . . . Various abstractions, including the "parts of speech" in grammar, seem, astonishingly, to be wired into specific regions of the brain (21, p. 72).

The proliferation of knowledge about the brain, however, does not satisfactorily answer the question of what intelligence is. Some psychologists claim that the ability of a person to make sound judgments is the most important aspect of intelligence. Others claim it is a person's capacity for directed, purposeful, and adaptive behavior. Still others say it is a combination of some genetically based potentiality, plus or minus the effect of our life experiences. In any case, everyone does agree that thinking and reasoning require intelligence.

Intelligence and Reading

Since success in reading requires directed, purposeful, and adaptive behavior, it appears obvious that there can be a positive correlation between intelligence and capacity for reading excellence. Severely mentally retarded people are incapable of learning to read, and people with I.Q.'s between 20 and 50 can learn to read only the simplest sorts of material. Individuals who have average or better intelligence can become good readers. It is well to remember, however, that intelligence is only one of the many factors that can influence learning.

Individual Intelligence Tests

There are several thousand tests that have been devised to measure aspects of intelligence, and since intelligence has not been defined to everyone's satisfaction, different tests measure different things. Modern intelligence testing began with the Frenchman, Alfred Binet, in 1905. He was asked by the French government to devise some tests to predict how well youngsters would do in school so that those identified as poor learners could be put into special education classes. His individually administered Binet Scale was a success and was later revised by Terman at Stanford University in 1916. This Stanford-Binet Intelligence Scale (26), whose most recent revision came out in 1960, is considered to be the granddaddy of I.Q. testing. It continues to be used extensively and is probably the best instrument for accurately measuring both the highest and lowest extremes of intelligence.

The Stanford-Binet is known as an age scale since there are subtests at each age level, and the person is given a certain number of months credit for each subtest passed. The test is heavily weighted toward verbal abilities and reasoning, but it also has tests for number skills, manual dexterity, and short-term memory. The score on the test is a compilation of months' credit converted into a mental age. This mental age, when contrasted with the subject's chronological age, yields an I.Q. score.

The other most prestigious individual I.Q. test was produced by David Wechsler in 1939. He began with an adult test called the Wechsler-Bellevue and has since enlarged his offerings to include the Wechsler Pre-School and Primary Scale of Intelligence (29) for children from four to six-and-a-half years old; the Wechsler Intelligence Scale for Children, Revised (28) for children from five to sixteen years old; and the Wechsler Adult Intelligence Scale (27) for people sixteen years and older.

The Wechsler tests, in contrast to the Binet age scale, is a point scale. Types of tasks are grouped into subtests so a point score can be assigned for each "aspect" of intelligence. There are six verbal subtests and six performance subtests, each yielding an I.Q., and a combined score yielding a Full Scale I.Q. On the WPPSI and the

WISC-R, a method is provided for figuring mental age. The verbal portion of the test measures a person's fund of general information, his meaning vocabulary, arithmetic reasoning, categorizing abilities, "common sense" reasoning, and short-term memory. The performance portion measures attention to detail, sequencing, manual dexterity combined with the ability to plan ahead, speed and accuracy in using a code, and maze tracing.

Both the Binet and Wechsler tests must be administered by a licensed psychologist, and they take from one to two hours to give. Both also require a large kit of test materials. It was because of these limitations that such tests as the Slosson Intelligence Test for Children and Adults (23) was produced. It is administered by a "responsible person" (23, p. iii) and takes about ten to twenty minutes to give and to score, and there are very few materials needed for testing. This test took most of its items from the Stanford-Binet (26) and the Gesell Development Schedules (11). Due to the abbreviated number of test items given to each subject this test should be used with caution, and the results should be considered as a screening device, rather than as a reliable indication of a person's intelligence.

Since most intelligence tests lean heavily on verbal ability, there is a large segment of the population who would be unnecessarily penalized by these kinds of tests: the deaf, the learning disabled, the speaker of a foreign language, and the mute. Thus, several tests have been produced that require nonverbal responses. The Leiter International Performance Scale (15) and the Chicago Non-Verbal Examination (4) are examples of this type of test. They both determine I.Q. performance by having the subject arrange things in sequence, pair items that are alike in some way, and demonstrate manipulative ability.

Group Intelligence Tests

Group intelligence tests are quite popular because any number of individuals can be tested in the same time it takes to test one person with an individually administered test. There are, however, serious limitations which should be carefully weighed before deciding on using one of these. They are, at the outset, tests that require reading ability and therefore penalize unfairly people with reading problems. They also contain only limited assessments of manipulative ability. In addition, they are usually even more culturally biased than individual I.Q. tests. They can, however, be a useful screening tool so long as no more is expected of them than that, and so long as testing procedures are carefully controlled. Two of the more popular ones are described below.

The Otis-Lennon Mental Ability Test (19), for grades K.5 to 12, includes items for classifying, following directions, using quantitative reasoning, verbal concepts, and analogies. The California Short-Form Test of Mental Maturity (3), for grades K to adult, measures logical reasoning, numerical reasoning, verbal concepts, and memory.

Observation of Intellectual Factors

Teachers should beware of making any judgments about the intellectual *abilities* of their students. They can make some guesses about their intellectual *functioning* in that particular environment, but even then it is a dangerous exercise. So many factors operate on an individual, such as personality factors, motivation, interest in a subject, and so on, that judgments can miss the mark by a wide margin.

The teachers can, however, notice whether their students are resourceful, creative, adaptable, and responsive. They can note comparative language ability and manual dexterity. But, primarily, they must realize that subjective judgments in this area are often wrong, and wrong judgments can have an extremely deleterious effect on their students.

EXERCISE
10.1. How can a wrong judgment of a child's intelligence hurt that child?

Mitigating Intellectual Problems

More teachers in regular classrooms are being assigned mentally retarded children than ever before. Mainstreaming is a fact, and it will undoubtedly be with us for a long time, if not forever. But it has always been true that teachers have had to deal with children with low average I.Q.'s—the ones whose problems are not severe enough to qualify them for special education.

Methods of treatment for both of these groups are similar.

1. Teach concepts in small units.
2. Use a great deal of redundancy since the principle of overlearning is especially important with these children.
3. Combine whenever possible the motor sense with the visual and aural senses. The more senses one uses the greater is the possibility of learning.
4. Provide ample opportunities for transfer of learning. Incorporate into the learning of a principle, the actual use of that principle.

5. Eliminate all unnecessary learning. For instance, if a child applies a phonic rule consistently, there is no need for him to learn to state the rule.
6. Teach the child how to go through the appropriate steps in solving a problem.
7. Maintain attention by using short, highly structured lessons, and by changing types of activities often.

MENTAL CONTENT

Experiential background or mental content comes from the environment of the individual. From the moment of conception until death, parents, relatives, other people, animals, physical setting, nutrition, teachers, and events, all have a vital influence on what the individual becomes.

The pervasive role that environment plays in the development of a child has been convincingly proved in study after study. One study, conducted back in 1937 (17), reported that a group of identical twins (who have the same hereditary makeup) reared in the same home had more similar I.Q.'s than another group of identical twins reared apart. There was as much as 24 I.Q. points difference in the second group of twins, in spite of their identical heredity.

Another research study showed that when rats were exposed to a rich and rewarding environment their brain size actually increased, and their problem-solving capacity was appreciably enhanced. Dr. Mark R. Rosenzweig, the principal experimenter, said, "Generally, a rich early training is good, and there is no reason why we can't extrapolate our laboratory results to humans to improve the learning ability of culturally-deprived children." (20)

EXERCISE
10.2. What is your position on the nature-nurture controversy? Is heredity or environment more important in developing cognition? Defend your answer.

Mental Content and Reading

The goal of reading is to get meaning from the writing of an author. In order to identify, interpret, and evaluate the ideas of the writer the reader must bring his whole background to the task. His past experiences with the alphabet and knowledge of word attack skills will help him identify the words. His experiences with the connotation of the ideas imbedded in the phrases and sentences will help him interpret what the author is saying, and his total background in the subject presented will make him able to evaluate what the author has said.

In Chapter 6 a story was presented about a makeshift school provided by our early settlers. The story contained the phrase, "In pioneer days . . ." The reader must first identify the words. He probably learned the word *in* as a sight word. Syllabic instruction perhaps helped him say the word *pioneer,* and a study of word families helped him to know how to pronounce *ay* words, so he could recognize the word *days.* Interpretation requires a background that includes the idea of olden times in the United States. It might evoke from memory pictures of wagon trains and battles of settlers and Indians. Evaluation would require that the reader judge the accuracy of the total concept: the need for a school, the dearth of materials for education, and the awareness of the pioneer spirit which would help the people make do with what they had.

There is no act of reading that does not demand an extensive background of experiences, either in the flesh or vicariously provided by hearing or reading.

Tests of Mental Content

All achievement tests are obviously measures of mental content, but so are I.Q. tests. As a matter of fact, any test that requires the subject to display his prowess is a test of learned behavior (with the possible exception of so-called creativity tests). Achievement tests such as the California Achievement Test, the Stanford Achievement Test, the Comprehensive Test of Basic Skills, the Peabody Individual Achievement Test (5), and the Metropolitan Achievement Test, all measure the accumulation of knowledge and reasoning ability that a subject has at his disposal (see Chapter 7). Every type of reading test is also in this category (see Chapters 6 and 7).

Some tests label themselves as measures of *aptitude,* which implies future ability and therefore might circumvent mental content, but on examination they, too, require a background of experiences. For instance, the Short Form Test of Academic Aptitude (22) measures vocabulary, analogies, sequences, and memory. Also, even the Detroit Test of Learning Aptitude (1) is largely a test of learned behavior. This test provides specific information about mental traits, motor speed and precision, social adjustment, and abilities or disabilities in learning.

The fact that it is almost impossible to exclude experiential background in any testing situation attests to the importance of this factor.

Observation of Mental Content

It is fairly easy for a teacher to recognize a dearth of enlightening experiences in a student. The word *enlightening* is important, because, strictly speaking, there is a difference between experiential background and mental content. A child on a motor trip who whiles away the miles by reading a comic book and at his destination enjoys only the swim in the motel pool will have that trip in his experiential background, but his mental content will be enlarged only by knowledge of the comic book character and whatever he learned about swimming in a pool.

Students display aspects of their mental content all during the school day. What they do and do not know about academic subjects, social situations, and the world in general can be discerned by an alert teacher. It is more a matter of keeping records on each child's fund of knowledge, general and specific, than it is recognizing the adequacies and inadequacies in the first place. Since excellence in reading can be acquired only by bringing a wealth of background to the reading act, this is an important duty of the teacher. If she finds that little Suzie cannot tell time, does not know what month or day it is, and does not know when she was born, the teacher might predict that Suzie will have great difficulty in any temporal sequencing task. If Steve has never heard of a camel or even seen a picture of one, it will do him little good to be able to pronounce the word on demand. In the notebook the teacher keeps on her students there should be a place for setting down her observation of specific areas of the mental content of each child that need to be bolstered.

Enhancing Mental Content

The field trip is a tried and true builder of experiential background, but its efficacy is measured by the degree of involvement of the children in the experience. It is necessary for the teacher to prepare her students beforehand so that they will become enthusiastic and curious. She must also maintain their attention during the trip, and finally she must guide them into gaining the concepts she deems important. Subsequent pooling of the children's reactions builds an even greater fund of information and reinforces their learning.

Previewing a subject is another traditional method of enlarging background which has withstood the test of time. The teacher should take a few minutes, or even longer if necessary, to focus the student's attention on the subject about to be covered. If there are several children who, like Suzie, have difficulty with temporal concepts, the teacher can preview that subject by asking them if it is cold or hot at Christmas time and on the Fourth of July. She can use a calendar to mark the special days, and the more identifications the children can make the greater are her chances of giving them a gestalt for the meaning of time.

Another means of building mental content is by "seizing the moment of interested curiosity." Byways leading away from the subject at hand because of sudden interest in a thought or question can be more rewarding than the prepared lesson itself.

Aside from these generalities there are many particular areas in which a certain child will need greater pre-knowledge. The teacher can make simple explanations, or can help the child search out information from reference books, atlases, history books, and even fiction. She can involve another child who already has a wealth of knowledge on the subject. If there are several students who need help in a certain area, she can portion out a search of different aspects to each of the students and have them instruct each other. The instruction can be in the form of inventing a play, constructing a bulletin board or an experience chart, or any number of other interesting activities.

EXERCISE
10.3. Gerry, a third-grader, is about to read a story about a kangaroo. He has never even heard the word before. What type of books might he read in order to gain knowledge of the animal?

PERCEPTION

Everyone has a basic sensory system for receiving data from both his external and internal environment. Thus, the basis for all communication lies in a person's perceptual awareness and understandings.
Our senses include

1. Auditory (hearing).
2. Visual (seeing).
3. Olfactory (smelling).
4. Gustatory (tasting).

147

5. Tactile (touching).
6. Kinesthetic (muscular activity).
7. Proprioceptive (stimuli arising from within the organism).

Each of these senses has three major properties.

1. *Sensation,* which is acuity, or the physical ability to receive the stimulus.
2. *Perception,* which is discrimination, or the identification and interpretation of the sensory stimulus.
3. *Cognition,* which has two components: synthesis, or the blending of the perception with previous mental content, and memory.

The way we perceive things is a combination of intellectual, environmental, maturational, and emotional factors. Perception is an elusive quality. There are machines which show brain wave activity when perception has taken place but exactly what was perceived can only be inferred from the reaction or response of the individual. Have you ever wondered if the color you see as red is exactly the same as what another person perceives? There is no way of knowing positively.

EXERCISE
10.4. How could you use the student's tactile sense to teach sight words?

Perception and Reading

The visual and auditory senses are the ones most immediately involved with reading. The other senses contribute in varying degrees, but they are secondary to the first two. Acuity is less important to the reading act than perception and cognition, although there obviously must be some ability to see and, usually, to hear in order to read. Growth in ability in perception is affected by maturation, and some people are quite slow to develop the skill. Others have a difficulty that appears resistant to learning. These are the people with central processing dysfunction who were described in Chapter 9.

Visual perception is the ability to identify and interpret visual stimuli. For reading this means, for instance, we can recognize a *b* as a *b,* and *was* as *was,* and that we know the meaning of the word or phrase we see. We are not born with the ability to see things from left to right or top to bottom. This is learned behavior. A bright three-year-old, Jenny, wrote her name for us. It looked like this:

$\angle N$ $\wedge$ $\exists$ $\cap$. A right-side-up model of her name was presented to her and she insisted that her rendition was exactly like the model. A year later she wrote her name in appropriate orientation without hesitancy.

An interesting anomaly occurs when we realize that conservation, in Piaget's terminology, is learned behavior, too. By about age seven we come to realize, for example, that when you pour a tall, thin glass of water into a short fat glass, the amount of water remains constant, also, that Mother is the same mother whether we see her from the front or back, or even upside down. Children must learn conservation as they grow, but they must also learn not to use it when it comes to our letters and words. A *b* does not remain a *b* if it is *p* or *d*, or *q*.

The importance of auditory discrimination to reading can be attested to by the popularity of phonics as an approach to reading instruction. Although it is possible to learn to read without any knowledge of the way the words are pronounced in oral speech, learning is made infinitely easier by the association of the sounds of words with their written presentation. If a person can identify and interpret the words *pin* and *pen* when he hears them, his chance of recognizing them in print is enhanced.

Kinesthetic perception is the awareness produced by the sense of movement. It is axiomatic that we learn by doing and therefore writing a word—using our kinesthetic sense—helps us learn to read that word. The visual and auditory modalities are primarily receptive, or passive channels, whereas the kinesthetic modality is generative, or active.

Visual-motor processes are considered by many people to be very important in the development of the child's academic progress. Training in eye-hand coordination, position in space, spatial relations, and form constancy, has been advocated by some educators, psychologists, optometrists, and parents. A problem arises, however, when training in these areas is used to improve the reading ability of the child, and yet the exercises are not based on the reading or writing act. Children who participate in the nonword perceptual training often—but not always—improve their scores on perceptual tests, but not on reading. These tests and training techniques include the Frostig-Horne Program for Development of Visual Perception (9) and the Kephart-Getman (14, pp. 187-207) visual-motor training techniques. In an attempt to assess their worth for improving children's learning Donald Hammill, Libby Goodman, and J. Lee Wiederholt conducted an exhaustive inquiry into results of research studies and performed some studies themselves. They concluded that

The results of attempts to implement the Frostig-Horne materials and Kephart-Getman techniques in the schools have for the most part been unrewarding. The readiness skills of children were improved in only a few instances. The effect of training on intelligence and academic achievement was not clearly demonstrated (12, p. 476).

Integration of sense modalities, when practiced during the reading act, however, has been found to facilitate learning. The visual, auditory, and kinesthetic modalities are the most relevant for educational purposes. We learn through these senses, and most of us learn better through one sense than another. Dr. William B. Barbe (2) and associates conducted a research project to measure the relative strengths of the visual, auditory, and kinesthetic modalities of almost one thousand children. Their findings suggest that the auditory modality tends toward being the strongest in early elementary children and the visual and kinesthetic modalities become ascendant by about fourth grade. But these are only generalities and each child should have his modality preference identified if the teacher wants to channel her teaching through the easier learning pathway.

Once the perception of a fact or idea has occurred the cognitive processes can take place. The perception is synthesized with previous mental content and thus is capable of being remembered.

Perceptual Testing

There are a great many tests of perception on the market. August J. Mauser in *Assessing the Learning Disabled* (16) lists eighty-seven of them, and even more have been published since his book came out in 1976. These tests are primarily, although not entirely, of more interest to special education teachers than to reading teachers. The types of perception tests most relevant to reading would include word recognition, auditory discrimination, phonics, writing, spelling, and learning methods tests. Some examples of these would be

1. The Jordon Written Screening Test (13), which deals mainly with visual perception in the reading act.
2. The Wepman Auditory Discrimination Test (30), as its name indicates, requires the student to identify likenesses and differences in paired syllables, presented orally.
3. The supplementary phonics subtests of the Spache Diagnostic Tests (25), and the Ekwall Phonics Test (7) are also examples of auditory discrimination assessment.
4. The Mills Learning Methods Test (17), by a process of teaching

and testing which occurs in fifteen-minute segments over a period of five days assesses whether the individual learns best by visual, auditory, kinesthetic, or a combination method.

5. Another learning methods test is the Gates Associative Learning Test (10) which takes only a few minutes, and compares the relative strengths of a person's visual-visual or visual-auditory associations.

What the Teacher Can Do

If a child is perceptually handicapped, he or she is a candidate for the ministrations of the school psychologist or the special education teacher. The major task for the classroom teacher is to provide stimulation in the use of visual, auditory, and kinesthetic perception. She should use her own modality sense strength while teaching, and she should help the student use his while learning, but the student will benefit also by the teacher's efforts to help him combine his strength with his less developed pathways for learning. If, for instance, the teacher's greatest strength is in the auditory sense she could talk to her students about the subject at hand and, at the same time, she could present visual cues with a picture or a word card. She also could add kinesthetic properties by having the children write what they see and hear.

One method of combining the pathways that has proven to be useful is that used by Grace Fernald (8). It combines the visual, auditory, kinesthetic, and tactual (haptic) systems in learning new words. The student looks at the word, says it, and traces it with his fingers. Then he or she attempts to write it without access to the model.

Another, less formal, way to combine visual, auditory, kinesthetic and tactual stimulation is to have students read plays aloud, with expression, and go through the actions that the words call for.

ATTENTION

Attention is basic to learning and memory. At any one time there are multitudes of stimuli bombarding an individual, and only a few of these can be attended to at the same time. Attention is created and sustained by novelty, familiarity, and motivation. It is most readily focused on signals that have significant pleasure and punishment connections. Punishment creates avoidance and pleasure creates the desire to continue the activity. Activities related to past successes tend to give pleasure and therefore encourage attention. Different children have different degrees of staying power when it comes to maintaining attention, and it is easy for the teacher to recognize these individual differences.

The lesson behind these facts are well known to teachers but are not always honored in the classroom. Some classic methods of sustaining attention in reading are

a. Give each child a feeling of success so he or she will be eager to pursue the activity.
b. Eliminate as many distractions as possible in the classroom.
c. Create novelty whenever it is appropriate. For instance, begin a lesson in a new way by challenging the children to debate an issue that is forthcoming, or deliberately write the name of the story upside down on the chalkboard.
d. Stop an activity while the children are still interested. Thus they will look forward to going back to it the next time.
e. Change the routine occasionally. Have the children teach you the lesson, or put the reading lesson after lunch instead of in the morning.
f. Alternate sedentary and active lessons. Draw hopscotch boxes on the floor with chalk and fill them with phonic pairings, or rhyming words. Have the children jump from one to another according to directions.
g. Above all, make each child feel that he or she can accomplish the task. Feed his or her self-concept with the "I can" spirit.

COGNITIVE STYLES

More and more is being discovered about the way we learn. One of the newer concepts is cognitive style, or the approach to problem solving. The factors to consider are

a. Whether the locus of control is within the individual or comes from the environment.
b. Whether the individual organizes his or her experiences in dependent or independent fashion.
c. Whether his or her reaction time reveals impulsivity or reflection.
d. Whether he or she processes stimuli by analysis or by relating them to other concepts.

Reading experts are attempting to correlate the learning of a student with his particular cognitive style. Awareness on the teacher's part of at least some of these factors can make it possible for him or her to utilize more effective learning techniques. The teacher might, for instance, approach a subject analytically for the student who prefers to process stimuli in this manner.

LANGUAGE

Language is an important aspect of cognition and, in the view of many people, the higher levels of intelligence would be impossible without languaging ability.

Babies learn very early to communicate orally. The sounds they make are quickly identifiable as conveying pleasure or discomfort. During the first few weeks of life they can distinguish human sounds from other noises. By about six months they can produce most of the phonemes of speech, and very soon afterwards their babbling includes intonational variations that mimic the speech they hear. They understand words before they can produce them. By the time a child is about two years old he has a growing repertoire of words, or pseudowords. By four years of age he has mastered amazingly complicated word constructions and the basic syntax of his language. This is remarkable because basic syntax (the rules of combination) is a complex structure. The child also begins to duplicate tense and plurality rules. This sometimes leads to overgeneralization. He will say, "I goed to grandma's," or "My foots is wet." One little girl of our acquaintance told her mother, "I don't have a single clo to wear." This was her interpretation for the singular form of the word *clothes.*

Young children perform an incredible task when learning their native language. A six-year-old child knows an estimated fourteen thousand words. In order to accomplish this he must master an average of nine new words a day from the onset of talking until his sixth birthday.

The child encounters other problems, too. As Frank Smith explains (24), we might say, "There is a dog," and "Here is a cat," but we never tell a child how to distinguish between the two. The distinction is difficult to explain unless one knows biology and so we leave the child to find out for himself. Also, our adjectival patterns are quite conventional, and only linguistic specialists can give us a rule for them. If there is a rock that is gray, and round, and large, almost everybody would say, "the large, round, gray rock." No other word order would do. "The gray, round, large rock" sounds awkward to us, as does any other order of the words. A child must learn this on his own. Hardly anyone bothers to teach it.

Language and Reading

Both the quantity and quality of a child's speech are important to reading. The more words he knows and the more concepts he can put into words, the more concepts he can recognize when he reads. The quality of speech is also a factor. Children with articulation disorders often have problems learning to read. If a child has problems with the *r* or *l* sounds, or if he distorts vowel sounds, those very same sound-letter matches are likely to be poor.

The child's early environment provides the foundation for language facility. Vocal play activities and oral interaction with others are vital. Hearing the same words spoken by different people and in different contexts undoubtedly helps the child in his eventual recognition of the meaning of the word. Parents who talk with their babies, and who use an extensive vocabulary with their children as they grow up, are far more likely to give them a sound background in languaging ability than the less interactive parents.

It is not always the families at the lower end of the socioeconomic scale who do not supply enough verbal stimulation. Sometimes the last child in the family or the nondominant twin might have someone habitually talking for him, leaving him verbally impoverished.

Formal and Informal Assessment

All manner of tests address themselves to language. Vocabulary tests, such as were described in Chapter 7, are language tests. Tests of grammar and word usage are, too. Due to the fact that language, strictly speaking, includes listening, reading, speaking and writing, there are few tests on the market that could not be considered to be assessing language.

There are also tests for speech disorders but these are usually more useful to speech therapists than to classroom teachers.

Teacher Observation

Inferences regarding an individual's ability to process information through language can be based on observations guided by the following questions.

1. Does the individual have a large, meaningful vocabulary?
2. Does he or she speak in complete sentences?
3. Can he or she produce a complex sentence?
4. Is he able to organize his ideas well when expressing himself orally?
5. Can he follow directions that are given orally?
6. Does he or she speak distinctly and clearly?
7. Does he or she have a good command of the phonemes of our language?
8. Is he resourceful and creative in his responses?

What the Teacher Can Do

Since language facility is so heavily dependent on a child's first five years, the teacher's role is necessarily limited. However, every effort to enlarge his or her student's verbal concepts should be made.

The teacher herself should have an interest and excitement in vocabulary growth. She should find unusual words to offer to the class. She could do as one teacher does; have a contest once a week in which each child brings to class the longest word he or she can find, or the most onomatopoeic, or the funniest.

She should have sessions in which the children must say a sentence in a different way, or reverse the entire meaning. Recently there has been a resurgence of interest in parsing sentences. This can be made more enjoyable by establishing a shape code for different parts of speech, such as having all nouns encased in rectangles and all verbs in triangles.

She should encourage conversations, especially with the shy, quiet child. She should play listening games, and games that require following oral directions. Anything and everything that encourages oral and written languaging should benefit her students.

SUMMARY

Cognitive factors are overridingly important in reading excellence. All of the cognitive factors are initiated before the child enters school. Intelligence, mental content, perception, attention, and language are appreciably molded in the first years of a child's life. This does not mean that the teacher is excused from attempting to alter the course of a child's early patterning. It is possible, but difficult, but it is necessary if that child comes to school with impoverished tools. The teacher can make a difference.

REFERENCES

1. Baker, Harry J., and Bernice Leland. *Detroit Tests of Learning Aptitude.* Indianapolis: Bobbs-Merrill, 1967.
2. Barbe, William B., R. H. Swassig, with M. N. Malone. *Teaching Through Modality Strengths.* Columbus, OH: Zaner-Bloser, 1979.
3. *California Short Form Test of Mental Maturity.* Monterey, CA: CTB/McGraw-Hill, 1963.
4. *Chicago Non-Verbal Examination.* New York: The Psychological Corporation, 1971.
5. Dunn, Lloyd M., and F. C. Markwardt. *Peabody Individual Achievement Test.* Circle Pines, MN: American Guidance Service, 1970.
6. Dyer, Henry. "Common Misconceptions About Tests and Test Results." in Don E. Hamechek, ed. *Human Dynamics in Psychology and Education* (Third Edition). Boston: Allyn and Bacon, 1977.
7. Ekwall, Eldon E., and Lowell D. Oswald. R_x *Reading Program.* Glenview, IL: Psychotechnics, Inc., 1971.
8. Fernald, Grace M. *Remedial Techniques in Basic School Subjects.* New York: McGraw-Hill, 1943.
9. Frostig, M., and D. Horne. *The Frostig Program for Development of Visual Perception.* Chicago, IL: Follett, 1964.
10. Gates, Arthur I. *The Improvement of Reading* (Third Edition). New York: Macmillan, 1947, 651-652.
11. *Gesell Development Schedules.* New York: The Psychological Corporation, 1943.
12. Hammill, Donald, Libby Goodman, and J. Lee Wiederholt. "Visual Motor Processes: Can We Train Them?" *The Reading Teacher* 27 (February 1974): 469-476.
13. Jordon, Dale R. *Dyslexia in the Classroom* (Second Edition). Columbus, OH: Charles E. Merrill, 1977.
14. Kephart, N. C. *The Slow Learner In the Classroom* (Second Edition). Columbus, OH: Charles E. Merrill, 1971.
15. *Leiter International Performance Scale.* Yonkers, NY: Special Education Materials, 1969.
16. Mauser, August J. *Assessing the Learning Disabled; Selected Instruments.* San Rafael, CA: Academic Therapy Publications, 1976.
17. Mills, Robert E. *Learning Methods Test.* Fort Lauderdale, FL: The Mills School, 1970.
18. Newman, H. J., F. N. Greenman, and K. J. Holzinger. *Twins: A Study of Heredity and Environment.* Chicago: University of Chicago Press, 1937.

19. *Otis-Lennon Mental Ability Test.* New York: The Psychological Corporation, 1967.
20. Rozenzweig, M. R. "Environmental Complexity and Behavior." Paper delivered at American Psychological Association Convention, September, 1965.
21. Sagan, Carl. *The Dragons of Eden: Speculation on the Evolution of Human Intelligence.* New York: Random House, 1977.
22. *Short Form Test of Academic Aptitude.* Monterey, CA: CTB/McGraw-Hill, 1970.
23. Slosson, Richard L. *Slosson Intelligence Test (SIT) for Children and Adults* (Revised reprint). Los Angeles: Western Psychological Services, 1977.
24. Smith, Frank. *Understanding Reading—A Psycholinguistic Analysis of Reading and Learning to Read* (Second Edition). New York: Holt, Rinehart and Winston, 1978.
25. *Spache Diagnostic Test.* Monterey, CA: CTB/McGraw-Hill, 1972.
26. Terman, Lewis M., and Maud A. Merrill. *Stanford-Binet Intelligence Scale,* (Form LM). Boston: Houghton Mifflin Company, The Riverside Press, 1960.
27. *Wechsler Adult Intelligence Scale.* New York: The Psychological Corporation, 1955.
28. *Wechsler Intelligence Scale for Children, Revised.* New York: The Psychological Corporation, 1974.
29. *Wechsler Pre-School and Primary Scale of Intelligence.* New York: The Psychological Corporation, 1967.
30. Wepman, Joseph M. *Auditory Discrimination Test* (Revised). Palm Springs, CA: Language Research Association, 1973.

SUGGESTED READING

Carey, S. "The Child as Word Learner." in M. Halls, J. Bressman, and G. A. Miller. *Linguistic Theory and Psychological Reality.* Cambridge, MA: MIT Press, 1978.
Robeck, Mildred Caen, and John A. R. Wilson. *Psychology of Reading, Foundations of Instruction.* New York: John Wiley, 1974, Chs. 2 and 8.
Wilson, Robert M. *Diagnostic and Remedial Reading for Classroom and Clinic* (Third Edition). Columbus, OH: Charles E. Merrill, 1977.

11

Environmental-
Emotional Factors

OBJECTIVES

This chapter will help you to

1. Understand the relationship between reading achievement and such factors as emotional maturity, personality characteristics, and self-concept.
2. Understand how the home, community, and school can contribute to reading retardation.
3. Discover ways to diagnose and treat emotional and environmental problems.

The environment in which a child lives has an impact on his personality, his self-concept, his attitudes, and his academic achievement. There are many interrelated factors in the environment which can contribute to a child's reading maladjustment. For example, the parents' attitude toward reading and school, their socioeconomic and educational levels, occupations, child-rearing practices, and their methods of coping with the problems of living have an effect upon a child's attitudes, values, and achievement in school. Diagnosis of emotional and environmental factors is not easy, but the teacher who is to help the disabled reader must be able to recognize and deal with them. In this chapter we shall emphasize the relationship between reading performance and the home, community, and school. Such factors as emotional maturity, personality characteristics, and the self-concept will be addressed.

EMOTIONAL MATURITY

Learning to read requires self-discipline and effort. Some children, in spite of adequate intellectual ability, have difficulty in learning to read because of immature behavior in the classroom. The emotionally mature individual has learned to do the thing that needs to be done when it needs to be done whether he wants to do it or not. He or she has the capacity for self-direction and social responsibility, and the will to become involved in tasks essential to the welfare of himself and others. Some characteristics of the emotionally mature child are listed below.

1. The child easily makes home-to-school adjustments.
2. The child accepts changes in routine quietly and calmly.
3. The child accepts opposition and defeat without becoming unduly upset.
4. The child assumes responsibility.
5. The child plans and does things on time.
6. The child attends to the task at hand.
7. The child takes care of his materials and equipment.
8. The child meets and talks to strangers without shyness or undue boldness.

Overprotection and domination of the child by his or her parents can lead to dependence on others, unwillingness to assume

160

responsibility, infantile behavior, and general immaturity. Studies by McGinnis (13) show that fathers and mothers of inferior readers express attitudes that contribute to a greater degree of dependence of their children on them than fathers and mothers of superior readers. Clinical experience and research findings suggest that some children fail to make satisfactory progress in reading chiefly because of emotional immaturity. Surely, this factor should be considered in the study of the disabled reader.

PERSONALITY CHARACTERISTICS

All efforts to find a type of personality characteristic of children with reading disabilities have failed. Harris and Sipay (8, pp. 318-321), however, list several types of emotional reactions that they suggest can contribute to reading disability.

1. Conscious refusal to learn.
2. Overt hostility.
3. Negative emotional response to reading.
4. Displacement of hostility.
5. Resistance to pressure.
6. Clinging to dependency.
7. Quick discouragement.
8. Belief that success in reading is dangerous. For example, the child with strong dependency needs may view learning to read as a step toward independence—something he fears.
9. Extreme restlessness or distractibility.
10. Absorption in a private world.

Spache (21, pp. 238-239) reports the following findings based upon his study of the personalities of poor readers.

11. Retarded readers, as a group, show significantly more hostility and overt aggressiveness toward others, and less ability to acknowledge or accept blame.
12. Their responses to the situation of adult-child conflict are characterized by resistance to adult suggestions, and lack of interest or passiveness toward solutions of conflict.
13. In dealing with other children, retarded readers show less tolerance, fewer efforts to find solutions for conflict, and greater defensiveness than do normal children.

Failure in reading has been attributed to emotional problems, and emotional maladjustment has been attributed to reading disability. Apparently emotional and personality maladjustment are both cause and effect. Frustration, resulting from failure to learn to read, frequently results in a lack of interest, inattention, discouragement, and maladjustment. Each individual is seeking satisfaction, security, and recognition. When these needs are threatened, emotional conflicts can impair the individual's ability to learn.

SELF-CONCEPT

Self-concept is important in the learning process. This statement is substantiated by the work of Herbert (9, p. 78) who found a direct relationship between high self-concept and high reading comprehension. Unfortunately, not all children enter school with high self-concepts. Some children are brought up in homes in which they do not develop the feeling of security that comes from trust, physical safety, and fulfillment of the need for love and belonging. If these conditions are characteristic of a child's life during the preschool years, he often comes to school with a negative self-concept. A self-concept of inadequacy, along with other factors, can be a cause of reading disability. An idea clearly entertained in mind works itself out in action. If a person firmly believes that he is inferior to others and that he is incapable of learning, he often gives up and becomes completely defeated by the task at hand. Thus, his self-prophecy of failure is fulfilled.

Failure to learn to read can also lead to a poor self-concept. The child who experiences difficulty in learning to read usually becomes frustrated and conspicuous in class. The child becomes convinced that he or she is inferior and loses confidence in his or her ability to learn. The child is hurt and often learns to dislike reading. His lack of success and his feelings of inadequacy may contribute to emotional and social maladjustment. He or she may become aggressive, put on a bold front, and become cruel and destructive. On the other hand, the child may become timid, passive, and withdrawn. In both instances, self-concept has been reduced.

Smith and Butler (20) in their study of the self-concept and its relation to speech and reading found that children with reading problems have lower self-concepts than children with speech problems. They concluded that the correlation between self-concept and poor reading is so clear that there can be no doubt that the goal of the teacher should be to improve the self-esteem as well as the communication skill.

Family, peers, and teachers play a significant role in the formation of a child's self-concept. Ketcham (10) has shown that such factors as the mother's use of the library, the number of magazines and newspapers in the home, and the father's occupational level affect the child's concept of himself as a reader and his concept of his reading progress. Spache (21, p. 246) has stated that such attitudes as "reading is feminine" and "only eggheads like to read" are negatively related to reading success as is the amount of TV viewing of parents which implies their lack of need for reading.

Porterfield and Schlicting (16) found that rejection by peers strengthens the low self-concept and withdrawal tendencies that many poor readers exhibit. Stevens (22) has reported that poor readers recognize and acknowledge their lack of acceptance by peers.

Palardy (15) studied the effects of teacher attitudes on the achievement of first-grade boys and girls. He found that when first-grade teachers reported that they believed that boys are far less successful in learning to read than girls, then the boys in these classes achieved significantly less than boys in classes where teachers believed that boys are just as successful as girls. Carter (3) also found that teacher expectations significantly affect student's level of confidence and scholastic performance. Rosenthal and Jacobson (17) in a series of extensive studies obtained similar results. Such studies suggest that self-concept is a major factor in learning to read and should be investigated in the study of the disabled reader.

THE HOME AND ITS EFFECT UPON READING ACHIEVEMENT

The socioeconomic level of the family influences a child's interest and achievement in reading. Many poor and working-class parents have unhappy memories of their school experiences. The language, sentence patterns, and concepts of the school were unfamiliar to them. Their teachers often made their lower class values seem inferior and gave them little encouragement to learn. These experiences made them uncomfortable in middle-class educational surroundings and in subtle, and not so subtle, ways they have conveyed these feelings to their children. Children from middle and upper socioeconomic levels are often handicapped by their parents' attitudes too. Some of these parents become overly anxious about their children's academic achievement and place pressure on the children to excel. This pressure interferes with rather than helps achievement in the classroom.

The high mobility of families is another factor to consider. Many families move frequently. The children have to adjust to different communities, different teachers, different peer groups, and different instructional programs in reading. Some children adjust readily to these changes. Others are not so fortunate and become confused and discouraged.

Conflict in the home, child neglect or abuse, overprotection, parental domination, and extreme rivalry among siblings produce feelings of insecurity which can interfere with adjustment in school. Seigler and Gynther (19) found that family conflict is greater in the homes of poor readers than it is in homes in which no child has a reading deficiency. They found that parents of poor readers more frequently describe their children as aggressive, distrustful, or dependent and devaluate their children's personalities more often than parents of good readers.

A study by McGinnis (13) shows that parents of superior readers express attitudes that are less dictatorial and more democratic than do parents of inferior readers. Mothers and fathers of superior readers manifest attitudes that foster independence rather than dependence, include outside influences rather than exclude them, place less emphasis on extreme respect for parental authority and more on group thinking and group participation. Parents of superior readers convey attitudes that encourage their children to voice their ideas and points of view rather than attitudes that discourage freedom of discussion. Furthermore, the McGinnis study indicates that parents of superior readers manifest attitudes suggesting that they refrain from attempting to hurry the growth and development of their children. Instead, the attitudes of these parents suggest that they appreciate the concept of readiness. Attitudes of parents of superior readers emphasize the value of communication and the development of language skills. This study also shows that the parents of superior readers and the parents of inferior readers differ significantly in their attitudes toward the importance of reading, the value of language development, and the importance of experiential background. Parents of superior readers place a higher value on reading, language development, and the building of mental content than do parents of inferior readers.

A study by Carter (4) shows that differences in attitudes exist between parents of superior and inferior readers at the college level. He found that parents of superior college readers, to a significant degree, placed a higher value on reading, the development of language skills, and the building of experiential background than did parents of inferior readers at the college level.

THE COMMUNITY

There are within our society large numbers of people who live in subcultures that do not prepare them adequately to adjust to academic requirements or to the demands of the world at large. Edwards (7) states, "Our American society has allowed many millions of its members to remain culturally isolated, locked in their own cultural cocoons, as it were, either by design or neglect." He points out that as a result of this segregation from contact with the predominant culture, they grow up culturally different. There is a tendency for them to feel inferior, rejected, and without a significant place in our society. Their experiences are limited. They speak a divergent dialect of American English or a different language. Their concepts are highly specialized and limited. Furthermore, their value systems differ from and frequently conflict with those of the dominant culture. Linguists also suggest that unfamiliarity with the standard English used by teachers and in school books may be a major source of difficulty for children who are not accustomed to standard English. Culturally different students come to school with language patterns, experiences, values, and problems that are different from those of children and teachers from middle socioeconomic communities. They frequently experience difficulty in learning to read when taught by teachers who make no attempt to adapt instruction to their specific needs. It is essential for teachers to help these children to maintain their pride in their heritage while teaching them the language of their new country or of the dominant social group.

Lewis (12, p. 25) estimates that approximately one-fifth of the population of the United States lives in a culture of poverty and that the largest numbers of this group are made up of Blacks, Puerto Ricans, Mexicans, American Indians, and Southern Poor Whites. According to Lewis' description, individuals who grow up in these cultures often develop attitudes of fatalism, helplessness, and inferiority. Their needs are immediate, and they exhibit a strong present-time orientation in their behavior. They tend to have little interest in postponing personal gratification or thinking about the future. They have learned through their experiences to avoid sources of authority, such as the police and the school principal. They view education as an obstacle course to be followed until they can go to work. They may use violence as a tool for living and as a way of getting the attention of those who won't listen. In such an environment the child sees few, if any, examples of individuals for whom reading is a highly desirable activity.

EDUCATIONAL FACTORS AND READING ACHIEVEMENT

Many school systems lack a unified educational philosophy. Many disagree about whether socialization or learning to read during the early years should be of primary concern to the school. Some teachers believe that the major goal of the school should be the development of well-adjusted and socially competent individuals, whereas others stress the idea that learning to read is the chief objective of education, especially in the early grades. Another area of conflict is whether the school should adhere to a competency-based educational program with its emphasis on skill development or a more creative program that stresses problem-solving, learning by discovery, experimentation, evaluation, and discussion.

Some schools have failed to modify the curriculum in accordance with their promotion policy. Children are promoted on the basis of seniority rather than achievement. Consequently, as poor readers are promoted from grade to grade, they become frustrated and are unable to keep up with their group. Eventually their reading disability leads to emotional and social maladjustment. Furthermore, until very recently, developmental instruction in reading was provided only for elementary school children. Obviously, both the school and the community failed to regard reading as a continuous process, having its beginning in the home and continuing throughout the elementary grades, junior high school, the secondary school, and beyond.

A contributing factor in causing and perpetuating reading disability is the selection of inappropriate materials and faulty teaching methods. Books and other reading materials which lack interest to the learner or which deal with concepts unfamiliar to the reader can be detrimental. Requiring children to attempt to read materials at or above their frustration level or well below their independent level is too common a practice and is an excellent way to impede progress in reading.

Most teachers base their instruction on commercial materials and employ a method of teaching dictated by the materials. They fail to question how effective these methods are for each individual and often do not adapt materials and methods to the needs of the individual. Other teaching practices that have a detrimental effect on learning are instructing the child at too rapid a pace and not observing and correcting problems before they become serious. Overemphasis on oral reading, too much meaningless drill, and the use of only the basal reader for instruction are additional teaching practices that interfere with the learning process.

Spache (21, pp. 124-127) points out that teachers are inadequately prepared to provide instruction in the area of phonics, comprehension, critical reading, and reading in the content areas. A major weakness is in the area of diagnosis of pupil needs. Yet Rupley and Blair (18, pp. 32-33) maintain that, on the basis of published research, the characteristics of the effective reading teacher are well known. The effective reading teacher utilizes ongoing diagnostic techniques, develops an individual prescription for each student, takes time and effort to prepare for each lesson, and differentiates instruction and materials according to the reading levels, interests, and needs of the students. Apparently, teachers in their preparation for the teaching of reading, have not been made sufficiently aware of the fact that they should focus their attention upon the child and adjust aims, materials, and procedures to his or her needs and way of learning. To improve reading instruction, it is essential that colleges of education do a better job in the preparation of teachers.

In addition, as was mentioned earlier, there is evidence that there is a relationship between teacher expectation and student performance. Carter (3), Herbert (9), Palardy (15), and Rosenthal and Jacobson (17) have studied this issue and have concluded that teacher expectations affect the self-concept of the learner and in turn his performance.

Personality clashes between a teacher and a student can have a detrimental effect upon the student's willingness to profit from the teacher's instruction.

EXERCISE

11.1. Rate yourself or someone else who is currently teaching reading on each of the following items. When you have completed the rating, indicate the areas which you think should be changed in order to provide an improved reading program.

Classroom Climate	Rarely	Sometimes	Frequently
1. The teacher provides a classroom environment which is conducive to learning.	_____	_____	_____
2. The teacher accepts, clarifies and supports the ideas and feelings of students.	_____	_____	_____
3. The teacher encourages and praises.	_____	_____	_____

	Rarely	Sometimes	Frequently
4. The teacher asks questions to stimulate pupil inter-action.	_____	_____	_____
5. The teacher shows consid-eration and respect for children whose language, cultural background, and values are different.	_____	_____	_____
6. The teacher imparts her own enthusiasm for read-ing through her behavior and verbal communication with students.	_____	_____	_____

Materials

	Rarely	Sometimes	Frequently
1. The teacher seeks out and uses a variety of materials during the reading period in order to teach the skills needed for learning.	_____	_____	_____
2. The teacher chooses and uses materials that are appropriate to the reading levels of students.	_____	_____	_____
3. The teacher uses materials that are of interest to the students.	_____	_____	_____
4. The teacher produces teacher-made materials in reading to assist in pro-viding instruction for the specific needs of students.	_____	_____	_____

Instruction

	Rarely	Sometimes	Frequently
1. The teacher attempts to match instruction to chil-dren's learning needs through flexible grouping.	_____	_____	_____
2. The teacher uses diagnostic procedures to determine the students' needs.	_____	_____	_____
3. The teacher attempts to provide one-to-one instruc-tion for students who need it.	_____	_____	_____

	Rarely	Sometimes	Frequently
4. The teacher attempts to adapt teaching procedures to the learning styles of the students.	_____	_____	_____

Record Keeping

	Rarely	Sometimes	Frequently
1. The teacher keeps a record of each student's strengths and weaknesses in reading in order to plan and implement instruction to meet each student's needs.	_____	_____	_____
2. The teacher keeps a record of the types of books read by each child in the classroom for enjoyment.	_____	_____	_____
3. The teacher maintains a folder for each student with samples of his or her work in reading.	_____	_____	_____

ASSESSING ENVIRONMENTAL-EMOTIONAL FACTORS

Environmental-emotional factors can be investigated by teacher observations and rating scales, interviews, projective techniques, and personality tests. The use of some of these methods requires the services of a school psychologist or counselor.

Teacher Observations and Rating Scales

The teacher who is with his or her students over a prolonged period of time has an excellent opportunity to observe the student on many occasions and in many different situations. She can observe his attitudes toward reading and toward his friends, his ability to concentrate, his ability to apply himself to a difficult task, and his ability to cope with stressful situations. She or he can observe such factors as impulsiveness, resistance toward change, aggressive behaviors, dependence on others, inability to concentrate, lack of self-confidence, tension and anxiety, impatience, lack of persistence, unwillingness to put forth effort to improve, and tendencies to withdraw from social activities. In our work with disabled readers we have used the following checklist as a guide to observations.

Analyzing and Treating Reading Problems

TABLE 11-1. Personality Checklist

Child's Name _____

Observer's Name _____

Personality Characteristics

	Yes	No
1. Does the child speak disparagingly of himself?	Yes	No
2. Is he or she unable to risk making a mistake?	Yes	No
3. Is she fearful of new situations?	Yes	No
4. Is he unwilling to try new or difficult tasks?	Yes	No
5. Is she excessively shy or withdrawn?	Yes	No
6. Does he or she lack self-confidence?	Yes	No
7. Does he show excessive concern with acceptance by others?	Yes	No
8. Is he or she unusually unhappy or depressed?	Yes	No
9. Does she have difficulty making decisions?	Yes	No
10. Does he have difficulty focusing attention on the task at hand?	Yes	No
11. Does he or she appear overly tense?	Yes	No
12. Is he too impulsive?	Yes	No
13. Does she react emotionally to failure?	Yes	No
14. Is he unable to evaluate his behavior realistically?	Yes	No
15. Does she react inappropriately to criticisms and guidance from others?	Yes	No
16. Does he or she have violent outbursts of temper?	Yes	No
17. Does he lack curiosity?	Yes	No
18. Does she daydream excessively?	Yes	No
19. Is she indifferent or passive?	Yes	No
20. Is he overactive and restless?	Yes	No
21. Does he lack confidence in most learning situations?	Yes	No
22. Does she become upset when things do not go her way?	Yes	No
23. Does he or she cry easily?	Yes	No

Attitude Toward Peers

	Yes	No
1. Does the child have few, if any, friends in his peer group?	Yes	No
2. Does he disrupt other children?	Yes	No
3. Do other children avoid him?	Yes	No
4. Is he destructive of other people's property?	Yes	No
5. Does she belittle the accomplishments of others?	Yes	No
6. Does she withdraw from group activities?	Yes	No
7. Does her behavior provoke unkind attitudes and expressions from others?	Yes	No
8. Does she complain that other people do not like her?	Yes	No

Attitude Toward Teachers and Parents

	Yes	No
1. Is the child antagonistic and defiant toward adults?	Yes	No
2. Does he encourage peers to disrupt the class?	Yes	No

3. Does he or she disobey classroom rules?	Yes	No
4. Does she manipulate adults?	Yes	No
5. Is he dependent on his teacher or parents?	Yes	No
Attitude Toward Reading		
1. Does the child hate reading?	Yes	No
2. Does she avoid reading activities?	Yes	No
3. Is he unwilling to put forth effort to improve his reading?	Yes	No

There are a number of rating scales which can be purchased. Some of them are listed below.

1. *Burks' Behavior Rating Scales* (2). Identifies patterns of behavior problems in children in grades one to nine.
2. *Child Behavior Rating Scale* (5). Provides a profile of a child's adjustment in five areas: self, home, social, school, and physical activities.
3. *Walker Problem Behavior Identification Checklist* (24). Identifies elementary grade children with behavior problems. Provides scores for five scales: acting out, withdrawal, distractibility, disturbed peer relations, and immaturity.

Interviews

Interviews with the parents, former teachers, and the student can yield useful information that will help the teacher to understand the student's environmental background and some of the emotional problems the child may be experiencing. Interviews can be used to investigate any area which appears to be significant (See Chapter 8). In talking with the student we stress the importance of getting him to talk about his reading and his problems through the use of open-ended questions. The goal is to secure enough information about the child so that the teacher better understands his or her problems, feelings, and attitudes.

Projective Techniques

The purpose of projective testing is to study and obtain an evaluation of the total personality. Unlike "paper and pencil" personality tests the individual is not asked questions about himself but is asked to tell what a stimulus looks like or to tell a story of a picture, inkblot, or design. Without realizing it, the individual reveals his inner self by what he says and how he reacts. Most projective techniques cannot be used by classroom teachers. The Rorschach (11), the Children's Apperception Test (1), and the Thematic Apperception Test (14) are projective tests which require considerable psychological background and training to administer, score, and interpret. A child's drawing of the human figure and of his family is often used by psychologists to investigate the individual's concept of himself and to provide some insights regarding the family and its impact on the child. These instruments should be limited to use by a psychologist or psychiatrist.

The Sentence Completion Test is a projective technique which teachers can use. It samples the child's feelings and attitudes. With disabled readers it will be necessary for the teacher to read the partial sentence to the child and to have the student respond orally. The teacher can write the child's responses in the space provided. Obviously, the teacher must have good rapport with the child. A sample incomplete sentence test is given below.

TABLE 11-2. An Incomplete Sentence Test

Child's Name _____

Examiner's Name _____

Date _____

1. When I read, I _____

2. I like to read _____

3. I worry over _____

4. I feel hurt when _____

5. I make believe that _____

6. I am afraid that _____

7. I feel sorry when _____

8. I feel proud when _____

9. I feel ashamed when _____

10. I like to _____

11. I hate to _____

12. Reading is _____

13. I am happy when _____

14. My parents _____

15. Most books are _____

16. Some teachers are _____

17. Someday I want to _____

18. Learning to read is _____

19. If I had three wishes, I would _____

_____

_____

20. If I had a million dollars, I would _____

_____

_____

Personality Tests

There are several personality tests that teachers can administer. There are some cautions one must consider in interpreting the results obtained from such tests. Students often answer the questions in terms of what they perceive to be "right" answers rather than in terms of how the questions apply to them. Many personality tests are affected by the mood of the person on the day he takes the test. The same personality test given to an individual on a day when he feels happy and on a day when he feels depressed will not provide the same results. In spite of these shortcomings, many clinicians and teachers find personality tests helpful in understanding the child. Since most of these tests require reading ability, it will be necessary for the teacher to read the test questions to the disabled reader.

The *California Test of Personality* (23) has two major sections: Personal Adjustment and Social Adjustment. The self-adjustment section is subdivided into self-reliance, sense of personal worth, sense of personal freedom, feeling of belonging, freedom from withdrawing tendencies, and freedom from nervous symptoms. The social adjustment category is subdivided into social standards, social skills, freedom from antisocial tendencies, family relations, school relations, and community relations.

For a number of years a group of research workers has been engaged in developing and substantiating an objective and comprehensive approach to the measurement of personality and cognitive behavior. Tests representative of the results of their efforts have been published by the Institute for Personality and Ability Testing. The IPAT personality inventories (6) measure sixteen personality factors.

TREATING ENVIRONMENTAL-EMOTIONAL FACTORS

The purpose of exploring the environmental-emotional factors that may be affecting the child's reading performance is to secure information that will help the teacher and the parents to understand the child and to meet his or her needs more adequately.

What the Teacher Can Do
1. Accept the child as a person with respect for his own individuality.
2. Have faith in the child's ability to learn and show this confidence to him or her and to the other students in the class.
3. Provide the child with suitable materials—materials which are at his independent and instructional levels and are of interest to him. Avoid all materials at his frustration level.
4. Build success into the reading program and help him to be aware of the progress he is making.
5. Avoid comparing the child with others.
6. Keep careful records of his progress and share these with him.
7. Encourage the child to keep a record of his progress.
8. Create a classroom environment where exciting things are happening. Develop centers of interest.
9. Use games to teach skills.
10. Integrate the teaching of reading with art and music.
11. Read exciting stories aloud to the child.
12. Let the child know the purpose of each lesson.
13. Avoid placing the child in a situation that he or she views as threatening, such as reading aloud to the class.
14. Make arrangements with a teacher of younger children for the student to help someone in his or her class, perhaps as a tutor.
15. Use stories to build understanding of people of different ethnic backgrounds.
16. Compliment the child when he or she shows kindness toward and cooperation with others.
17. Arrange time for the child to talk with you about his or her concerns, problems, and feelings.

18. Respond to the student each day in a warm, personal way.
19. Reward the child when he or she engages in desirable behavior. Do not reinforce undesirable behavior.
20. Inform parents of the nature of your reading program.
21. Write notes of commendation about the child to his parents.
22. Build the parents' confidence in the child.
23. Help the parents understand the child's needs.
24. Reduce the parents' feelings of anxiety and guilt for the child's problems.
25. Conduct parent conferences and send letters to the home about ways to build good reading habits at home.

What Parents Can Do

1. Let the child know that you love him, that you have confidence in his ability to learn, and that he is an important member of the family.
2. Read to the child at home and make the activity an enjoyable one for him or her.
3. Let the child see you reading books, newspapers, and magazines for your own pleasure and share the information you obtain from reading with the child and other members of your family.
4. Take your children to the library regularly and get books for yourself and for them. If your budget permits, buy books for your child.
5. Listen to your child. Show an interest in what he has to say and the way he puts his ideas into words. Encourage him to talk freely about stories he has read and about experiences he has had.
6. Encourage his special interests and continue to enlarge his areas of interest by calling attention to things in which you think he might be interested.
7. Create a home atmosphere of friendly quiet comfort that will encourage reading and studying at home. Allow your child to have paper, pencil, crayons, paste, and paints to work with at home.
8. Answer your child's questions well. Do not be too busy.
9. Do not compare your child with other children.
10. Encourage your child's association with other children in school, play, clubs, and at home. This will help him to mature socially.
11. Encourage him or her to participate in family discussions of current events and everyday activities. Take time to explain

words and incidents to your child.

12. Develop the idea that every member of the family has responsibilities for doing daily tasks. Be consistent and firm in your expectations.

13. Give your child experiences that are meaningful and interesting to him. This increases his general knowledge and builds a better background for reading.

14. Help your child add words to his speaking vocabulary. Take time to explain meanings of words to him. The larger number of words he can use naturally in everyday conversations, the more meanings he will have for the words in a book.

15. Be interested in but not anxious about his progress in learning to read.

16. Display a positive attitude toward school. If parents are interested and enthusiastic about school and respectful of teachers, their children are apt to be also.

17. Help the child understand his own problems. When he makes progress, praise him for his efforts. Build his self confidence and his feelings of security.

18. Cooperate with the child's teacher and do not criticize the school or the teacher in the child's presence.

19. Encourage your child to read aloud to you. If he is willing to do so, give him an opportunity to read the material silently before reading aloud. If the child encounters a word he does not know, tell him the word immediately.

20. Provide the child with nourishing meals. Be sure he or she eats a good breakfast.

21. Arrange for your child to have plenty of rest and sleep.

22. Send your child to school each morning happy, well prepared, and ready to start his day in school.

23. Praise the child for the effort and progress he or she makes in learning to read.

EXERCISE

11.2. Below is a brief summary of one boy's school experiences. Identify and describe the factors which you believe have adversely affected Tom's progress in reading. Assume that you are Tom's present teacher. Describe how you would attempt to help him overcome his reading problems.

Tom is ten years old and a student in the fourth grade. He entered kindergarten at the age of five. School records indicate that his kindergarten teacher considered Tom to be a bright boy who at the end of the year was not ready to be promoted to the first grade. Nevertheless he was permitted to enter the first grade. He was introduced to formal instruction in reading and experienced difficulty in learning to read. He was retained in the first grade and spent another school year with the same teacher. He did not like her and became quite rebellious in school. Even though he made little progress in reading, he was permitted to enter the second grade at the age of eight. His second-grade teacher used a basal reader approach. The children were divided into three groups, and Tom was placed in the slow group where he remained throughout the year. He showed little interest in reading and balked at being in what he called "the dummy" group. Tom's group "read" the readers intended to be used with second-grade students at a slower rate than the other two reading groups. Similar materials and procedures were followed in the third and fourth grades. Tom's attitude toward reading and school in general is one of dislike.

1. What are the factors which you believe have adversely affected Tom's progress in reading?

2. If you were Tom's present teacher, what would you do to help him overcome his reading problems?

In these next exercises you will find excerpts from interviews with parents of disabled readers. Identify the factors in the home environment that you believe have adversely affected each child's progress in reading. Indicate what the parents can do to help the child make a more satisfactory adjustment.

EXERCISE

11.3. John is a twelve-year-old boy in the sixth grade of a public school located in a small rural community. His father is a well-to-do farmer. His mother is a former teacher who, in addition to co-managing the farm, is active in many community organizations. At the mother's request and with the school's cooperation, they have brought their son to a university reading clinic for diagnosis and treatment. A small portion of the clinician's interview with the parents is given.

Interviewer: Why did you bring John to the Reading Clinic?

Mother: I'm worried about his school work. He can't read, and he doesn't want to learn to read. I've tried everything. I've pleaded with him, bribed him, nagged him, but to no avail. He's twelve years old. He's getting older. What's going to happen to him in the future if he can't read?

Father: Well, I can't read, at least not very well. I get along all right.

Mother: Yes, and you're always telling John that, and he believes you. You just can't get along in this world if you can't read.

1. What factors in the home may be related to John's reading problems?

2. What can the parents do to help John?

11.4. Bill is nine years old and a fourth-grade student. He is short, thin, and frail in appearance. In the classroom he is polite, quiet, and well-mannered. He seldom participates in class discussions. His classmates, although kind to him, ignore him. Bill seems to like his teacher and often stays after the other children have been dismissed to talk with her. He is reading at approximately second-grade level. Bill's father died when Bill was in the first grade. The mother has not remarried. Bill's teacher has been concerned with his academic and social adjustment and has invited the mother to a school conference.

Mother: Billy is a good boy. He and I have a close relationship. He is my only child. My husband died when Billy was six years old, and I've raised him alone since then. He is very intelligent, and we have many happy times together. We don't know many people in the city although we've lived here for years. Billy has never been well. When his Daddy died, I kept Billy home with me the rest of the year. He's very frail, don't you think? That's why I try to protect him all I can. I don't let him play with the other children in the neighborhood. They are so rough! I try to make it up to him though—his not having friends his own age—by always being with him. We play all kinds of games together, and I know he's happy.

I don't understand why he hasn't learned to read better. He likes to have me read to him. I read to him every night. He enjoys this so much. So after I've given him his bath and helped him into his pajamas, I read to him. This is our happy hour.

1. What factors in the home may be related to Bill's academic and social adjustment?

2. How would you counsel the mother?

11.5. Joe is nine years old. He has been referred to the school's diagnostic center by his fourth-grade teacher. While Joe was being examined by the diagnostician, the mother was interviewed.

Mother: I'm worried about Joe. He has had trouble with reading since first grade. And, frankly, I think his teachers haven't been firm enough with him. They passed him from grade to grade even though he didn't do the work. It didn't take him long to figure out that no matter what he did in school, he'd be promoted to the next grade. The teachers don't care. Well, I care and I've tried to teach him to read. We sit down for one hour when he gets home from school and we read, but it doesn't do any good. He just sits there and holds the book. I get so mad at him. I know it's wrong, but I can't help myself. I yell at him when he won't try. He acts so dumb and so stupid. He's not. He's very bright. He must be to fool his teachers year after year, but I won't put up with that. I have called him a dumbbell and said he was stupid, but he knows I don't mean it. He won't do his homework. He won't read any books. He won't even look at the newspaper! I get so exasperated with him.

1. In what ways do you think the mother has been an influence on Joe's school adjustment?

2. If you were to counsel the mother, what objectives would you attempt to accomplish?

11.6. Ron is a fourth-grade student who is having difficulty in the class-room. His teachers have been concerned about his lack of interest, his limited experiential background, and his inadequate performance in reading. The fourth-grade teacher made a home visit. A brief excerpt of the mother's and teacher's conversation is given. It is typical of the total interview.

Teacher: I've come today to talk with you about Ron.
Mother: Yeah. Well, come in. Set down.
Teacher: Ron is having difficulty in school, especially in reading.
Mother: Yeah. Well, that's your job.
Teacher: I think if I knew Ron better I could help him more.
Mother: Yeah.
Teacher: Tell me about him.
Mother: Well, uh, what do you want to know?
Teacher: How does he spend his time at home?
Mother: Well, he plays.
Teacher: What else?
Mother: Uh, he works.

1. What inferences can you make regarding Ron's home?

2. In treating Ron's reading problem, would you counsel the parents in an attempt to bring about a change? Why?

SUMMARY

The environment in which a child lives significantly affects his personality, his self-concept, his attitudes, and his academic achievement. In order to help the individual whose reading performance is adversely affected by environmental-emotional factors, cooperation between parents and teachers is essential.

Analyzing and Treating Reading Problems

REFERENCES

1. Bellak, Leopold, and Sonya S. Bellak. *Children's Apperception Test*. New York: C.P.S. Company, P. O. Box 83, Larchmont, 1971.
2. Burks, Harold F. *Burks' Behavior Rating Scales*. Los Angeles: Western Psychological Services, 1977.
3. Carter, Dale L. "The Effect of Teacher Expectations on the Self-Esteem and Academic Performance of Seventh Grade Students." Doctoral dissertation, University of Tennessee, 1970.
4. Carter, Homer L.J. "A Study of Attitudes Toward Certain Aspects of Reading Expressed by Parents of Inferior and Superior College Readers." *The Philosophical and Sociological Bases of Reading*. Fourteenth Yearbook of the National Reading Conference. Milwaukee: The National Reading Conference, Inc., 1965: 188-194.
5. Cassel, Russell N. *Child Behavior Rating Scale*. Los Angeles: Western Psychological Services, 1962.
6. Cattell, Raymond B. *IPAT—The Sixteen Personality Factor Test*. Champaign, IL: Institute for Personality and Ability Testing, 1972.
7. Edwards, Thomas J. "Cultural Deprivation: Ideas for Action." in *Forging Ahead in Reading*: Conference Proceedings of the International Reading Association, Vol. 12, Part 1, 1968: 357-363.
8. Harris, Albert J., and Edward R. Sipay. *How to Increase Reading Ability* (Seventh Edition). New York: Longman, 1980.
9. Herbert, D. "Reading Comprehension as a Function of Self-Concept," *Perceptual and Motor Skills* 27 (1968).
10. Ketcham, C. A. "Factors in the Home Background and Reader Self-Concept Which Relate to Reading Achievement." in *Proceedings College Reading Association*, Vol. 6, 1966: 66-68.
11. Klopfer, Bruno. *The Rorschach Technique*. New York: Grune and Stratton, 1942.
12. Lewis, Oscar. "The Culture of Poverty." *Scientific American* 215 (October 1966): 19-26.
13. McGinnis, Dorothy J. "A Comparative Study of the Attitudes of Parents of Superior and Inferior Readers Toward Certain Child Rearing Practices, the Value of Reading, and the Development of Language Skills and Experiential Background Related to Reading." Doctoral dissertation, Michigan State University, 1963.
14. Murray, Henry A. *Thematic Apperception Test*. Cambridge, MA: Harvard University Press, 1943.
15. Palardy, James M. "The Effect of Teachers' Beliefs on the Achievement in Reading of First-Grade Boys." Doctoral dissertation, Ohio State University, 1968.
16. Porterfield, A. V., and H. F. Schlicting. "Peer Status and Reading Achievement." *Journal of Educational Research* 54 (April 1961): 291-297.
17. Rosenthal, R., and L. Jacobson. *Pygmalion in the Classroom, Teacher*

Expectations and Pupils' Intellectual Development. New York: Holt, Rinehart and Winston, 1968.

18. Rupley, William H., and Timothy R. Blair. *Reading Diagnosis and Remediation.* Chicago: Rand McNally College Publishing Company, 1979.
19. Seigler, Hazel G., and Malcolm D. Gynther. "Reading Ability of Children and Family Harmony." *Journal of Developmental Reading* 4 (Autumn 1969): 17-24.
20. Smith, Dorothy Edna, and Katharine G. Butler. "The Self Concept and Its Relation to Speech and Reading." *Reading Horizons* 7 (Winter, 1967): 59-63.
21. Spache, George D. *Investigating the Issues of Reading Disabilities.* Boston: Allyn and Bacon, 1976.
22. Stevens, Deon O. "Reading Difficulty and Classroom Acceptance." *Reading Teacher* 25 (October 1971): 52-55.
23. Thorpe, L. P., W. W. Clark, and E. W. Tiegs. *California Test of Personality.* Monterey, CA: CTB/McGraw-Hill, 1953.
24. Walker, Hill M. *Walker Problem Behavior Identification Checklist.* Los Angeles: Western Psychological Services, 1976.

SUGGESTED READING

Austin, Mary, and C. Morrison. *The First R: The Harvard Report on Reading in the Elementary Schools.* New York: Macmillan, 1963.

Brookover, W. B. *Self-Concept of Ability and School Achievement.* East Lansing, MI: Michigan State University Press, 1965.

Charters, W. W. "Social Class Analysis and the Control of Public Education." *Harvard Educational Review* 23 (Fall 1953): 268-283.

Davis, A. *Social Class Influences on Learning.* Cambridge, MA: Harvard University Press, 1962.

Larrick, Nancy. *Parent's Guide to Children's Reading* (Fourth Edition). New York: Doubleday, 1975.

Mercer, Jane R. *System of Multicultural Pluralistic Assessment, Technical Manual.* New York: The Psychological Corporation, 1979.

Morrison, C., and Mary Austin. *The Torchlighters Revisited.* Newark, DE: International Reading Association, 1977.

12

Making a Diagnosis and Planning Treatment

OBJECTIVES

This chapter will help you to

1. Integrate the results of the investigative procedure.
2. Make a diagnosis.
3. Plan treatment.

No matter how lengthy the assessment procedure has been it is merely the first step toward the goal of helping a retarded reader. Results of tests, interviews, and observation must be analyzed and then synthesized. A diagnosis should be formulated, and from this should come the mapping of the treatment which is appropriate for that particular student.

WHERE TO START

Before taking on the job of analysis and synthesis the reading teacher or clinician should take into consideration the three elements involved in the process. She should know her student; she should know herself; and she should know what to collect.

Know Your Student

The more you know about your student the greater are your chances of helping him. You should know how well he reads, how great his potential for reading is, what reading difficulties he is having, and what might have caused the problems. You should know his interests and what motivates him. Also, you should know his modality strengths and his cognitive style. In addition, you should know which of his inadequacies are impeding his progress and which needs have priority. If a student cannot identify the parts of speech but always speaks grammatically, it would seem sensible to concentrate on some more immediate need, at least for the present. And, finally you need to know how to coordinate all of this into a program specifically designed to make that particular person into a successful reader.

Know Yourself

We all have our cognitive styles and our biases. We must keep in mind that the reliability and validity of our conclusions are, to a considerable degree, dependent on our awareness of our own prejudices, preconceptions, and emotional bias (2, p. 79). We need to be aware of these tendencies so that we can use them to the best advantage or change them when they need to be changed.

Beware of specializing in a particular diagnosis. There is an urge to find the disability that one has learned to cure. A renologist looks for a diseased kidney, and a pancreologist looks for a malfunction of the pancreas, and so on. It is the same for reading teachers and clinicians. If minimal brain damage is the area of specialty, they might find it more often than not in a child with a reading difficulty. Years ago, Joseph R. Royce said, "The dilemma of the specialist as truthseeker is that he has not seen much of the universe from the black bottom of his nicely furrowed rut, but he proceeds to proclaim his world view anyhow and in many cases with considerable vigor" (9, p. 3).

The trick is to keep an open mind; to look for any and all possibilities, and when the problem is found, to solve that problem. Eclecticism sometimes appears to be capriciousness, but it is, in fact, the most difficult principle for a diagnostician to follow.

Know What to Collect

Beware of too cursory an assessment. Diagnosis must take into account the whole individual. Each of the aspects of the person must be related to the rest of him. If a new child joins a second grade class and does not know the alphabet, it might not mean that he is lagging far behind. He may have come from a school where the initial teaching alphabet was used. He may be as far advanced as the other children when he uses the system that he has been taught. Thus, only a bridging process between the two reading systems is called for. Too cursory an assessment might lead to reaching a wrong conclusion.

It is even more important not to collect too much information. Many teachers collect so much material that the jumble never gets organized. The essence is lost in a morass of the irrelevant. If, for instance, a child is an obviously happy, gregarious member of the class, there should be no need to give him a personality test.

ORGANIZING THE DATA

In the clinic the assessment of an individual is usually carried on in a single time frame, whereas in the classroom data for a complete diagnosis might take months to gather. In either case having an organizational system makes the job easier. An analysis sheet, such as was presented in Chapter 4, or as shown here, might be adapted. Every teacher in every grade will need his or her own list of skills, and the following sample includes more categories than any one teacher would need.

Whatever type of summary is used for each student, it should be followed by another paper that contains three widely spaced items: Observations, Inferences, and Special Notes. Remarks made on this portion of the summary will contribute heavily to the diagnosis and eventual treatment of the student.

TABLE 12-1.   Student Reading Analysis Sheet

Name _____ Teacher _____

Age _____ Grade _____

Standardized Test Scores _____

Informal Reading Inventory

	Oral	Silent
Independent	_____	_____
Instructional	_____	_____
Frustration	_____	_____
Listening Capacity	_____	

Skill	*Degree of Mastery*

Sight Words _____

Phonics _____

    Consonants _____

    Consonant Clusters _____

    Vowels _____

    Vowel Clusters _____

Structural Analysis _____

    Word endings _____

    Compounds _____

    Affixes _____

    Contractions _____

    Possessives _____

Skill	Degree of Mastery
Syllabication	_____
Contextual Clues	_____
Word Meaning	_____
Literal Understanding	_____
Main Idea	_____
Detail	_____
Sequence	_____
Comparisons	_____
Cause-Effect	_____
Character Traits	_____
Interpretative Meanings	_____
Inferring Main Idea	_____
Inferring Details	_____
Inferring Sequence	_____
Inferring Comparisons	_____
Inferring Cause and Effect	_____
Inferring or Predicting Outcomes	_____
Figurative Language	_____
Evaluation	_____
Fact-Opinion	_____
Reality-Fantasy	_____
Validity	_____
Acceptability	_____
Reading-Study Skills	_____
Special Vocabulary	_____
Following Directions	_____
Organizing	_____
Summarizing	_____

Skill	Degree of Mastery
Reference books _____	
Chart, Graph Reading _____	
Skimming, Scanning _____	
Outlining _____	
Notetaking _____	
Using a Dictionary _____	

FILLING OUT THE ANALYSIS SHEET

Any comprehensive assessment program will contain some duplication, and occasionally the conclusions or scores will be at odds with each other. Data from the tests, inventories, and observation should be entered on a summary sheet, but what do you do when two tests give conflicting results? You might average the scores or you might temper those scores with your own knowledge of the student, and of the instruments themselves. For instance, if Timmy's reading grade score on one test was 2.5 and on another was 3.5, you would consider Timmy himself before deciding what score to use. How was his mood on each of those occasions? Did one test have selections that were more interesting to him than the other? Were there distractions during one testing situation which could have inhibited his success? You should also consider the tests themselves. Is one more reliable or valid? Do they both test essentially the same thing? Are the scores on one test consistently higher or lower than on the other? These questions and others can help you decide what score to record in the summary.

Another problem that arises is how much weight to give to specific errors the student makes. On a sight word list Bobby says *was* for *saw, for* for *of,* and *pat* for *tap.* Would this indicate a reversal problem? Maybe, and maybe not. The flashing of individual words for instant recognition is artificial to the reading process and is therefore less obviously a left-to-right exercise to the young student. If Bobby also made those kinds of reversal errors in a real reading situation, it would suggest that this is indeed a problem for him.

It should be remembered that there should be *copious* evidence that a certain reading skill is inadequate before making a judgment of inadequacy. Everyone occasionally makes a mistake through carelessness or inattention. Such errors can be discounted if the examiner always insists on multiple evidence of inadequacy. Every notation on the Summary Sheet should be made after combining and coordinating all of the information that has been gathered on that particular subject.

MAKING A DIAGNOSIS

After all of the information has been gathered, why go any further? Why not simply work on the skills which are inadequate and let it go at that? The reason we cannot take this apparently obvious, straightforward approach is because each student is a complex, unique individual, and much more must be known about him or her than a list of his strengths and weaknesses. Diagnosis does enable the examiner to prescribe the right materials and procedures, but in order to do that successfully, the diagnosis should reveal the cause of the difficulty.

The person making a diagnosis must examine the information, see the relationships among the specifics, and unify the results as best as possible. She can *identify* the students who need help, she can *classify* their problems by noting their degree of retardation and how this affects their learning in general, and she can identify their *reading needs* through the data-gathering process. This information coupled with background data on the students should make it possible for her to infer *causal factors.*

Finding Causal Factors

In most cases making an interpretation of causal factors is a vital step in the process because, as is true in medicine, curing the cause is more effective than merely alleviating the symptoms. If, for instance, the cause is a physical one it might be unproductive to concentrate on reading until the original problem has been corrected. Or, if the student is just learning English as a second language, the treatment of his problem will need to take this into account.

The possible physical, cognitive, environmental and emotional factors (see the preceding three chapters) should each be considered in relation to every student being examined. Sometimes a totally unexpected cause will be uncovered by close scrutiny. For example, a charming little girl in the third grade was still having trouble reading primers, and the teacher was at a loss to explain the reason for her difficulty. She enlisted the help of the school psychologist who found that the child's IQ was in the low 80s. The little girl's delightful personality had made the teacher assume that she was at least of average intelligence.

Some people find that a checklist of causal factors can be valuable. Each item on it should be considered carefully before deciding whether or not in fact it could be causing the problem. A suggested checklist is presented here.

TABLE 12-2.   Checklist of Causal Factors

Physical Factors
   Vision
   Hearing
   Speech
   General Health
   Neurological Deficits
Cognitive Factors
   Intelligence
   Mental Content
   Perception
   Attention
   Language
Environmental–Emotional Factors
   Home
   Community
   School
   Emotional Maturity
   Emotional Adjustment
   Self-Concept

More often than not, the examiner will find that there is a combination of factors affecting a particular student rather than a single one. The factors may be related to each other, such as a perceptual difficulty combined with a resultant low self-concept, or they may be disparate, as in the case of a hard-of-hearing individual who also comes from a bleak home environment. In any case, all the causal factors that are impeding the person's progress should be recorded so that they can direct the plan of treatment.

How to Make a Diagnosis

There are certain steps to follow in making a diagnosis whether it is done by a teacher or a clinician. First, decide what is *relevant* to the problem, but then decide what is *significant* to the future success of the student. In Chapter 5 the case of Trudy was presented. She was the tiny girl who was born with wryneck. Both her size and her neonatal physical difficulties were relevant to her problem but not to the solution. The *significant* factor was the overprotective attitude of the parents. The one led to the other but correction involved the changing of the parents' behavior toward Trudy rather than any need for physical improvement. The steps to follow in making a diagnosis are listed below.

1. Study all of the relevant findings.
2. Reject immaterial information.
3. Identify the problems.
4. Interpret rather than evaluate.
5. Take into account the interests, needs, and capabilities of the student.
6. Use intuition in developing a hypothesis.
7. Temper tentative judgments with facts.
8. Abandon the hypothesis if it does not stand up under the weight of the evidence.
9. Keep diagnosis open-ended; change as the child changes, or as new evidence comes to light.

What Kind of Diagnosis to Make

Diagnosis can be informal or formal. The teacher should make an informal judgment of the causal factors whenever possible. This may take the form of notes on the diagnostic sheet, such as "Molly's problem seems to stem from her poor auditory perception." Another might say, "Ed's whole family seems to go through life never talking to each other. Ed needs vocal stimulation."

Formal diagnosis is the kind produced when a written report is required. It is usually done by the reading specialist or the school psychologist. It is the result of team effort, and consensus is reached before the diagnosis is formulated. The presumed causal factors are stated in formal language and as succinctly as possible. Since parents probably will be reading it the statement should be made in as kindly a manner as is consistent with the truth as the clinician sees it.

A formal diagnosis might go something like this: "J.J. is a girl of average intelligence who is experiencing difficulty in learning to read primarily because of the confusion arising from exposure to four different reading programs in the four schools she attended during the first and second grades."

Other examples of formal interpretations, culled from the authors' files, are reproduced here:

> Ann B. is experiencing academic difficulty primarily because of inadequate intellectual functioning. Her reading skills are commensurate with her level of ability.
>
> Bruce M. is not reading at the expected level because he is in an orally based reading program despite his lack of fluency and his inadequate meaning vocabulary.
>
> Laurie S.'s reading problem is caused by a combination of factors. Reading instruction has been inconsistent. Insufficient opportunities for social interaction have contributed to a low self-concept, and her teachers, parents, and Laurie herself no longer expect reading success from her.

EXERCISES

12.1. Ed's informal diagnosis mentioned earlier, was "Ed's whole family seems to go through life never talking to each other. Ed needs vocal stimulation." Change this into a formal statement.

12.2. Devise a formal diagnosis for Trudy, using only the information provided on page 191.

12.3. Assuming that the following information contains the essence of the problem, write an appropriate formal interpretation or diagnosis.

> Billy is twelve years and eight months old and is in the sixth grade. He and his parents feel that his reading is not progressing adequately. The parents insisted that he be given speech therapy when he was four years old. He was dismissed after five months as having adequate speech, and no other agency could be persuaded that he had a speech problem. The parents also insisted that he repeat first grade. When the school authorities refused, the parents moved to a new school district and succeeded in having him held back in the first grade. At present the teacher reports that he is reading at low sixth-grade level.

The collection of the test results and the formulation of a diagnosis is a time-consuming job and, to make matters worse, it is part of a process, not a culmination. As Fabricant (4, p. 332) said, "Diagnosis is a working hypothesis and is useful in planning and prediction but is not an end in itself." As soon as the hypothesis has been made, it is time to begin adding to the collection of data and even altering the diagnosis as new evidence appears.

PLANNING TREATMENT

Once the interpretation of causal factors has been made and the needs of the student have been identified, the teacher or clinician has the material necessary to begin planning treatment.

It should be noted that strategies used for treatment are similar for both classroom and clinic. The clinic may have fewer students at one time, but techniques and procedures are essentially the same.

Principles of Remediation

There are certain principles which should guide the teacher in planning treatment for the student.

- Provide a program that is appropriate for the needs, reading level, and interest of the student.
- Provide a well-structured, sequential program.
- Provide for instruction that is balanced between skill acquisition and actual reading activities.
- Select materials that are unfamiliar to the student. The practice of having him "reread" a book he has already failed in violates psychological and common sense principles.
- Provide for transfer of learning to everyday reading tasks.
- Provide for enhancement of the student's self-concept by beginning with material at his independent reading level and slowly incorporating more difficult activities as he exhibits the ability to handle them.
- Provide a program which emphasizes his learning modality strength and his cognitive style.
- Plan for immediate assistance in mastering the abilities that he needs in order to move forward quickly.

Long-range Goals

The goals one sets for the semester or year should be made in terms of what reasonably can be expected to be accomplished with that particular student in that amount of time. These long-range goals should be realistic and as precise as possible. Many reading teachers couch their long-range goals in behavioral language. A behavioral objective states the exact kind and degree of improvement the learner should display by the end of the term. It must be observable behavior, the instrument by which it is measured must be identified, and the degree of accuracy the student must attain is stated. Such a statement might be: By June 10, Gerry will identify with 100 per cent accuracy the diphthongs *ou* and *oi* when presented with a list of twenty words made up of five *ou* words, five *oi* words, and ten words without diphthongs.

The reasoning behind the use of behavioral objectives is sound. They provide specifics to aim for and they keep the daily lessons on track. Their weakness arises from their mechanistic nature. They tend to direct the therapy toward skill drill. It is practically impossible to concoct a behavioral objective to measure any increase in enjoyment of reading. It is also impossible to measure precisely the degree of transfer of learning to a regular textbook that may have taken place. It would seem sensible then, for long-range goals to be in the form of behavioral objectives whenever possible and to state the remainder in more general terms.

Example

Dan, an eleven-year-old boy in the fifth grade, whose instructional grade level in reading was fourth grade, had the following problems identified: His sight word vocabulary measures at 3.5. He uses decoding skills on tests but seldom uses anything but contextual clues when reading connected discourse. He has difficulty in drawing conclusions and in finding the main idea of what he reads. He does not enjoy reading.

The long-range goals which were made up for him were

a. To increase his sight word vocabulary.
b. To teach him to use decoding skills when reading a book at the fourth-grade level of difficulty.
c. To stimulate an interest in reading.
d. To improve his skills in finding the main idea and in drawing conclusions from what he reads.

Some of these goals can be put into behavioral objective terms and others can not. The first one could be, "By the end of the therapy term Dan will recognize 90 per cent of the Barbe fourth grade sight word list." Goal number two might say, "By the end of the term Dan will decode all of the words in the first chapter of *Space Pirate* (by Henry Bamman, Benefic Press, Westchester, IL, 1970).

Number three would be difficult to change into a behavioral objective, but number four could say, "By the end of the term Dan will read the first story in Alfred Hitchcock's *Solve Them Yourself*

Mysteries (Random House, NY, 1963). He will identify the main idea of each paragraph with 95 per cent accuracy and will be able to draw all of the conclusions the author asks the reader to make as the story progresses."

EXERCISE

12.4. Andy's problems are identified for you. Decide how to phrase long-range goals to help solve these problems, then convert into behavioral objectives any that you feel can be in that form.

Andy is a second-grader whose instructional reading level is 1.5. His major difficulties are

a. Lack of confidence.
b. A very limited meaning vocabulary.
c. Lack of vowel sound identification.
d. Inability to blend sounds to decode words.

SELECTING MATERIALS

There is an almost infinite variety of materials that can be used for teaching reading. Catalogues, newspapers, comic books, the Bible, street signs, grocery store items, and so on, are all valid materials, but the most usual ones are specific skill acquisition materials and regular books.

Skill Acquisition Materials

Practically all retarded readers need some work on skill acquisition, and it is the teacher's or the therapist's challenge to make it as interesting as possible. Frank Smith (10, p. 184) says, in relation to meaningless drills and exercises, "There are so many candidates for this category ranging from deciding which of three ducks is facing the wrong way to underlining silent letters in words, that I shall not attempt to make a list. Children may learn to score high on boring, repetitive, and nonsensical tasks . . . but such a specialized ability will not make readers of them."

Skill drill material should be as interesting as possible, and should be geared exactly to the skill the student needs help with. Published materials are becoming more and more interesting, but often the teacher can create an activity which follows these principles even more exactly. If an impetus to creativity is needed, the teacher might find some excellent suggestions in the following—highly incomplete—list of books.

Reading Activities for Today's Elementary Schools. Burns, Paul C., and Betty D. Roe. Chicago: Rand McNally College Publishing Company, 1979.

Learning Activities for Reading (Second Edition). Selma Herr. Dubuque, IA: Wm. C. Brown Company, 1970.

Teaching Reading Vocabulary. Johnson, Dale D., and P. David Pearson. New York: Holt, Rinehart and Winston, 1978.

Teaching Reading Comprehension. Pearson, P. David, and Dale D. Johnson. New York: Holt, Rinehart and Winston, 1978.

Reading Activities for Child Development (Second Edition). Spache, Evelyn B. Boston: Allyn and Bacon, 1976.

Books

Therapy has the goal of making the person become a lifelong reader and the best way to do that is to make him view books as his friends. Thus, therapy material should include a wealth of interesting books. Where does the teacher get them? As Jeanette Veatch (12, p. 3) says, "Research the attic . . . buy 'em . . . swap 'em . . . hunt for 'em anywhere . . ."

Instruction should be conducted in books that match the student's instructional reading grade level, and free reading should be done in books at his or her independent level. Once we know what grade level books a child is capable of reading it is necessary to find books at that level. Libraries can be helpful for this, and there are many published lists available which estimate the reading level of popular trade books. Basal series, of course, indicate the difficulty level of their books (not always accurately), but there is a wide world of interesting material outside of these series which the children should have the opportunity to read.

In spite of these helps it is often the teacher who must decide how easy or hard a particular book is to read. Even textbooks, at least those written before 1975, have often been inappropriate for the grade level intended. Many high school science books, for instance, are written at college level of difficulty.

Readability formulas, ways to figure how difficult printed materials are to read, began to proliferate after Rudolph Flesch (5) published the first one in 1943. Two of the most popular formulas have been concocted by Dale and Chall (3) and George Spache (11). The Flesch and Dale-Chall formulas are for fourth-grade level and up, and Spache's is for the earlier grades.

Most of the extant readability formulas consider such things as sentence length, number of syllables per word, vocabulary difficulty and diversity, and occasionally other aspects of the selections. And,

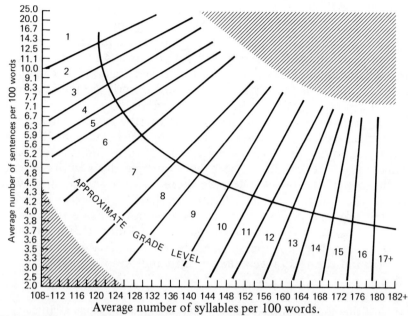

Average number of syllables per 100 words.

Figure 12-1. Graph for estimating readability—extended (Fry). Dr. Edward Fry, Rutgers University Reading Center, New Brunswick, N.J. 08904. Note: This "extended graph" does not outmode or render the earlier (1968) version inoperative or inaccurate; it is an extension (Reproduction Permitted— No Copyright).

Expanded Directions for Working Readability Graph
1. Randomly select three (3) sample passages and count out exactly 100 words each, beginning with the beginning of a sentence. Do count proper nouns, initializations, and numerals.
2. Count the number of sentences in the hundred words, estimating length of the fraction of the last sentence to the nearest one-tenth.
3. Count the total number of syllables in the 100-word passage. If you don't have a hand counter available, an easy way is to simply put a mark above every syllable over one in each word, then when you get to the end of the passage, count the number of marks and add 100. Small calculators can also be used as counters by pushing numeral 1, then push the + sign for each word or syllable when counting.
4. Enter graph with *average* sentence length and *average* number of syllables; plot dot where the two lines intersect. Area where dot is plotted will give you the approximate grade level.
5. If a great deal of variability is found in syllable count or sentence count, putting more samples into the average is desirable.
6. A word is defined as a group of symbols with a space on either side; thus *Joe, IRA, 1945,* and *&* are each one word.
7. A syllable is defined as a phonetic syllable. Generally, there are as many syllables as vowel sounds. For example, *stopped* is one syllable and *wanted* is two syllables. When counting syllables for numerals and initializations, count one syllable for each symbol. For example, *1945* is four syllables, *IRA* is three syllables, and *&* is one syllable.

most of the formulas are complicated, nerve-racking exercises that take too much of the teacher's time to figure out. Some school systems and clinics have solved this problem by programming computers to perform this chore. But this is not always available to every teacher, so the goal is to find as simple and accurate a readability formula as possible. Two which meet these criteria are the Fry Readability Formula (6) and the Raygor Procedure (8).

There are two basic principles involved in the Fry formula. One is that longer words are harder to read than short ones and therefore a greater number of syllables per hundred words indicates a higher grade level of readability. The other principle deals with sentence length, so that the *fewer* sentences there are in a one-hundred-word passage the greater is the difficulty level. It should also be noted that the dot one places on the graph does not indicate that precise point but rather a three grade range of readability. If, for example, a dot is placed within the sixth-grade boundaries this can be construed as indicating a range between fifth and seventh grades.

EXERCISE

12.5. Using the Fry Readability Formula, compute the reading difficulty level of this book. Choose

    a. The first one hundred words in the preface, beginning with the word "Analyzing . . ." and ending with the phrase "significant findings to the diagnosis and treatment . . ."

    b. In Chapter 3 the first one hundred words under the title "Underachievement in Reading," on page 25, begining with "The underachiever . . ." and ending with "However, Dick is not reading . . ."

    c. The first one hundred words under the title, "Setting Instructional Goals," in Chapter 4, page 45, beginning with "Test results . . ." and ending with "should involve the student in the . . ."

	Number of Syllables	Number of Sentences
The first 100 words	_____	_____
The second 100 words	_____	_____
The third 100 words	_____	_____
Average	_____	_____
Estimated Difficulty Level	_____	

Alton Raygor felt that too many errors were made when people were asked to count the number of syllables in three one-hundred word selections. His solution was to have them count the number of words which contained six or more letters instead of syllables.

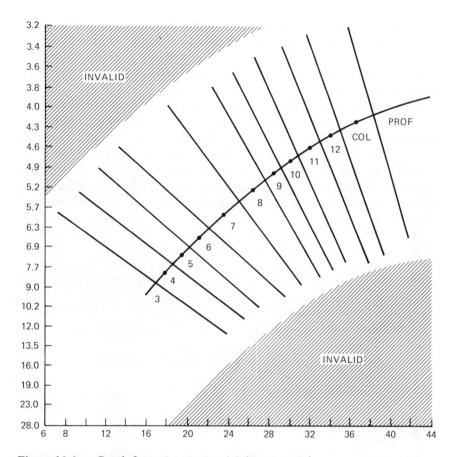

Figure 12-2. Graph for estimating readability (Raygor).

Directions:

Count out three 100-word passages at the beginning, middle, and end of a selection or book. Count proper nouns, but not numerals.

1. Count sentences in each passage, estimating to nearest tenth.
2. Count words with six or more letters.
3. Average the sentence length and word length over the three samples and plot the average on a graph.

Example:

	Sentences	6+ Words
A	6.0	15
B	6.8	19
C	6.4	17
Total	19.2	51
Average	6.4	17

Note mark on graph. Grade level is about 5.

This graph is not copyrighted. It may be reproduced. Copies can also be obtained from Dr. Alton L. Raygor, University of Minnesota, 192 Pillsbury Drive S.E., Minneapolis, Minnesota 55455.

Baldwin and Kaufman (1, p. 151) made a comparison study of the Raygor and Fry techniques and found that Raygor's took less time to compute and yet correlated highly with Fry's technique. On page 199, for comparison with the Fry Readability Formula, is Raygor's graph and directions.

As useful as readability formulas are, they do have some drawbacks. One of these is the universal use of sentence length as a criterion of difficulty. Marshall and Glock (7, pp. 10-56) found that poor readers had more difficulty understanding or remembering the relationship between two ideas when they appeared in separate sentences than when they were linked together in a single sentence with cue words, such as *because, since, after,* etc. This suggests that shorter and simpler sentences are not always more comprehensible.

Another drawback to readability formulas arises from the fact that there are some factors that contribute to the relative difficulty of a particular book that are almost impossible to measure. The organization of the material, the format, and the number of incidental helps such as headings, margin notes, and graphic aids, all affect the readability. The conceptual level of the content is another factor that defies measuring. Reading a simplified description of Einstein's Relativity Theory might contain only easily understood words but the conceptual level would be an insurmountable barrier to many of us.

It should be kept in mind, too, that it is quite possible for a person to understand material that is beyond his estimated reading grade level if he has an interest in the subject and some background knowledge of it.

The solution to these problems is to temper readability results with common sense.

PROCEDURES FOR REMEDIATION

Remediation usually involves the teaching of fundamental skills. It should be stressed, however, that they be taught within the framework of a goal-oriented process, and not as separate entities.

The overall plan for remediation should be constructed around the following guidelines.

- Decide how often the therapy sessions will be held. This is dictated by the constraints on the teacher or specialist, but the greater the frequency of the meetings, the more possible is improvement.

- Decide how long each session will be. Younger children need shorter sessions, usually no longer than forty-five minutes, and older children often can stay on task for an hour.
- Decide on how many different aims can be accomplished in each session. Two or three quite different activities are probably enough. The therapist should follow the principle of a balanced program. For instance, a word attack skill, a comprehension exercise, and a study skill could make up a session.
- Provide an opportunity for success for the child. Begin with material that he can read easily, and slowly work up into more difficult things. Also make use of the teaching method with which the child is most successful.
- Keep the student informed of the reasons for each activity, and keep him aware of the progress he is making.
- Convince the student that he or she is a worthwhile individual who can learn.

SUMMARY

This chapter has discussed the reasons for integrating all of the information that is gathered about a student with reading problems. The things that the teacher must know about her student, about herself, and about the kinds of information she should collect are set forth. Next are suggestions for organizing the mass of material and for making a diagnosis. Finally, suggestions are made for formulating aims, selecting materials, and deciding on procedures for the entire therapy term.

REFERENCES

1. Baldwin, R. Scott, and Rhonda Kaufman. "A Concurrent Validity Study of the Raygor Readability Estimate." *Journal of Reading* 23 (November 1979): 148-153.
2. Carter, Homer L. J., and Dorothy J. McGinnis. *Diagnosis and Treatment of the Disabled Reader.* New York: Macmillan, 1970.
3. Dale, Edgar, and Jeanne S. Chall. "A Formula for Predicting Readability." *Educational Research Bulletin* 27 (January 11 and February 17, 1948): 11-20 and 37-54.

4. Fabricant, Benjamin. "Aspects of Teaching Clinical Diagnosis in an Academic Setting." *Academic Psychology Bulletin* 2 (November 1980): 403-405.
5. Flesch, Rudolph. *How to Test Readability.* New York: Harper & Row, 1951.
6. Fry, Edward. Rutgers University Reading Center, New Brunswick, NJ, 1977.
7. Marshall, M., and M. O. Glock. "Comprehension of Connected Discourse: A Study into the Relationships Between the Structure of Text and Information Recalled." *Reading Research Quarterly* 14 (1978-79): 10-56.
8. Raygor, Alton L. University of Minnesota, Minneapolis, 1977.
9. Royce, Joseph R. *The Encapsulated Man.* Toronto: Van Nostrand, 1964.
10. Smith, Frank. *Understanding Reading.* New York: Holt, Rinehart and Winston, 1978.
11. Spache, George. "A New Readability Formula for Primary Reading Materials." *Elementary School Journal* 52 (March 1953): 410-413.
12. Veatch, Jeannette. *How to Teach Reading with Children's Books.* New York: Citation Press, 1965.

SUGGESTED READING

Bader, Lois A. *Reading Diagnosis and Remediation in Classroom and Clinic.* New York: Macmillan, 1980.

Carducci-Bolchazy, Marie. "False Prerequisites in Learning to Read." in Kenneth Vandermeulen, ed. *Reading Horizons: Selected Readings.* Kalamazoo, MI: Western Michigan University Press, 1979: 380-385.

Waller, T. Gary, and G. E. MacKinnon. *Reading Research Advances in Theory and Practice.* Vol 1. New York: Academic Press, 1979.

Winkley, Carol. "What Do Diagnostic Reading Tests Really Diagnose?" *Diagnostic Viewpoints in Reading.* Newark, DE: International Reading Association, 1971: 64-80.

13

Correcting Word Identification Problems

OBJECTIVES

This chapter will help you to

1. Understand the basic principles underlying the teaching of word identification skills.
2. Discover ways to improve sight word skills.
3. Discover ways to improve contextual analysis.
4. Discover ways to improve structural analysis.
5. Discover ways to improve letter-sound correspondence.
6. Discover ways to improve spelling.

Words have three aspects, form, sound, and meaning, and the third aspect is the most important. It avails a person very little to recognize the form and sound of a word if he does not understand its meaning. On the other hand, if he cannot recognize either its sound or its form, he has no way to understand what the word means. Since words are the elements that combine to indicate meaning, the separation between word identification and reading comprehension is somewhat artificial but is necessary for organizational purposes. In this chapter we will be dealing primarily with that aspect of meaning called word identification, and the following chapter will discuss reading comprehension and meaning vocabulary.

WHY TEACH WORD IDENTIFICATION TECHNIQUES?

The goal in teaching word identification techniques is to provide ways for a person to identify an unfamiliar word in its written form. Learning to read is more difficult than adults often realize. The process must begin with an awareness that the squiggles on a page represent words. Next comes the ability to differentiate one word from another. Acquiring word identification skills gives a child the means for "cracking the code."

There are four different strategies used for this acquisition. The first, sight word identification, means the immediate recognition of a word upon presentation. The second, contextual analysis, requires the use of semantics and syntactics to assume the meaning of a word and then, with typographic or pictorial clues, identify it. Number three is structural analysis in which the individual examines the morphemic elements in a word in order to identify the whole word. Finally, letter-sound correspondence, or phonics, is a skill that permits the reader to approximate the pronunciation of the written word and thereby identify it.

All four of these word identification strategies are important for the learner. If he does not immediately recognize a word, he might try using the context of the surrounding material. If that does not work, he might turn to analyzing the word either structurally or by its letter-sound correspondence.

SIGHT WORDS

Learning to recognize a word on sight is, in effect, identifying the word by some combination of size, shape, and peculiarities (essentially, configuration and association). For instance, many children say they know the word *look* because it has two staring eyes in the middle.

Any word that is immediately identified by the reader is a sight word, no matter what word identification strategy was used originally to figure it out. But "sight words" also refers to the several hundred basic sight words that account for most of the words we find in connected writing. These are the words that the beginning reader needs in order to make sense of anything he or she reads.

How to Choose Candidates for Instruction

Some ways to identify the individual who needs to build up his or her collection of sight words are listed below.

1. Reads word by word.
2. Has poor phrasing.
3. Hesitates over individual words.
4. Omits words.
5. Mispronounces words.
6. Substitutes words.

When to Teach Sight Words

Poor readers, almost by definition, have an inadequate supply of sight words and the high-frequency, basic sight words should be given precedence in correcting their reading problem. From the very beginning of instruction these words should be taught, retaught, and reinforced.

The ultimate goal is to make tens of thousands of words become immediately identifiable to the reader. It is estimated that the average adult can recognize on sight over twelve thousand words and their derivatives. The groundwork for this goal should be started immediately and should be continued throughout the student's academic life.

How to Teach Sight Words

Many reading experts have compiled lists of the basic sight words and have arranged them in order of ascending difficulty. Dolch, for instance, in 1936, listed seventy-five words found in preprimers, forty-five more for primers, and another fifty each for the first and second readers (5). This list is still used fairly extensively, but there are more modern ones to choose from, such as the Cunningham List (3, pp. 351-352). Another popular list, Johnson's Basic Vocabulary for Beginning Reading (9, pp. 15-16) contains 180 first-grade words and 126 second-grade ones. He chose his words from the speech of children themselves, thus ensuring their utility.

One category of basic sight words is called *marker* or *glue* words. They are the utterly necessary ones such as *the, a, of, in, at, to,* and *it.* These words are in constant evidence and yet do not lend themselves to being represented in a picture, or even to being described. They are usually taught by the "whole word approach" since they are so necessary for understanding printed passages and since many of them cannot be analyzed structurally or phonically. Besides the use of flash word cards, one of the most effective ways to teach them is by including them in flash phrases: *the ball* or *in the room.*

As for other basic sight words, nouns are ordinarily the easiest to teach because often the object itself can be labeled, such as *table, desk,* or *window.* When labels are used, the teacher should point to the printed word whenever she or he mentions it. Other nouns, such as *sky, water,* and *children,* cannot easily carry a label, so pictures might be used.

One highly effective method is called the visual-visual-auditory technique. A plastic overlay is placed on an interesting picture and the student is asked to name certain items in the picture. The teacher prints these words with a grease pencil, directly on the items. Then she asks the child to identify each of the words she has printed—an easy task since the picture of the item is right there. Next, she removes the picture and again asks him to identify each word. His memory of the picture itself helps him in this task, but if he hesitates, the teacher can put the picture back in place. Next, each of the words should be printed on a 3 x 5 card or on the chalkboard, to see if the printed word itself is identified. Finally, the student is asked to describe what is going on in the picture, using his newly recognized words. The teacher writes what he says and then asks him to read it. This technique can also be used by projecting a slide onto the chalkboard and turning the projector on and off as needed.

There are many other activities for teaching and reinforcing sight words. Board games lend themselves to an almost infinite variety of learning tactics. The drill words can be taped onto checkers and the child may move a checker only if he can say its word. To jump his opponent's checker he must use his word in a sentence. Race tracks with words on different points, and toy cars can be used. Spinners or dice can indicate how many sections of the race track the contestant may move and how many words he must say. (It is our experience that dice are more lasting and less ambiguous than spinners which can land between two numbers.) Card games, such as Old Maid and Go Fish, can easily be adapted for sight word practice.

Verbs, adjectives, and adverbs can be practiced by using board and card games too. Matching games are also popular. For verbs, pictures of the activity can be matched to the word or the student can be challenged to do the action of the verb, such as *write,* or *hop,* or *laugh.* Adjectives and adverbs, too, can be acted out. Children often enjoy this game. Basic concept, or function words, such as *under, behind, after, above,* and so on can also be acted out. One player takes a card, says, "Put the pencil _____ the table." He exposes the word card to his opponent rather than saying the word. The opponent then performs the action.

Marker words are most often taught by the use of flash cards, board and card games, and by flash phrases. These words need a great deal of repetition to ensure that they are learned.

A more novel means for supplying basic sight words than the lists described earlier is proposed by Sylvia Ashton-Warner (1, p. 35) and is not a list at all. She calls it the Key Vocabulary, and it is the basis for the language experience approach. Her idea is to have the children themselves provide the words they will learn. Each child is asked to tell the teacher his "best" word, or the "scariest," or anything else that provides a highly meaningful word to the child. The teacher talks about the word with the child and asks him to say what it means to him. That word is the one the teacher writes on a card and very often it becomes a sight word for that child by the very next day.

This system has much to recommend it since the child's emotions are involved, which provides him with real motivation. The drawbacks are that it is time-consuming, and it does not usually produce marker words or other necessary but uninteresting ones. Used sparingly, and in combination with other techniques, this could be one of the most edifying beginning sight word activities.

There are two principles involved in the teaching of sight words: that the student learn to identify them immediately every time he sees them and that the identification is carried over into actual reading activities. Transfer of learning cannot be assumed, but must be proved. One intermediate step between the learning of the word and its transfer is the use of phrase cards rather than single words.

After that, the student should be given multiple exposure to the words in actual reading situations.

EXERCISE

13.1. You have two second-grade children who are just beginning to recognize the basic sight words: *in, around,* and *beside.* Devise an activity to reinforce their identification of these words.

CONTEXTUAL ANALYSIS

Contextual analysis is the bridge between word attack skills and word meaning. Whereas sight words, phonics, and structural analysis are used to figure out words, and from that determine the meaning, contextual analysis lets the person figure out the general meaning first and from that, determine the specific word.

Types of Context Clues

Contextual analysis is made up of typographic and pictorial clues, and two aspects of language, syntax and semantics.

Syntactic Clues. The English language is highly dependent on word order in communicating meaning. Syntax is word order, or sentence structure. "Alice hit Fred" does not mean that Fred hit Alice. The parts of speech in our language fit in certain places. For example, in the sentence, "The _____ watched television," the missing word must be a noun. In the sentence, "We _____ to the playground," the missing word must be a verb. And in the sentence, "Tom fell down the _____ flight of stairs," the missing word must be an adjective. A proficient reader uses his knowledge of word order to predict what is coming next.

Semantic Clues. There are several types of semantic or meaning clues which help the reader to predict the meaning of an unknown word.

Definition. The unknown word is defined in the context.
   Example: *Fresco* is the art of painting on a surface of plaster, especially while the plaster is still moist.

Experience. The reader's experiences and mental content help him to supply the meaning of the unknown word.

Example: John attends *elementary* school.

Synonym. The clue consists of a known synonym for the unfamiliar word.

Example: She behaved in a *fatuous* or silly and foolish way.

Summary. The clue to the unknown word may be a summary of the ideas which precede it.

Example: The doctor was able to revive John from apparent death. John was *resuscitated.*

Mood. The clue may be a reflection of a situation or mood.

Example: I can hear the sounds of footsteps outside my window. Who can it be? I am alone in the house and afraid. There's that noise again. What is it? Is someone trying to open the window? I am filled with *apprehension.*

Comparison and Contrast. The meaning clue consists of a comparison or contrast of the unknown word with a well-known word.

Example: John who is usually receptive to new ideas was *impervious* to my suggestion.

Familiar Expression. The clue consists of an association of the unfamiliar word with a familiar expression that is a part of the reader's language pattern.

Example: Einstein is known for his theory of *relativity.*

EXERCISE

13.2. Determine the type of contextual aid used to find the meaning of the italicized words in the following sentences.

1. The *omnivorous* reader sat immobile in her chair. Her insatiable appetite for books had her in its grasp.
2. *Apodal* means lacking feet or legs.
3. In spite of his *orthodoxy,* he suddenly refused to conform.

Semantics has another value. It permits the reader to identify the precise meaning of a multimeaning word. Consider the words "She ran. . . . . ." What synonym can be used for the word *ran?* There is no way to tell without the rest of the sentence or phrase.

Sentence	Synonym
She *ran* the truck.	operated
She *ran* away.	fled
She *ran* the meeting.	conducted
She *ran* for office.	competed
She *ran* down the street.	moved swiftly
She *ran* with a snobbish crowd.	consorted with

She *ran* down his ideas.	disparaged
She *ran* down the list of figures.	read rapidly
She *ran* on and on.	talked continuously
She *ran* the ad in the paper.	caused to be published

These are only ten of the fifty or sixty different definitions that can be found in dictionaries for the word *run* and only context can determine which meaning is the right one.

EXERCISE
13.3. Look up the word *spirit* in a dictionary. See if you can make up at least five sentences, using the word with *a different meaning in each one.*

Typographic Clues. The major typographic aids, besides the letters themselves, are definitional footnotes and parentheses. For example, if the word *audiometer* is unknown to the reader, notice how typographic clues can help in understanding the meaning of the word.

Carlos is using an audiometer.[1]

[1] An audiometer is an instrument for measuring the sensitivity of hearing.

Carlos is using an audiometer (an instrument for measuring hearing) to determine whether or not Sally has a hearing loss.

Pictorial Clues. Pictures, charts, and diagrams are often provided in written material to clarify the concepts being discussed. For example, John looked through the *periscope* and saw the approaching ship.

Such graphic devices as charts, graphs, tables, diagrams, time lines, and maps are very useful contextual aids in the content areas. However, in the initial stages of learning to read they must be used with caution so that the reader does not become overly reliant on them.

How to Choose Candidates for Instruction

Any student who exhibits the following behaviors should be given instruction in using contextual analysis.

1. Omits unknown words.
2. Substitutes words similar in appearance but with different meaning.
3. Overuses configuration to guess at a word.
4. Overuses letter-sound correspondence to guess at a word.
5. Recognizes words in isolation but not in context.
6. Uses poor phrasing when reading orally.
7. Makes senseless insertions.
8. Ignores punctuation.

When to Teach Contextual Analysis

Contextual analysis is a skill children already are using when they first come to school. They know and produce word order in phrases and sentences. They say, "I fell down" (or "I falled down,") but never "Fell down I." They also understand much that is said to them even though there is a word here and there that is unfamiliar to them. If on the first day of school the kindergarten teacher says, "Hang your coat on this hook," as she points to the hook, they will understand and quickly add the word *hook* to their speaking vocabularies. Even before children can read anything, they can be learning to use contextual clues in what they hear, which will give them a mind set to the use of this skill when they do begin to read.

How to Teach Contextual Analysis

The teacher can prepare many activities to help the student develop the habit of examining surrounding context to make sensible predictions about the meanings of unfamiliar words. Several instructional activities are briefly described below.

Using Experience or Mental Content. The teacher or therapist can play oral guessing or mystery games by saying, "Finish what I want to say.

Our flag is red, white and _____.
I have one brother and two _____.
When I'm sleepy, I go to _____.
I hear a barking _____."

Any well-worn phrases or traditional word pairs, such as *salt and pepper, lock and key, side by side, sink or swim, boys and girls,* can be used. At first only the last word should be the mystery so that the child does not become confused.

Using Teacher Questions and Directions.   Once the child has begun to read a little on his own the teacher can assist him in making the right choice for any word that is unknown to him. She should stress that it is not a guessing game where any answer will do, but rather it is a way of *thinking*. It requires real detective skill to ferret out the word that the author used. She can help him by saying such things as the following.

1. What word would it have to be to make sense?
2. Read the rest of the sentence before you decide.
3. Say the sentence out loud with your word in it. See if it sounds right.
4. What has been happening in the story up to this point? Does your word fit in with that?
5. If you were telling the story to someone else, what word would you use there?

Cloze Procedure.   The cloze procedure refers to the practice of providing individuals with passages in which some words have been deleted. There are two major types of the cloze procedure. One type systematically deletes every fifth, eighth, or tenth word. The second type deletes certain parts of speech. The individual completing the cloze passage must supply the missing word. This requires the student to read the surrounding context in order to determine the appropriate missing word.

In using cloze, it is essential that the passage selected be relevant and at an appropriate level of difficulty for the student. The first sentence should be left intact. Beginning with the second sentence, words are deleted. A line should be drawn in place of the missing word. Sometimes letter clues are given. Below are examples of the cloze procedure presented from least to most difficult (6, p. 186).

1. I enjoy eating g - ng - rbr - - d for dessert.
   (Delete all the vowels)
2. I enjoy eating g - - - - - - - - - d for dessert.
   (Delete the middle of the word and retain only the first and last letters)
3. I enjoy eating g - - - - - - - - - for dessert.
   (Retain only the first letter of the word)

4. I enjoy eating - - - - - - - - - - - for dessert.
   (Number of letters is indicated by the number of blank spaces)
5. I enjoy eating _____ for dessert.
   (A line is provided)

There are variations on the cloze procedure that can be used for teaching purposes. The teacher can take cartoon strips and black out some of the words, or use familiar nursery rhymes with some words missing.

There is an entertaining game that requires the use of the parts of speech, and therefore should not be introduced before second or third grade. A story is written with many words omitted, and beneath each omission the part of speech is indicated. The child or group of children are asked to choose a word for the blank. As with most contextual analysis activities, any answer that makes semantic and syntactic sense should be accepted. Paragraphs and stories for this are easily concocted. Here is an example.

Once there was a big _____ who wanted to _____ some
                  noun   verb

flowers. These flowers were so _____ that he decided to
                          adjective

_____ before going into the _____.
verb   noun

Homographs. Another activity that points up the fact that context helps to indicate the sound and meaning of words is to contrast homographs. A homograph is a word identical with another in spelling, but differing from it in origin and meaning and sometimes in pronunciation. The student must use context in order to pronounce the word correctly and to determine the appropriate meaning. Here are some examples.

He will *sow* the seeds today.
The *sow* is in the pen.

I received a *present* for Christmas.
The high school band will *present* a program today.

I *wound* the clock last night.
The *wound* is deep.

Matching Definitions. Words can have many different meanings. Only the context can reveal the precise meaning intended by the writer. Children can profit from exercises in which they compare the different meanings according to the use of the word in a sentence. For example, have the students match the use of the word *count* in each of the following sentences with the appropriate meaning (*a, b* or *c*).

Can I count on you? (The best meaning is _____)
He is the Count of Monte Cristo. (The best meaning is _____)
Count your marbles. (The best meaning is _____)

a. sum up
b. rely
c. nobleman

Scrambled Sentences. In this activity the student is presented with scrambled sentences and is asked to reconstruct the sentence so that the words are in the correct word order. For example:

we go will city the to.
car Joe new has a.

Commercial Activities. Many basal readers and other published materials, such as those listed in Chapter 12, provide excellent ideas for helping students to become more adept in using context clues.

EXERCISE

13.4. Make a list of other instructional activities that could be used to help students use context clues more effectively. Consult basal readers and other published materials for ideas.

The efficient reader is one who can make educated guesses when necessary but who uses all the evidence available before guessing. His knowledge of the subject under discussion, typographic, pictorial, syntactic, and structural clues, all are taken into account. The teacher must try to promote good, not wild, guessing.

STRUCTURAL ANALYSIS

Structural analysis is recognizing the morphemic elements of a word. A morpheme is a meaning unit. The word *girls* contains two morphemes: *girl*, a young human female, and *s*, which means "more than one." The use of structural analysis in word identification permits the reader to identify the known parts of a word in order to approximate the meaning of the whole word. If a person knew that *bio* means "life," *graph* means "written," and *y* often signifies a noun, he would have little trouble understanding the word *biography.*

Aspects of Structural Analysis

There are both bound morphemes and free morphemes. A bound morpheme cannot stand alone. The *un* in *unhappy* is a bound morpheme. Free morphemes can stand alone. Most root words are in this category. *Unendingly* has one free morpheme—*end,* and three bound morphemes—*un, ing, ly. End* is the only morpheme in this word that is a word in itself. The word *itself* is made up of two free morphemes and is therefore a compound word.

Morpheme units in words consist of affixes, roots, inflectional endings, compound words, and contractions.

EXERCISE

13.5. Segment the following words into either free or bound morphemes.

Words	Free Morphemes	Bound Morphemes
Oblong	_____	_____
Floorwalker	_____	_____
Artistic	_____	_____

Prefixes, Roots, and Suffixes. Prefixes, roots and suffixes are examples of meaningful parts of words and are very useful in working out the meaning of an unfamiliar word. For example, the word *misogamist* is a difficult appearing word. With a knowledge of the meaning of the parts of this word, it is easy to determine its meaning. *Miso-* is used as a prefix and means "to hate." The suffix *-ist* refers to a *person* and indicates that the word is a noun. The root *gam* means "marriage," thus a *misogamist* is "a person who hates marriage."

Table 13-1 presents a list of common prefixes. Table 13-2 presents a list of common suffixes.

TABLE 13-1. Common Prefixes

Prefix	Meaning	Prefix	Meaning
ab-	away from	mis-	wrong
ante-	before	multi-	many
anti-	against	non-	not
auto-	self	op-	against
bi-	two	out-	over, surpass
circum-	around	poly-	many
com-, con-, ⎫	together	post-	after
co- ⎭		pre-	before
contra-, ⎫	against	pro-	⎰ in front of,
counter- ⎭			⎱ before
de-	from, down	re-	back
dis-	not, away	semi-	half
en-	in	sub-	under
ex-	out	super-	above
hemi-	half	syn-, sym-	together
hyper-	above	trans-	across
hypo-	under	tri-	three
in-, im-	into, not	ultra-	above
inter-	between	un-	not
il-, ir-	not		

Inflectional Endings.   Structural analysis also includes inflectional endings. Examples of these are plural endings as in *dogs, radishes,* and *ponies;* verb tenses as in *walks, walking, walked;* comparisons as in *small, smaller, smallest;* and possessives as in *Bill's* and the *girls'.* Suffixes and inflectional endings differ in that suffixes usually change the part of speech (*porter, portable*) whereas inflections do not (*run, runs, running*).

Compound Words.   Another form of structural analysis involves compound words such as *daytime, bluebird,* and *mailman.* Compound words consist of two words that have been joined to form a new word. Each of the two words usually maintains its own pronunciation and the meanings of the two words are connected to express the meaning of the new word. Compound words are usually easy to teach.

TABLE 13-2. Common Suffixes

Suffix	Meaning	Suffix	Meaning
-able	capable of being	-ity, -ty	state of being
-age	act or state of	-ly	like, in manner
-al	relation to	-less	without
-able, -ible	capable of being	-ment	state or quality
-cy	state of	-ness	state of being
-den, -dom	state or condition	-ship	relationship
-ful	capable of being	-some	state of being
-ian	relating to	-ster	one who
-ise, -ize	to make	-tion	{ state or condition
-ish	state of being	-tude	{ state or condition
-ism	act of	-ure	act or process
-ist, -ite	one who	-ward	direction of

Contractions. Another form of structural analysis is contractions. Examples of contractions are *let's* for let us, *isn't* for is not, *she'll* for she will, *they're* for they are, and *you've* for you have. Contractions often are difficult for children to learn and can, therefore, be an inhibiting factor in reading.

How to Choose Candidates for Instruction

A student needs to learn to use structural analysis if he or she displays the following behaviors.

1. Does not look for meaning units within an unrecognized word.
2. Does not recognize the root or stem of a word.
3. Ignores prefixes.
4. Ignores such word endings as suffixes or inflectional forms.
5. Does not recognize the individual morphemic elements in compound words.
6. Does not recognize apostrophes signalling either possessives or contractions.

When to Teach Structural Analysis

After the teacher identifies what aspects of structural analysis the learner lacks, she concentrates on those areas rather than on the entire list of those skills. If she needs to teach more than one of these aspects, she can follow the sequence, suggested here, that is the generally accepted practice in reading education.

Children reading at the first-grade level can be introduced to compound words such as *snowman, cowboy,* or *sunburn.* Next they learn about stem or root words and the inflectional forms for plurals, tenses, and comparisons. When these are mastered, the other word endings such as suffixes, possessives, and contractions are taught. Prefixes are usually the last element of structural analysis to be introduced. This is because a prefix changes the meaning of the whole of the remaining word. In the word *unhappiness,* the root *happy* has *ness* (the state of being) added to it, to indicate the part of speech, and finally the *un* is added to indicate the opposite of the derived word *happiness.*

How to Teach Structural Analysis Skills

One of the best ways to help students acquire skill in structural analysis is through word building activities. A few examples are provided.

Compound Words
- List words in two columns and have the student combine them to form a new word which he is to write in column 3.

1	2	3
foot	ball	_____
black	bird	_____
mail	man	_____

- Present the child with several compound words and have him draw pictures or use the words in sentences.

Roots and Plural Endings
- Provide the student with noun words that take the simple addition of -*s* to indicate plurality. Have him create a sentence using the plural version of the word.
- Give the student cards with either -*es* or -*ies* written on them and have him match these plurals to words such as *baby, glass, match,* and *ruby.*
- Provide the student with several root words such as *move* and *entertain.* Have him make as many new words as he can by adding suffixes to them.

Other Inflectional Endings and Suffixes

- Provide the student with a number of sentences and have him indicate whether or not the italicized words show "belonging or ownership." For example,

    The *boy's* shoes were dirty.
    The *boys* took off their shoes.

- Ask the student to underline the correct word in sentences that contain a choice of various forms of words. For example,

    Sam was (skip, skips, skipping, skipped) rope.
    The movie was (enjoy, enjoyment, enjoyable).

Contractions

- Have the student match the contractions in column 1 to their meanings in column 2 by drawing a line from each contraction to its meaning.

1	2
you'll	is not
won't	will not
let's	you will
isn't	let us

- Present the student with a short paragraph in which several contractions have been used. Have him underline the contractions and explain their meanings.

Prefixes

- Have the student find pictures that illustrate word meanings. For example,

active	inactive
usual	unusual

- Have the student take a common root word and see how many prefixes will go with it. For example,

    port (*com-, de-, ex-, im-, re-, trans-*).

SYLLABLES

Breaking words into syllables can be considered as an element of structural analysis or as part of phonics. The structure of a word is made up of syllables, each of which may or may not be a meaning unit, but syllables also are units which determine the pronunciation of a word, thereby belonging to the phonics category. In any case, recognizing syllables is an integral part of learning to read.

We all "know" what a syllable is but many people have difficulty putting the definition in words. A syllable is a unit of pronunciation which always includes either a single vowel sound, a diphthong, or a syllabic consonant. It also may include one or more consonants. It is important to remember that syllables are made up of vowel *sounds*, not vowel letters. The word *piece* contains three vowel letters but only one vowel sound.

Syllabication can be vital to the analysis of an unknown word. The letters of the alphabet are not trustworthy pronunciation units, syllables are. When context clues do not help to identify an unknown word, the student should try to pronounce it by syllables and thereby decide if it is a word he or she recognizes.

How to Choose Candidates for Instruction

Some ways to identify students who need help in breaking words into syllables are listed below.

1. Omits words with more than one syllable.
2. Mispronounces many words.
3. Can read only primers.
4. Mispronounces the final syllable in words that end in *le*.
5. Breaks words within consonant blends (for example, *reply* is pronounced as *rep ly*).
6. Does not recognize compound words, even though he can read each of the words separately.
7. Mispronounces prefixes and suffixes.

When to Teach Syllabication

Since beginning phonics deals almost exclusively with one-syllable words, the teaching of syllabication should be put off until the student has a basic grounding in phonics. The words a child learns in beginning reading will be teaching him preliminary syllabication principles by example, and the rules can come later, if necessary. As the child is required to read more and more multisyllabic words, this basic grounding will make it easier for the child to generalize syllabic principles.

How to Teach Syllabication

There are some rules to show how to break words into syllables. These rules can be taught by the inductive or deductive method. For the deductive method the teacher gives the rule and has the students find examples. The inductive method is more effective since the student himself "invents" the rule. This, in turn, makes it more likely that the concept is internalized. The statement of the rule itself is not the goal; the *use* of the rule in pronouncing a word is. For example:

- *Rule 1.* There are usually as many syllables in a word as there are vowel sounds.
  Induction: Can you hear that the word *ba by* has two beats, *BA by*. How many beats are there in these words? *Frog, banana, before.*
- *Rule 2.* When there is a single consonant between two vowels, the consonant goes in the second syllable.
  Induction: Here are some words you know how to say: *pa per, mo tor, la dy.* Say them the way I did. Now, how would you say the words I put on the board? *Labor, basin, crazy, pupil.*
- *Rule 3.* When there are two consonants following the first vowel sound, the syllable break is between the two consonants.
  Induction: Here are some words you know how to say. Sound them out and put a line through them where you hear them break. *Ladder, after, puppet.*
- *Rule 4.* Prefixes and suffixes are usually syllables in themselves, such as *con/struc/tion, de/pend/ent.*
- *Rule 5.* If a word ends in *le,* preceded by a consonant, that consonant begins the last syllable; *lit/tle, sam/ple, ta/ble.*
- *Rule 6.* An *x* or a *v* in the middle of a word will go with the preceding vowel to form a syllable; *trav/el, tax/a/tion.*

EXERCISE
13.6. Make up an inductive method for teaching one of the last three rules.

Other Suggestions for Teaching Syllabication

The real goal is to develop the student's sensitivity to syllables. Rather than teaching rules, the teacher might follow some such sequence as this. When introducing a new word she would say, "This new word has two parts to it; *feel—ing.* Can you hear the two parts?" Stressing auditory and visual discrimination, along with copious examples from words the child already knows, he should become able to generalize to new words on his own. Once the concept is understood, the division of compound words, double letter words, roots and affixes, should all become easy for him.

PHONICS

The word *phonics* means letter-sound correspondence in words, and it also means the strategies used to convert the arrangement of letters in a written word into an oral word. The purpose of phonics is to teach beginning readers that letters and letter combinations represent speech sounds and to teach them to blend sounds into pronounceable words. A child cannot learn every word in English as a sight word, and context can contribute only plausible alternatives. The use of phonics can help supply the exact word by reducing the uncertainty that might still exist when using context alone.

The teaching of phonics has an important role in education today although some reading teachers wish that this were not so. It seems to us that teaching phonics is valuable to beginning readers so long as certain cautions are observed. As Gyles Brandreth (2, p. 7) says, "The English language is rich because it isn't pure."

1. Phonics is useful only on regularly spelled words.
2. Many phonic rules are useful less than half of the time. For instance, the rule, "when two vowels go walking the first one does the talking," is correct in fewer than 45 per cent of the words with two-vowel combinations (4, p. 426). Most experts agree that a rule should not be taught unless it has at least a 75 per cent utility rate.
3. Studies indicate that children who are taught a great many phonic rules take longer to decode words than those taught only a few rules (8, p. 12).
4. Most children cannot define phonic terms, nor can they supply examples of them, even though much classroom time was spent in learning them. Those same children, however, usually can use phonics successfully (10, pp. 431-437).

In order to make phonics a useful tool to the beginning reader, the teacher should help the student to generalize only the rules that are useful and she should know what phonic terms to use.

It is our opinion that more phonic labels are used than are absolutely necessary (see p. 226) but we present here the full list of terms taught in most phonic programs.

- Single consonants
    (one pronunciation, usually):
        b, d, f, h, j, k, l, m,
        n, p, r, t, v, w, y, z
    (two or more pronunciations):
        c (come, city)
        g (go, giant)
        s (kiss, rose, sugar, vision)
        x (extra, exact, xylophone)
- Consonant blends
    (A combination of two or more consonant phonemes in a syllable in which the *regular sound* of each letter can be distinguished.)
bl	*br*	*sk*	*tr*
cl	*cr*	*sm*	*tw*
fl	*dr*	*sn*	*str*
gl	*fr*	*sp*	*spr*
pl	*gr*	*st*	*str*
sl	*pr*	*sw*	*spl*
- Consonant digraphs
    (Two-letter combinations that represent a single sound.)
    (one pronunciation):
        ph   sh   ng
    (two pronunciations):
        th (these, think)
- Consonant clusters
    (Two or more consonants, occurring together in a syllable, which may or may not have their regular pronunciation.)
nk	*ch*	*shr*
wh	*thr*	*sch*
- Silent letters

*k*n (knee)	*t*en (hasten)
m*b* (bomb)	gn (gnaw)
*w*r (wrong)	g*h* (ghost)

- Short vowel sounds
- Long vowel sounds

- r-Controlled vowel sounds
  (When a vowel sound is followed by an *r* in a syllable, the vowel is given an irregular pronunciation.)
  ear, *air*, f*ur*, *are*, p*oor*, *or*
- Vowel digraphs

ai (fail)	*ie* (pie)
ay (say)	*oa* (oat)
ea (each)	*oo* (boot)
ee (keep)	*oe* (toe)
ei (receive)	*ue* (blue)

- Vowel diphthongs
  (The smooth joining together of two adjacent vowel sounds in the same syllable.)

oi (boil)	*ew* (few)
oy (toy)	*eu* (feud)
ow (cow)	*u* (music)
ou (bough)	

The above list does not include many of the alternative pronunciations that can occur in our language. For instance, even some of our most regular consonants occasionally are pronounced in other ways; *d* can be pronounced as *t* in place*d*, and as a soft *g* in words such as indivi*d*ual, and the letter *f* has a *v* sound in *of*. Another variation to note is the fact that *ph, sh,* and *ng* are digraphs only when they occur in a single syllable not as in such words as ha*ph*azard, mi*sh*ap, and u*ng*ainly.

There is common agreement that a consonant digraph is a combination of two consonants which lose their own identity and form a single new sound. However, there may be confusion in identifying them. Some of the two-letter combinations mislabeled as digraphs, even on phonic tests and phonic books published as late as 1981, are *ch, wh, nk,* and *qu.* All of these combinations, in their regular pronunciation, produce two sounds each, rather than one. *Ch* is a combination of a *t* and a *sh* to produce the sounds heard in the words *ch*urch and *ch*allenge. The *irregular* pronunciations of this combination are digraphs; the *k* sound in *ch*aracter, *ch*asm, and *ch*olesterol, and the *sh* sound in *ch*arlatan.

Wh regularly is "supposed" to be pronounced as *hw;* *wh*en, *wh*y, *wh*ere, but this is slowly dying out from disuse. If a teacher pronounces those words as *wen, wy,* and *ware,* they can be called digraphs. Also, the *irregular* pronunciation of *wh,* occurring in such words as *wh*o, *wh*ole, and *wh*olesome, where only the *h* is heard, can be called a digraph. *Nk* is a combination of *ng* and *k,* and is therefore not a digraph, but a cluster, and the regular form of *qu* also results in a cluster; the *kw* sounds in *qu*ick, *qu*een, *qu*erulous. The combination is pronounced as *k* in the irregular words uni*que*, pi*que*, par*qu*et.

EXERCISES

13.7. For a quick review place each of these underlined letters in the appropriate column:

bum	crow	flutter	listen	thing	think
share	chair	triphammer	knack		graph

Consonant	Consonant Blend	Consonant Digraph	Silent Letter	Consonant Cluster
___	___	___	___	___
___	___	___	___	___
___	___	___	___	___
___	___	___	___	___

13.8. Now place each of these underlined sounds in the appropriate column:

goes   pewter   choice   mask   partner   mouse   worm   poke

Short Vowel	Long Vowel	r-Controlled Vowel	Diphthong	Vowel Digraph
___	___	___	___	___
___	___	___	___	___
___	___	___	___	___

13.9 Just about everyone knows which speech sounds are consonants and which are vowels. It is a little more difficult to *define* these two words. Define *vowel*:

_____

_____

Define *consonant*:

_____

_____

Some Suggested Alternatives

Since children typically have difficulty remembering labels and since there is confusion even in the literature on assigning the labels to regular speech sounds, it might be appropriate to do some consolidation. The most inclusive label for two or more consonants occurring together is *cluster*. Why not simply use the term *cluster* for consonant digraphs, blends *and* clusters? An alternative solution might be to provide rules without including labels at all. This can become unwieldy, of course, when a person tries to talk about phonic elements without giving them names.

How to Choose Candidates for Instruction

Some of the behaviors exhibited by individuals who could benefit from phonics instruction are listed here.

1. Does not attempt to sound out words.
2. Guesses wildly at words.
3. Guesses at words, using only the beginning letter as a guide.
4. Overuses context.
5. Substitutes words.
6. Mispronounces words.
7. Finds rhyming difficult.
8. Has difficulty breaking words into syllables.

When to Teach Phonics

Since visual and auditory discrimination are necessary prerequisites to sound-symbol relationships, phonics should, of course, follow this discrimination learning. Teach the sounds of consonants in the initial and final positions first, followed by the medial consonants. After that, short vowels can be taught, and finally, the long vowels.

It is usually sometime during the teaching of first-grade skills that phonics is introduced, and it should be accompanied by practice in actual reading situations. It is helpful if children are taught from the very beginning that a combination of context and phonics is a good way to figure out unrecognized words. One of the authors of this book tested a six-year-old boy who had been given intensive training in phonics. In response to a word card he said, "mmmmaaaannnn," but he was unable to identify the word as *man.*

When Not to Teach Phonics

When a student consistently uses phonic principles to unlock unrecognized words in an actual reading activity, he should not be given instruction in phonics. Only those phonic elements that give him trouble should be taught.

How to Teach Sound-Symbol Relationships

Phonics can be taught by a synthetic or analytic approach. The synthetic method (part-to-whole) is the teaching of letter sounds in isolation before incorporating them into words. It is, in essence, the same as the deductive method since the rules of pronunciation are the vehicles for teaching. This method appears to be merely an exercise in rote learning that offers no referents to the student.

The analytic approach is a whole-to-part strategy, which might also be called the inductive method. The student is taught to use his sight words as samples for speech sounds. With this system the student learns not only the typical sounds of letters but the reason for learning them by seeing them used in the words themselves.

Children should be taught from the very beginning that sound-symbol relationships can be predicted only some of the time. If this is not done, they will feel betrayed when they run into an irregularly pronounced word.

Teaching Auditory Discrimination of Words. Listening and rhyming are considered to be the bridge between auditory discrimination and phonics.

1. Teach the children some simple poems. Discuss how the words at the end of the lines rhyme with each other. Then say something like, "I'm thinking of a word that rhymes with *bake.* It is something good to eat. Can you think of a word that rhymes with *bake?*"

2. Have the students make up sentences in the Dr. Seuss tradition, such as, "The tan fan ran and ran."
3. The printed word should then be incorporated into the auditory games. The teacher can have the rhymes and sentences printed on the board and can indicate the words with her finger as she and the children say them.

Teaching Beginning Consonants.   Using the words that start with the same sound, such as *boy, ball,* and *baby,* say them, emphasizing the first sound. Ask students if any parts of the words sound the same. Then write the words on the board and have students see that all these words start with the letter *b.* Have them think of other words that start with that letter. They also can make a picture dictionary illustrating each letter page with words that start with that letter.

Teaching Final Consonants.   Use a board game with marked-off spaces. Most spaces should have pictures on them. Children roll dice to see how many spaces they should move. Each time they pass a picture they must give a word that rhymes with the word they pass. For instance, a picture of a bat should evoke such words as *fat, sat, hat,* or *rat.*

Teaching Medial Consonants.   Have the children underline the word that fits in the sentences.

              many
    We have   toys.
              Mary

                     wager.
    I will drink the
                     water.

Teaching Short Vowel Sounds.   Make a round smiling face with a wide open mouth. Slits are cut at the top and bottom of the mouth so a strip of paper can be threaded through, revealing a different vowel as the strip is moved up or down. Letters, such as *p—n* are printed on either side of the mouth. The child pronounces the word that is revealed as he moves the strip. He must say which, if any, is not a real word.

Teaching Long Vowel Sounds.   Have cards with a short vowel word on each, and a poster with a slit in it and a final *e* at the end.

As the child places the card in the slit, he pronounces the resulting word. The words used would be pairs such as *mat* and *mate, bid* and *bide.*

Teaching Consonant Clusters.   Print a consonant cluster on each segment of a dart board. The child must say a word using the cluster which his dart hits. He wins a point for each correct word.

Teaching Diphthongs.   Label ten ping-pong balls either with *ow, ou, oi,* or *oy.* Place them in a box. The child reaches in, and throws a ball to his opponent, who must say a word containing that diphthong. If he does, he gets a point. Each child throws five balls; then it is the other child's turn.

Teaching r-Controlled Vowels.   Draw a train on folded cardboard. Each car has a different vowel-plus-r printed on it. The child must match words with the appropriate car.

Teaching Vowel Digraphs.   Bingo cards are made up with many vowel digraphs placed at random on the squares. The teacher says words from a mixed-up pile of word cards. The children use buttons to cover the digraph contained in the word.

Other Ways to Teach Sound-Symbol Relationships.   Besides the teaching of phonics by the analytic method, there are two other approaches used in many phonics programs. These are the teaching of rules that govern pronunciation and teaching word families.

Teaching Phonic Rules.   A search of the literature reveals only twelve rules that hold true in at least 75 per cent of the words that have a particular combination of letters.

1. When there is one vowel followed by a consonant in a syllable, the vowel is usually short.
2. When there is only one vowel in a syllable and it is at the end of the syllable, it is usually long.
3. When *c* or *g* comes before *a, o,* or *u,* it has the hard sound. Otherwise, it usually has the soft sound.
4. When *y* is the final letter in a word, it has a vowel sound (whether it is preceded by a vowel *or* a consonant).
5. When the letters *oa* are together in a syllable, the *o* has its long sound and the *a* is silent.

6. Vowels followed by *r* are often given a pronunciation that is neither long nor short.
7. When *ght* come together in a word, the *gh* is silent.
8. When a word begins with *kn,* the *k* is silent.
9. When a word begins with *wr,* the *w* is silent.
10. When a syllable ends in *ck,* the *c* is silent.
11. Doubled consonants almost always produce a single sound.
12. Words having a double *e* often have the long *e* sound.

EXERCISE
13.10. Provide a sample word for each of the above rules.

Teaching Word Families.   Many people feel that the best way to teach sound-symbol relationships, at least at the beginning, is to teach typical phonic patterns, or *word families.* They are also called "common letter clusters." These are patterns such as are found in the words *sat, mate, tin,* and *sing.* Word family lists usually contain about seventy-five of these typical patterns. One comprehensive list has been compiled by Gerald Glass (7). Proponents of this teaching method acquaint the students with the list of words and help them practice making other words that rhyme with those on the list.

The teaching of common letter clusters should avoid any suggestion that students should, on their own, look for little words in big words. There are so many times when this is ineffective that it creates more problems than it solves. There are such mismatched little word-big word pairs as: he—her, father—fat her, am—among, and as—aside.

SPELLING

One of the best reasons for teaching phonics is the fact that it enhances spelling ability. If phonics teaches an individual how to pronounce an unknown written word, by the same token it helps him write a word he can pronounce.

Most spelling lessons are of the skill-drill variety and are closely allied with phonic principles. It is considered important for the teacher to pronounce the word carefully and use it in a sentence when children are asked to spell words. Many teachers feel that there is a real advantage in having the children correct their own spelling papers after their first attempts and then to try the same words again. Having children become "editors" and proofread material is another spelling lesson which sometimes appeals to the students.

One method of teaching spelling that is used extensively with people who have difficulty with auditory discrimination is the Fernald method or some adaptation of it. This is the VAKT method which utilizes a variety of senses to learn to spell a word. The student should

1. Look at the word all the way through.
2. Say it as he looks at it.
3. Spell it as he looks at it.
4. Trace the word with his fingers as he looks at it and says it.
5. With the stimulus word removed, he writes the word.
6. He checks to see if he is correct. If he is, he uses it in a sentence, but if he is not, he goes through the entire procedure again.

One variation of this system, to be used with younger children, is pictured below.

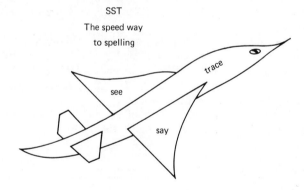

Spelling is one school subject for which many interesting commercial games can be used to reinforce the learning. Some of these are *Scrabble* (Selchow and Righter Co.), *Perquacky* (Lakeside Industries), and *Spellbound* (Hasbro Co.).

SUMMARY

Although reading is the process of getting meaning from what is written, it is necessary to be able to decode the written words in order to understand the message they contain. This chapter has discussed sight words, contextual analysis, structural analysis, and phonics. Ways to identify the students who need help in these areas and techniques for improving student performance have been suggested.

REFERENCES

1. Ashton-Warner, Sylvia. *Teacher.* New York: Simon and Schuster, 1963.
2. Brandreth, Gyles. *The Joy of Lex.* New York: William Morrow, 1980.
3. Cunningham, James W., Patricia M. Cunningham, and Sharon V. Arthur. *Middle and Secondary School Reading.* New York: Longman, 1981.
4. Dauzat, Jo Ann, and Sam V. Dauzat. *Reading: The Teacher and the Learner.* New York: John Wiley, 1981.
5. Dolch, E. W. *A Manual for Remedial Reading* (Second Edition). Champaign, IL: Garrard Press, 1945.
6. Emans, Robert. "Use of Context Clues." *Teaching Word Recognition Skills.* Newark, DE: International Reading Association, 1971.
7. Glass, Gerald. *Teaching Decoding as Separate from Reading.* Garden City, NY: Adelphi University Press, 1973.
8. Inselberg, Rachel, Beverly Holland, and Uldis Smidchens. "Determining the Minimum Amount of Phonetic Analysis Needed for Word Decoding Using the Co-Twin Method." ERIC Document #ED176233, 1980.
9. Johnson, Dale D., and P. David Pearson. *Teaching Reading Vocabulary.* New York: Holt, Rinehart and Winston, 1978.
10. Tovey, Duane R. "Children's Grasp of Phonic Terms vs. Sound Symbol Relationships." *The Reading Teacher* 33 (January 1980).

SUGGESTED READING

Durkin, Dolores. *Strategies for Identifying Words.* Boston: Allyn and Bacon, 1976.
Heilman, Arthur W. *Phonics in Proper Perspective.* Columbus, OH: Charles E. Merrill, 1976.
Herr, Selma E. *Learning Activities for Reading* (Second Edition). Dubuque, IA: Wm. C. Brown Co., 1970.
Ives, Josephine P., Laura Z. Bursuk, and Sumner A. Ives. *Word Identification Techniques.* Chicago: Rand McNally College Publishing Co., 1979.
Johnson, Dale D., and P. David Pearson. *Teaching Reading Vocabulary.* New York: Holt, Rinehart and Winston, 1978.
Van Riper, Charles, and Dorothy E. Smith. *An Introduction to General American Phonetics.* New York: Harper & Row, 1979.

14

Correcting Vocabulary and Comprehension Problems

OBJECTIVES

This chapter will help you to

1. Understand some of the causes of an inadequate vocabulary and poor comprehension.
2. Become aware of instructional strategies and methods for treating individuals with vocabulary and comprehension problems.

Many students are experiencing difficulty in reading because they are deficient in two essential areas. They do not possess a powerful meaning vocabulary, and they lack competency in basic comprehension skills. It is the purpose of this chapter to present some of the causes of an inadequate vocabulary and poor comprehension and to suggest strategies for helping students to overcome these deficiencies.

CAUSES OF AN INADEQUATE VOCABULARY AND POOR COMPREHENSION

There are many factors which contribute to an inadequate vocabulary and poor comprehension. In order to help children and adults overcome these inadequacies, it is essential that the teacher be aware of these factors.

Insufficient Mental Content

A major cause of an inadequate vocabulary and poor comprehension is limited experiential background. Vocabulary development is basically concept development and is the result of one's actual or vicarious experiences. If one has had limited experiences and opportunities for concept development, vocabulary will be limited. The environment in which one lives plays an important role in vocabulary development. Because of different experiences the vocabularies of inner-city children differ from the vocabularies of farm children. The vocabularies of minority groups or subcultures differ from the vocabularies of the larger, dominant cultural group. For example, an inner-city child who has never visited a farm or heard people talking about farm life will be deficient in his knowledge of farm words and will have difficulty understanding a story about farm life.

Inappropriate Instruction

Some children fail to comprehend what they read because of inappropriate instruction in reading. For example, children whose reading instruction has overemphasized isolated word study and phonics often have difficulty in reading longer units of material. Frequently these children perceive reading as a word-calling process and pay little attention to meaning. An overemphasis on oral reading often has a detrimental effect on comprehension since it often

234

focuses the student's attention solely on precise reproduction of the words. Teachers contribute to their students' poor comprehension when they fail to set purposes prior to reading and when they over-emphasize literal understanding and neglect interpretation and evaluation.

Poor Concentration

Inability to concentrate while reading obviously interferes with comprehension. Some of the major reasons for inability to sustain attention are immaturity, lack of interest, unresolved personal problems, and poor physical health. Ability to concentrate can also be hindered by such environmental factors as noise, inadequate lighting, and poor ventilation.

Difficulty of Material

Many children experience difficulty in reading comprehension because they are expected to read materials that are too difficult for them. The materials may be written at their frustration level or carry a conceptual load which is far above their developmental and intellectual levels.

Lack of Flexibility

The individual who lacks versatility in his approach to reading materials often encounters difficulty. All materials cannot be read in the same way. The nature and difficulty level of the material being read and the reader's purpose determine one's approach to the material. For example, a *Reader's Digest* article which is being read for pleasure and enjoyment should not be read in the same way or at the same rate as one would read directions for a science experiment or a complicated mathematics treatise. Difficulty can occur when the student approaches all reading materials in the same way and at the same rate.

VOCABULARY DEVELOPMENT

Vocabulary development is essentially concept development. A concept is a generalized idea formed by combining the elements of a class into a category. To form a concept the individual must have many experiences with the elements of the category to be able to distinguish the characteristics that are common to it. For example, a child must have many experiences with different animals in order to understand the concept of animals. Concepts and the words that represent them grow out of the individual's experiences and are essential to effective reading. Therefore, to help a child improve his meaning vocabulary, the teacher or therapist must be concerned with concept building. Rentel (5, pp. 111-119) suggests that in developing concepts the teacher should (1) establish the proper word label for the concept or attribute, (2) place emphasis on significant differentiating characteristics, (3) provide examples of the concept, (4) encourage the child to discover the essence of the concept, and (5) provide for application of the concept.

TYPES OF VOCABULARIES

The successful student needs an adequate and effective receptive and expressive vocabulary. A receptive vocabulary is composed of the words understood through reading and listening. It is usually larger than the expressive vocabulary which is made up of words used in speaking or writing. Without words a student seldom can understand what is being communicated to him nor can he express his thoughts to others. Success in the content areas, especially, depends upon ability to master and use the fundamental vocabulary of the subject. There are two types of vocabularies: the general vocabulary that is used in all subjects and the technical vocabularies that consist of words having special meaning in particular areas such as mathematics, social studies, and the sciences. Many students have difficulty in reading because of an inadequate knowledge of technical terms rather than a limited general vocabulary. Both, however, are essential to effective reading.

SUGGESTIONS FOR VOCABULARY DEVELOPMENT

There are many ways in which the teacher or therapist can assist the child in building a meaning vocabulary. The ultimate goal is for the child to develop independence in vocabulary study. This can be accomplished by teaching him or her how to recognize word meanings through the use of contextual clues, structural or morphemic analysis, and the dictionary (See Chapters 13 and 15).

Provide the Child with Experiences

Vocabulary is built upon experience. Therefore, one of the best ways to help a child develop a meaning vocabulary is to provide him or her with many concrete experiences so that words to be learned are associated with real situations. Direct experience, however, is not always possible so vicarious experiences can be provided to build the child's mental content. Examples of vicarious experiences are using filmstrips, records, and pictures, reading aloud to the child, and talking about a subject.

Encourage the Child to Talk About His Experiences

Help the child to develop his speaking and listening vocabularies. He needs many opportunities to use the words he is learning. One effective way to relate this to reading is to use the language experience approach which is described later in this chapter. This allows the child to talk about his experiences and shows him that his experiences and ideas can be recorded and that he and others can read, understand, and discuss what he has written.

Help the Child to Understand Relationships

A child needs an opportunity to classify and compare experiences, build concepts from them, and associate words with them. Provide the child with an opportunity to categorize words according to their semantic features. For example, have the child list all the animals that belong to the *category* of things called animals. Have him make a list of *examples* of furniture. Have him make a list of *attributes* or *properties* of dogs. Russian preschools and Montessori schools emphasize this learning. For example, they provide the child with a variety of items and an assortment of bags. Each bag is labeled by class. The child categorizes each item by putting each one in the appropriate bag.

Help the Child to Appreciate the Precise Meanings of Words

The study of synonyms, antonyms, and homonyms can help the child to develop the range and depth of his concepts and to appreciate the precise meanings of words. A synonym is a word having the same or almost the same meaning as another word. *Car* and *automobile* are examples of synonyms. By comparing synonyms the child is helped to see the relationship between words of similar meanings and to appreciate shades of meaning which best fit the context.

An antonym is a word that is the opposite of another in meaning. *Loud* and *soft* are antonyms. Antonyms help the child to think in terms of contrasting statements and concepts.

Homophones and homographs are homonyms. A homophone is a word identical with another in pronunciation but differing from it in origin, spelling, and meaning. *Fair* and *fare, cite, site,* and *sight* are examples of homophones. A homograph is a word identical with another in spelling but differing from it in origin and meaning and sometimes in pronunciation. Examples are: the *wound* is not deep. I *wound* my watch this morning. Please *read* this aloud. I *read* it yesterday. Only through the use of context can the reader determine correct pronunciation and meaning.

A knowledge of synonyms, antonyms, and homonyms is very important in using context clues. An understanding and appreciation of them can be developed by teacher-made exercises. For example, the student can be asked to list all the words he can think of that mean about the same as *beautiful* and to use each word in a sentence that brings out its particular meaning. She can ask the child to choose from several choices the word which means the opposite of a certain word. She can ask the child to define words such as *beech* and *beach* and to use each in a sentence to show its meaning.

Help the Child to Recognize and Understand Verbal Analogies

An analogy involves relationships among words. For example, dog is to puppy as cat is to kitten is an analogy. The relationship is established in the first set of words. The same relationship applies in the second set of words. In order to deal with analogies the child must know word meanings and word functions and must be able to see and use various types of relationships. Blake (1, pp. 288-290) lists ten types of relations that can be used in verbal analogies. The most common ones are listed and illustrated below.

1. *Purpose Relation.* Plane is to fly as car is to ride.
2. *Whole-Part Relation.* Hand is to finger as foot is to toe.
3. *Part-Part Relation.* Leaf is to blossom as wings are to feathers.
4. *Concept-Class-Member Relation.* Fruit is to apple as vegetable is to potato.

5. *Cause-Effect Relation.* Sleep is to rest as study is to learn.
6. *Synonym Relation.* Pretty is to beautiful as homely is to ugly.
7. *Antonym Relation.* Hot is to cold as high is to low.
8. *Place Relation.* Kalamazoo is to Michigan as Chicago is to Illinois.
9. *Sequence Relation.* Spring is to summer as May is to June.
10. *Numerical Relation.* 1 is to 4 as 10 is to 40.

A child can be taught to deal with analogies by having him look at the first set of words and figuring out the relationship between them. Then he applies this relationship to the second set of words.

Help the Child to Understand the Relationship Between a Substitute Term and Its Antecedent

Many children experience difficulty in understanding written material because they do not recognize the relationship between a substitute term and its antecedent. One of the best ways to help a child who is experiencing difficulty in this area is to use questions that provide the reader with practice in relating the substituted term to its antecedent. In the following example, substitute terms have been italicized.

Kay drove to the grocery store. While *there she* met Rita.
They talked for a long time.

Questions such as the following could be asked. Who met Rita? Where did they meet? Who talked for a long time?

Another instructional activity is to provide the child with sentences in which each substitute term has been underlined. The child is asked to find the antecedent for each substitute term. For example, what are the antecedents for each of the italicized substitute terms?

Richard and Robert are brothers. The *former* is an excellent athlete. The *latter* is not.

The weatherman on television reports that a severe ice and snow storm is headed in our direction. We already have three feet of snow on the ground. *For these reasons* we will stay at home tonight.

John went to the movie. *So did* Judy.

Pearson and Johnson in their book, *Teaching Reading Comprehension,* present a discussion of eight ways in which words are used as grammatical substitutes for a preceding word or group of words. They also suggest a variety of ways to teach this relationship (4, pp. 122-125).

Teach the Multiple Meanings of Words

Many words have more than one meaning. For example, notice the different meanings of the word *ring* in the following sentences.

She wore a beautiful diamond *ring.*

The boxers entered the *ring.*

Look at that *ring* of trees.

I hear the *ring* of a bell.

If a child knows only one meaning for the word, *ring,* he will encounter difficulty in understanding sentences in which the word is used to convey a different meaning. One of the reasons why some children have difficulty in reading in content areas is because they know the general meaning of a word but not its technical meaning. For example, a child may know the general meaning of the word *mean* but not as it is used in mathematics to denote the arithmetic average.

Children can be helped to understand the multiple meanings of a word by discussing the various meanings with them and then having them make up sentences using the word to convey its different meanings.

Help the Child to Understand the Denotative and Connotative Aspects of a Word

The denotation of a word is the literal meaning of a word. The denotation of the word *lemon,* for example, is a small, yellow citrus fruit. The connotation of a word is the interpretive meaning, an added emotional meaning that the word implies. For example, in the sentence, My car is a *lemon,* it is obvious that the connotative meaning of the word is intended. The best way to build the literal meanings of words is through direct experience or through indirect experience by using pictures, filmstrips, and discussion. Structural analysis, the use of context clues, and the dictionary also aid in understanding the denotation of words. The connotative meanings of words can be developed through questions such as, "What does it mean when I say I feel *blue*?" "What does it mean when I say he's a *worm*?" "What does it mean when I say she lost her temper and made a *scene*?"

Develop an Interest in Words

One of the ways to create interest in vocabulary development is to study word origins. Words have a history just as people have a history. An appealing way to begin is to study the origin of names. What does the child's name mean? Where did it come from? For example, if the child's name is Annabel Baker, she may be interested in learning that Annabel comes from Latin and means "beautiful Ann" and that Baker probably was derived from the occupation of an earlier ancestor. What is the origin of the names of the months? the days of the week? the different kinds of cloth? Studying the origin of such words as *maverick, quixotic, sandwich, pasteurize,* and *boycott* often helps the child to visualize the word in a setting and to remember its meaning.

Many of the words in the English language have been borrowed from other languages. For example, from the Hindi we have borrowed the words *pajamas, bungalow,* and *shampoo.* From American Indian, we have taken the words *moccasin, toboggan,* and *raccoon,* and from the Spanish the words *patio, taco,* and *mosquito.*

New words come into our language almost daily, chiefly by coining. One of the ways that we coin or create a new word is by combining morphemes. Examples are *television, astronaut,* and *cosmonaut.* Another way of coining new words is by blending the first part of a word with the last part of another word as in the word *smog* which comes from *smoke* and *fog,* and as in the word *brunch* which is a blend of *breakfast* and *lunch.* Many words are formed from the first letters of several words. These are called acronyms. Examples are *scuba* which comes from the expression, *s*elf *c*ontained *u*nderwater *b*reathing *a*pparatus and UNESCO which comes from *U*nited *N*ations *E*ducational, *S*ocial, *C*ultural *O*rganization.

Interest in words can also be developed by having the child demonstrate the meaning of a word by the way he writes it. This is sometimes called graphic writing. For example,

Encourage the Child to Keep a Record of Words Learned

The words that are taught to a child should be those which have permanent value. They should be the ones that he wants to learn and will use. He should be encouraged to keep a notebook of the new words he has learned along with their definitions and an example of their use in a sentence. These words can then be reviewed frequently and available for use in stories or accounts of personal experiences which he may write.

Show Your Enthusiasm for Words

The teacher's interest in words and vocabulary development is essential. Her enthusiasm can be contagious so that the child becomes equally excited about the study of words.

MATERIALS FOR VOCABULARY DEVELOPMENT

There are many commercial materials that are useful in helping children to increase their vocabularies. A few are listed below.

- *Developing Your Vocabulary.* Offers techniques for learning new words, use of the dictionary and thesaurus, and discusses homonyms, figurative language, meanings and connotations of words. (Science Research Associates, 259 East Erie St., Chicago, IL. 60611).
- *Homonym Cards, Antonym Cards, Homophone Cards.* Games in which the player matches pairs of pictured words. (Developmental Learning Materials, 7440 Natchez Ave., Niles, IL. 60648).
- *Macmillan Reading Spectrum: Vocabulary Development.* Series of six programmed workbooks for grades 4 to 6. (The Macmillan Publishing Co., 866 Third Ave., New York, NY 10022).
- *Peabody Language Development Kits.* Stresses the development of overall oral language skills through reception, expression, and the cognitive processes. (American Guidance Service, Inc., Publishers' Building, Circle Pines, MN. 55014).
- *The Plus Ten Vocabulary Booster Program.* A structured vocabulary program for intermediate grade students. (Webster Division of McGraw-Hill Book Co., 1221 Avenue of the Americas, New York, NY 10020).

- *Reading Homonyms.* Five sets for grades 1 to 3. Each set contains 8 booklets, a teacher's manual, and spirit masters for duplicating worksheets. (Dexter and Westbrook, Ltd., 958 Church St., Baldwin, NY 11510).
- *Scope-Visuals.* Series of spirit masters for junior high students reading at 4-6 grade levels. (Scholastic Magazines and Book Services, 50 W. 44th St., New York, NY 10036).
- *Target Green.* Emphasizes use of context, homonyms, synonyms, antonyms, roots and affixes for grades 4-6. (Field Enterprise Educational Corp., 510 Merchandise Mart Plaza, Chicago, IL. 60654).
- *Target Orange.* Deals with the use of context, figurative language, and connotations. Suitable for grades 7-9. (Field Enterprise Educational Corp., 510 Merchandise Mart Plaza, Chicago, IL. 60654).
- *What's In A Name? Podunk and Such Places, They Gave Their Names.* Series of booklets dealing with the etymology of words. (Barnell Loft, Ltd., 958 Church St., Baldwin, NY 11510).

WHAT IS READING COMPREHENSION?

Reading comprehension is a complex process in which the reader uses his mental content to obtain meaning from written material. He must be able to recognize and decode words, obtain meaning from these words, and be able to relate the ideas to his previous knowledge. The goal of all reading instruction is to help individuals develop skill in comprehending or understanding what they read. There are three basic teaching strategies which can serve as the framework for improving comprehension. They are (1) the language experience approach, (2) the directed reading approach, and (3) the directed reading-thinking approach.

Language Experience Approach

In the language experience approach, the experiences of the child are used as the basis for reading materials. The child is encouraged to dictate an account of his experiences to the teacher who transcribes his story on the chalkboard or chart paper. When the story is complete, the teacher reads it aloud. As she reads, she moves her hand under each line to emphasize left-to-right reading of the story.

Then she asks the child to read the story orally as she moves her hand under the words. The teacher usually prepares duplicate charts of the story. One copy is left intact, and the other is cut into sentence strips. The sentence strips are used by the child to match each sentence with the sentence on the chart. He can also use the sentence strips to reconstruct the story. He is encouraged to read the sentences aloud as he performs these two activities. Words learned by the child are written on word cards and are placed in his word bank. When a sufficient number of word cards has been accumulated, they can be used to compose new stories. The language experience approach can culminate in a book written and illustrated by the child. The book can be shared with the child's friends and read to his parents. Suggestions for making books are described in *Diagnosis and Treatment of the Disabled Reader* (3, pp. 224-229).

The language experience approach is a highly successful remedial technique because it provides the student with reading material that is interesting to him and that is written in a language that is familiar to him. It has some disadvantages. It is an unstructured approach and lacks a sequential development of reading skills. The charts can be memorized rather than read by the child. In addition, there is a lack of vocabulary control and often little repetition of new words. Nevertheless, for some remedial students, especially those who do not view reading as a meaningful process, it can be a very effective approach.

Directed Reading Approach

The directed reading approach consists of five parts.

1. *Readiness.* During this stage the teacher creates interest in the material to be read, develops the necessary background, and introduces new vocabulary.
2. *Directed Silent Reading.* Before the child reads the story, the teacher provides the reader with a purpose for reading. The child then reads silently to seek answers to the purpose-questions asked by the teacher.
3. *Discussion.* The teacher raises questions to stimulate discussion of the material read and to determine whether or not the student has accomplished the purpose set for reading.
4. *Oral Re-Reading.* The student rereads aloud parts of the selection for a new purpose suggested by the teacher or to verify a point made during the discussion.
5. *Follow-Up Activities.* During this portion of the lesson, experiences can be provided for building and extending skill develop-

ment, and activities can be introduced to enrich the student's understanding and appreciation. For example, teacher-made worksheets or commercial materials can be used to reinforce comprehension skills or to build vocabulary. Enrichment activities such as role playing, art activities, and creative writing can be included.

The Directed Reading Approach has several advantages. It provides the basis for a systematic presentation of word identification and comprehension skills. It teaches the child to read for a purpose and encourages him to read for meaning. One of the major disadvantages of the Directed Reading Approach is that it is teacher dominated. The child can become too dependent upon the teacher's direction rather than learning to rely on his own ability to think for himself.

Directed Reading-Thinking Approach

In the Directed Reading-Thinking Approach, the teacher encourages the child to preview the material, to identify purposes for reading, and to make predictions concerning the material he is about to read. The teacher does not set purposes nor does she introduce vocabulary. She encourages the child to make his own predictions by formulating questions such as, What do you think this story is about? What do you think will happen in this story? The student then reads to verify his predictions. If, during reading, the child encounters an unknown word, he is told to read to the end of the sentence to see if he can figure out the unknown word. If this does not work, he is to use picture clues if they are available. He can also sound out the word. If none of these methods help to unlock the unknown word, then he is to seek assistance from the teacher. Following the silent reading of the material, the teacher asks the child how accurate his predictions were. The child produces proof by orally reading the sentences that revealed the answer. After this, follow-up activities are introduced. Many of the follow-up activities are skill building exercises and activities for enrichment.

The Directed Reading-Thinking Approach places emphasis on the relationship between reading and thinking. The child sets his own purposes for reading and reads to verify his predictions. He is encouraged to become independent in figuring out unknown words, to rely on context clues rather than on his teacher. The disadvantage lies in the fact that some children are unwilling or unable to make predictions. In addition, vocabulary development is not emphasized.

GUIDING PRINCIPLES FOR THE TEACHER

No matter what instructional strategy is followed by the teacher, the following principles should be given careful consideration.

- It is essential that the materials being used for remediation be meaningful to the reader and at his or her instructional level.
- The teacher should be certain that the student has the necessary mental content so that he can read with understanding.
- Factors that interfere with concentration should be eliminated if possible.
- Words for which the child has a well-defined need should be studied in context.
- Purposes for reading should be established prior to reading.
- The student should be encouraged to discuss what he or she has read. Discussion can be stimulated by thought-provoking questions posed by both the teacher and the student.
- Questions asked by the teacher should be well designed so that they stimulate higher levels of thinking.

THE ART OF ASKING QUESTIONS

The key to developing comprehension is to stimulate thinking while reading. This requires appropriate and varied questioning techniques on the part of the teacher. There are seven types of questions which are useful in guiding reading (6). Each type is described and an example is provided.

1. *Memory Questions.* These questions require the reader to recognize and recall facts and ideas explicitly stated in the material.
    Example: What are the names of the main characters in the story?

2. *Translation Questions.* These questions require the reader to put explicitly stated material into another form.
    Example: In your own words, tell me what happened right after . . . .

3. *Interpretive Questions.* These questions require the reader to draw an inference concerning information that is implied but not stated explicitly in the material.

> *Example:* What lesson, if any, is to be learned from this story?

4. *Application Questions.* These questions require using information gained from reading in problem-solving situations.

> *Example:* Have you ever had a problem like that of the person in the story? How did you solve the problem?

5. *Analysis Questions.* These questions require the student to separate the whole of what has been read into its parts.

> *Example:* Show how the writer has made this a humorous story.

6. *Synthesis Questions.* These questions require the reader to put the parts together to create a new whole.

> *Example:* What do you think happened to the main character after the story ended?

7. *Evaluation Questions.* These questions require the student to make judgments about the material.

> *Example:* Do you think you would enjoy being like the main character? Why or why not?

EXERCISE

14.1. Identify each of the following questions as to type.
1. What evidence of faulty thinking can be found in this article?
2. What techniques has the author used to create suspense?
3. In what year was Pearl Harbor attacked by the Japanese?
4. Draw a picture to show the inside of the sheepherder's wagon.
5. What is meant by the expression, "I'm so hungry I could eat a horse?"
6. If you were the author, how would you have ended the story?
7. What similarities do you see between problems faced by the main character in the story and the problems which you have?

The teacher can improve his or her questioning techniques by:

1. Asking a variety of questions designed to stimulate thinking. The teacher should avoid asking too many memory and translation questions.

2. Asking the child to support his opinion by answering the question, "Why do you think that?"
3. Asking questions that do not necessarily have a right or wrong answer.
4. Avoiding questions that can be answered with a simple yes or no.
5. Making sure that questions are properly stated; that is, do not give the answer in the question.
6. Avoiding questions which ask about insignificant aspects of the material.

HELPING STUDENTS TO READ IN THOUGHT UNITS

Meaning is conveyed through words, phrases, sentences, paragraphs, and whole selections. In this section we shall suggest ways in which children can be taught to read more effectively in thought units.

Phrase Reading

Many disabled readers need help in reading by phrases. The child who is a word by word reader especially needs assistance. Some of the ways to help children who need to improve in this area are

1. Use very interesting and easy material so that the child does not encounter difficulty in word identification and word meaning.
2. Mark off phrases in the material to be read by the child. For example, The squirrel/is climbing/the tree.
3. Use phrase cards instead of word cards for flashcard activities.
4. Have the child read simple poetry with feeling.
5. Read a sentence aloud to the child, phrase by phrase, and then have him read it aloud phrase by phrase.
6. Have the child read in unison with the teacher.
7. Have the child underline phrases in a sentence and then read it aloud phrase by phrase. Emphasize the meaning of each phrase.

Sentence Reading

Every sentence has a surface structure and a deep structure. Surface structure is essentially the words and the order of the words in the sentence. Deep structure involves the basic meaning of the sentence. It takes into account the *relationships* among the elements of the sentence, some of which are unstated and must be understood by the reader's application of his own mental content. For example, the surface structure of the following sentences is similar, but the deep structure is not.

He ate the orange last.

He ate the last orange.

One day two children arrived home from school to find a freshly baked cake on the table with a note from their mother saying, "Please ice the cake." One child wanted to put the cake in the refrigerator. The other child argued that the cake should have frosting applied to it. Both children correctly read the surface structure but imposed their own differing understandings on what the message required.

Often errors in oral reading occur because the reader understands what is meant by the passage even though he misreads some of the words. For example, two children read a sign that stated, "Please remove your boots." Ed correctly read every word on the sign but did not understand the meaning of the word, *remove,* and consequently did not know what action was requested. He was able to read the surface structure correctly but did not have the background to understand the deep structure. Dick, on the other hand, read the sign aloud as follows, "Please take off your boots," and did so before entering. He understood the deep structure even though he made an error in the surface structure.

In teaching a child to read, the deep structure should be emphasized. One of the best ways to help students understand the deep structure of a sentence is to ask questions about the sentence: Who, what, where, when, how, why.

Some children experience difficulty in understanding sentences that contain dependent clauses and embedded phrases and clauses. This may be due to the child's limited competence in language comprehension and may require exposing the child to oral language that is more complex. It may be due to his failure to make use of punctuation as an aid to reading. If this is a problem, simple explanations and examples of punctuation marks should be provided. Periods are used at the end of statements. A question mark is used at the end of an interrogative sentence. An exclamation point is used at the end of an emphatic statement. Commas and dashes are used to separate parts of a sentence and indicate pauses within a sentence. They are used to separate explanatory material from the main thought of the sentence, to separate items in a series, and to separate main clauses. Sometimes it is necessary to color code punctuation marks to emphasize them. Punctuation carries some of the meaning which speech conveys. Show the student how a period, exclamation point, or question mark can change the meaning of identical sentences. Have the student explain what a writer intends when he uses these different marks.

Some children encounter difficulty in understanding sentences because they have difficulty with connectives that qualify the meaning of the sentence. For example, in the sentence, We were going ice skating, but Mother popped corn, so we decided to stay home with her, the words *but* and *so* are connectives. Questions to help the reader might include: Did they go ice skating? Why did they change their minds? What words tell us that they did not go? Another way to help children understand sentences which contain connectives is to provide them with several sentences in which connectives such as *if, unless, however, moreover, until,* and *because* are used. Have them rewrite the sentences expressing the same idea.

In order to understand sentences, the reader must be concerned with meaning. He must learn to predict what is coming next. The use of the cloze procedure, described in Chapter 13, can serve this instructional purpose.

Paragraph Reading

A paragraph is a group of sentences organized around a main idea. To read paragraphs effectively, the student must be able to understand the relationships between the sentences in the paragraph and the general organization of the paragraph. Most paragraphs contain a central thought which may or may not be stated in a topic sentence. The reader needs to understand that the topic sentence, if there is one, states the main idea of the paragraph. The other sentences should support this main idea. The topic sentence is usually the first sentence in the paragraph, but sometimes it is the last sentence and sometimes it is imbedded in the middle of the paragraph.

The following list of questions can be asked by the teacher to assist the child in reading paragraphs.

1. What is the topic being discussed in this paragraph?
2. What does the paragraph tell about the topic?
3. What is the main idea of the paragraph? State the main idea in your own words.
4. What sentence states the main idea?
5. What supporting facts or details are provided in the paragraph?

Help the child to visualize the relationship between the main idea and supporting details by having him or her write the main idea in the large rectangle and each supporting detail below.

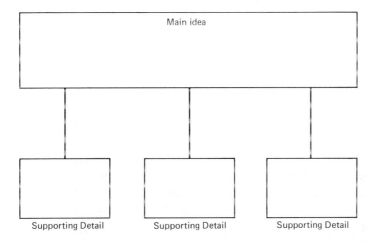

Students also need to understand that different types of paragraphs serve different purposes. For example, there are *introductory paragraphs.* These paragraphs generally occur at the beginning of a selection or major divisions of a long selection. They introduce the topic to be covered and stimulate interest in the material. *Transition paragraphs* indicate a change from one idea to another. *Illustrative paragraphs* contain examples to clarify ideas. *Summary paragraphs* usually occur at the end of a selection and summarize the main ideas.

Whole Selections

In order to read effectively a nonfiction selection the student should be taught to

1. Skim the introductory paragraphs so as to determine what the writer intends to do.
2. Skim the summary at the end of the article if there is one to discover what the author says he has accomplished.
3. Scan the major headings if the article contains these. Determine how the material is organized. Some materials are organized in chronological order; that is, events are presented in the way in which they occur. Some are organized according to topics, and some are arranged in causal relationships. The reader should try to determine the kind of organizational pattern utilized by the author because this information should aid him in relating the parts of the selection to the whole.

4. If there are no headings, scan carefully the topic sentence of each paragraph. Determine its contribution to the main idea of the whole selection.

Some teachers find it helpful to teach the student various techniques for representing his understanding of a whole selection. Some examples of representational format techniques, or graphic ways to represent the entire selection, are drawing a series of pictures or a comic strip to show the sequential events in the story, making charts or graphs to show cause-effect relationships, and producing a play to show character and plot development. For each selection the student chooses his representational technique, providing him with an opportunity to engage in creative and flexible thinking.

EXERCISE
14.2. Tressa dislikes reading as evidenced by her acknowledgment and behavior during reading activities. She is a word caller and only intermittently reads in meaningful units. She seldom corrects her miscues while reading orally, and most of the miscues do not make sense. She relies heavily on grapho-phonic clues and seems adept in using syntactic clues. She exhibits an awareness of, yet slight confusion about, contractions. She seems unsure of herself when asked to read and conveys the impression that she does not expect much either from the story or from her efforts. When she is asked to retell a story which she has read, she can recall only a few ideas. With this brief information, outline what you would do to help Tressa become a better reader.

SUGGESTIONS FOR DEVELOPING SPECIFIC COMPREHENSION SKILLS

Someone once defined reading as "thinking triggered by print." We agree with this concept. Reading *is* a thinking process. The teacher can facilitate the development of reading proficiency by helping the reader to set purposes for his reading that encourage the higher mental thought processes and by fostering discussion following silent reading by raising questions that involve interpretation, analysis, synthesis, and evaluation. To clarify these points, let us begin by listing Bloom's Taxonomy of Cognitive Skills (2) and relating the skills to three types of reading.

Bloom's hierarchy of cognitive skills sets forth seven levels of thinking.

Evaluation.
Synthesis.
Analysis.
Application.
Interpretation.
Translation.
Memory.

Memory and *translation* are the cognitive skills involved in reading for *literal understanding.* This type of reading involves recognizing and recalling what the author has explicitly stated. If the reader, for example, responds to a question concerning the material he has read by recalling just what the author has said, he is probably functioning only at the memory level. If the reader puts this information into another form, his own words for example, he is probably functioning at the translation level.

Interpretive reading involves the cognitive skills of *interpretation, application, analysis,* and *synthesis.* Interpretation involves recognizing unstated relationships. It involves drawing inferences from implicitly stated material. Application occurs when the reader uses the material to solve a lifelike problem. Analysis, in a sense, involves dissection. It involves analyzing the parts that compose the whole. Synthesis occurs when the student puts together separate pieces of information and shows the relations among them. It requires original creative thinking on the part of the reader.

A third type of reading, *evaluation,* involves all seven levels of thinking. To evaluate what one reads or to read critically, the reader makes a judgment according to standards he designates.

Literal and Interpretive Reading

Literal reading involves understanding information that is directly stated in a selection. Many disabled readers have difficulty in understanding material when it is explicitly stated, and they need a great deal of assistance in reading at this level. Recognizing and recalling stated main ideas, details, sequence, comparisons, causes and effects, and character traits involve literal reading. Interpretive reading involves making inferences based on information implied in the material. Interpretive reading includes drawing inferences concerning main ideas, details, sequence, comparisons, causes and effects, character traits, and figurative language. Activities for developing both literal and interpretive understanding are outlined here.

Main Idea

1. After the student has read a paragraph, ask him to underline the topic sentence.
2. Have the student state the main idea of a paragraph in his own words.
3. Have the child read a descriptive paragraph and make a drawing of the object, person, or event described.
4. Have the student select from a list of questions the one that the paragraph answers.
5. Have the child create a new title for a story.
6. Have the student read a passage in which the main idea is not directly stated. Have him infer the main idea of the passage.
7. Have the student read a newspaper article without a headline and select from several headlines, the most appropriate one for the article.

Details

1. After the student has read a paragraph, ask him questions concerning the details directly stated in the paragraph.
2. Have the child select from a paragraph the sentence that includes one irrelevant detail.
3. Have the student read newspaper articles and ask him questions which involve who, what, where, when, why, and how.
4. Give the child detailed written directions of some object and have him draw a picture of it.

Sequence

1. Teach the child the meaning and use of words such as *first, next, last,* and *finally.*
2. Have the child place in sequence events related in a story.
3. Cut up comic strips and have the child arrange them in the proper order.
4. Supply the child with a group of related sentences. Have him arrange them in proper sequence.
5. Supply the student with a story that has been cut so that each paragraph forms a separate section. Have the child place the paragraphs in sequential order.
6. Have the child make a series of drawings which show an interesting sequence from a story he has read.

7. Give the student a sequential type paragraph where one detail is out of place. Have him identify it.

Making Comparisons

1. Have the student read two articles dealing with the same subject. Ask him to compare the ideas in the two articles as to whether they are similar, different, or contradictory.
2. Have the student compare the main characters from different selections to see how they are alike or different.
3. Have the student explain how a character in a story he has read handled an emergency and have him compare it with how he thinks he might handle a similar situation.

Cause-Effect Relationships

1. Have the child read a paragraph that contains a cause and effect relationship. Have him state the cause and identify the effect.
2. Use questions that probe the student's ability to understand causal relationships in a passage.
3. Have the students paraphrase sentences so as to express a causal relationship in another way.
4. Have the student change the character in a story to see how the change effects the events in the story.

Following Directions

1. Use written instead of oral directions. Have the child read the directions and then explain in his own words what he is to do.
2. Have the child follow directions for making something of interest to him.
3. Give the child a picture and supply him with directions for coloring the picture.
4. Have a treasure hunt in which the student has to follow directions in order to find the treasure.

Identifying Character Traits

1. Have the student identify statements about a character which help to indicate the type of person he is.
2. Have the child hypothesize about the personality traits of a character in a story he is reading.
3. Have the student identify the events in a story which contribute to the development of a character.
4. Help the student become aware of the devices an author has used in a story to develop a character.

Predicting Outcomes
1. Have the student read a story and at appropriate places in the story, stop the child and have him answer the question, "What do you think will happen next?"
2. Have the child read part of a story and tell or write an ending for the story.
3. Have the child devise a new ending for a story he has read.

Inferring the Meaning of Figurative Language. Figurative language is language that conveys a meaning different from the literal meaning of the words. It is used to arouse sensory images and to show the feeling of a situation. The most common types of figurative language are defined and illustrated here.

Idiom. An idiom is an expression that has come to have a figurative meaning from common usage. The meaning of the expression cannot be understood from its grammatical structure or from the meanings of its parts.
Example: She has her *head in the clouds.*

Simile. In a simile a comparison between two unlike things or actions is made using *like* or *as.*
Example: Her skin felt *like velvet.*

Metaphor. A metaphor is an analogy or comparison without the words *like* or *as.* One thing is spoken of as if it were another.
Example: She's a *rock.*

Personification. In personification the characteristics of a human being are given to something nonhuman.
Example: The river *ate away* the bank.

Onomatopoeia. Onomatopoeia is using words with sounds that suggest their meaning.
Example: The wheels *screeched* as he turned the corner at a record-breaking speed.

Hyperbole. Hyperbole is an exaggeration or overstatement.
Example: I'm so hungry I could eat a *hundred* pizzas.

Synecdoche. Synecdoche is an expression in which the name of a part is used to mean the whole or the whole is used to mean the part.
Example: *All hands* on deck.

Irony. In irony an expression is used in a humorous or sarcastic way to mean exactly the opposite of what it says.
Example: *This has been a perfect day.* Everything has gone wrong.

In order to help an individual understand figurative meanings, the teacher must help him or her to become sensitive to figurative language. Some specific suggestions for helping a reader to infer the meaning of figurative language are listed below.

1. Provide the student with sentences in which figurative language has been used. Underline the figurative language. Provide three possible meanings for each expression. Have the student choose the correct meaning from the list of possible meanings you have provided.
2. Have the student draw pictures illustrating the literal meanings of figurative expressions. Then have him explain the intended meaning.
3. Provide the student with several sentences, each of which contains a figure of speech. Have him identify the figure of speech in each sentence and explain what it means.
4. Have the child "act out" the literal meaning of an idiom. Then have him explain its intended meaning. For example, a common idiom is "Step on it." Provide the child with a card on which the word *it* is written. Have him step on the word *it*. Then have him explain that this is not the intended meaning of the expression. If this activity is used with a group of children, have each child act out the literal meaning of an idiom and have the others guess what it is.
5. Have the student use figurative expressions to describe events, objects, or people.
6. Read a short poem that contains figurative language. Have the student underline the figures of speech and express the ideas in different language.

Evaluation

Evaluation, or critical reading, involves making judgments about the material. It includes distinguishing between facts and opinions, distinguishing reality from fantasy, detecting propaganda, and judging the adequacy, validity, worth, or acceptability of written material.

The critical reader does not accept every idea expressed in written form. He identifies, interprets, and evaluates ideas in terms of his background and previous experience. If an idea expressed by a writer appears unusual, overdrawn, or without support, he stops and investigates. He senses evidence of cloudy thinking and is alert to the techniques used by writers to trip the naive reader. The critical reader must read with a questioning attitude.

Distinguishing Facts and Opinions

1. Explain and illustrate the difference between a fact and an opinion. A fact can be verified. An opinion cannot.
2. Explain to the student that such phrases as "it seems," "it appears," "it may," "I believe," and "I think" are often used to denote an opinion.
3. Provide the child with a series of sentences, some of which are facts and some opinions. Have the child identify which statements are facts and which are opinions.
4. Have the student read newspaper editorials and underline each statement that is a fact. Have him circle each statement that is an opinion.

Distinguishing Reality from Fantasy

1. Have the child read a story. When he has finished, ask him questions such as, "Do you think this story really happened? Why or why not? Is the description in the story realistic? Why or why not? Are the characters in the story believable? Why do you think this? Was the ending of the story reasonable? Why or why not?
2. Provide the child with an opportunity to read stories that are factual and stories that are fantasy. Help him to see the differences in the two types of writing.
3. Have the child read a story for the purpose of determining whether or not the events in the selection could have occurred in real life.

Detecting Propaganda

- Acquaint the student with the seven types of propaganda techniques.
  1. *Glittering Generalities.* Use is made of vague phrases that promise much. The use of terms such as "clean," "new," and "advanced" are appealing to most of us.
  2. *Testimonials.* Some prominent person endorses an idea or product. A famous movie star or sport hero says he uses a certain product. If it is good enough for him, it must be good enough for us.
  3. *Card Stacking.* This technique presents only facts that support one side. Deception and half truths are used to keep us from learning the real truth.
  4. *Bandwagon.* Claim is made that "everyone is doing it."
  5. *Name Calling.* Use is made of labels which arouse negative emotions. Instead of dealing with truths, expressions such as

as "communist," "capitalist," and "warmonger" are used to arouse the prejudice of the reader.

6. *Plain Folks.* Appeals are made to the common man suggesting that an important person is ordinary like the rest of us and therefore can be trusted.

7. *Transfer.* The attraction of a respected organization or symbol is associated with a particular person, product, or idea, thus transferring the respect of the symbol to the new product or person.

- Supply the child with several newspaper and magazine ads. Have him identify and explain the propaganda techniques being used.
- Have the child observe a number of television ads for the purpose of spotting and identifying propaganda techniques.
- Have the child write ads to illustrate each of the propaganda techniques.
- Have the child evaluate various forms of propaganda by answering the following questions.
  1. Who is the propagandist?
  2. Whom is he serving?
  3. What is his purpose?
  4. To what human interests, emotions, desires is he appealing?
  5. What techniques does he use?
  6. Are you persuaded by him?

Judging Adequacy, Worth, or Acceptability

- Explain and illustrate to the child how the following questions can help him to read critically.
  1. What is the author's purpose in writing this article or book?
  2. What are his qualifications for writing on this topic? Is he a recognized authority in this field?
  3. Is the material timely? When was the article or book copyrighted?
  4. How appropriate is the material to the topic being discussed?
  5. Are the facts presented in the material true?
  6. Does the author differentiate clearly between facts and opinions?
  7. Does the author show evidence of prejudice or bias?
  8. Is the author's thinking sound and reasonable?
  9. Does the material contain propaganda?
  10. Does the author approach the material logically or emotionally?
- Have the student read an article for the purpose of judging it. Use the questions listed above as a guide for discussion.

EXERCISE

14.3. Joel is an unusually intelligent fifth-grade student who reads well orally but has difficulty in comprehending what he reads silently. He often memorizes material that he has read and when questioned by the teacher responds in terms of the exact words from the written material. His independent reading level is third grade, his instructional level is fourth grade, and his frustration level is fifth grade. His listening level is eighth grade. What would you do to help Joel?

SUMMARY

This chapter has endeavored to show the teacher or therapist how to treat individuals having vocabulary and comprehension problems. Strategies and methods have been suggested to overcome specific deficiencies. Emphasis has been placed on the importance of concept building in vocabulary development, on the setting of purposes prior to reading, and on the skillful use of questions to simulate thinking.

REFERENCES

1. Blake, Kathryn A. *College Reading Skills.* Englewood Cliffs, NJ: Prentice-Hall, 1973.
2. Bloom, Benjamin S., ed. *Taxonomy of Educational Objectives: Handbook 1, Cognitive Domain.* New York: McKay, 1956.
3. Carter, Homer L. J., and Dorothy J. McGinnis. *Diagnosis and Treatment of the Disabled Reader.* New York: Macmillan, 1970.
4. Pearson, P. David, and Dale D. Johnson. *Teaching Reading Comprehension.* New York: Holt, Rinehart and Winston, 1978.
5. Rentel, Victor M. "Concept Formation and Reading." *Reading World* 11 (December 1971): 111-119.
6. Sanders, Norris M. *Classroom Questions: What Kinds?* New York: Harper & Row, 1966.

SUGGESTED READING

Allen, Roach V. *Language Experiences in Communication*. Boston: Houghton Mifflin, 1976.

Burns, Paul C., and Betty D. Roe. *Teaching Reading in Today's Elementary Schools* (Second Edition). Chicago: Rand McNally College Publishing Co., 1980, Ch. 4.

Dale, Edgar, and Joseph O'Rourke. *Techniques of Teaching Vocabulary*. Palo Alto, CA: Field Educational Publications, Inc., 1971.

Pearson, P. David, and Dale D. Johnson. *Teaching Reading Vocabulary*. New York: Holt, Rinehart and Winston, 1978.

Ransom, Grayce A. *Preparing to Teach Reading*. Boston: Little, Brown and Company, 1978, Chs. 8 and 11.

Stauffer, Russell G. *Directing Reading Maturity as a Cognitive Process*. New York: Harper & Row, 1969.

Stauffer, Russell G. *The Language-Experience Approach to the Teaching of Reading*. New York: Harper & Row, 1970: 132-176.

15

Correcting Reading- Study Problems

OBJECTIVES

This chapter should help you to

1. Diagnose a student's difficulties in applying reading to study activities.
2. Treat individuals experiencing difficulty in reading-study activities.
3. Treat individuals having difficulty reading in specific content areas.

Reading problems often become evident when the student is expected to apply his reading skills to study activities and is required to read in various content areas. Teachers and therapists need to know how to diagnose a student's reading-study habits and how to help students develop basic reading-study skills.

DIAGNOSIS IN THE AREA OF READING-STUDY SKILLS

The development of skill in applying reading to study activities is often a neglected area in corrective and remedial teaching. Diagnosis of the student's ability to study should involve investigating cognitive, physical, and environmental-emotional factors and specific reading-study skills. Otto and McMenemy (2, pp. 192-193) point out that it is very important to determine the pupil's "will to learn." They state that the student's capacity for self-direction must be known if a realistic remedial program is to be successful. Investigating this factor is not easy. Therefore, the teacher probably will have to rely on her own subjective judgment based upon information gained from observing and working with him over a period of time. Informal inventories can be designed by the teacher to determine the student's skill in performing each of the reading-study skills discussed in this chapter. The checklist on page 265 may be helpful in summarizing data resulting from teacher observations and informal inventories.

There are standardized tests that measure various study skills. A few of them are listed here.

- *Iowa Tests of Basic Skills, Multilevel Edition.* Measures vocabulary, reading, spelling, capitalization, punctuation and usage as well as map and graph reading, and general reference skills. For grades 3-8. (Boston: Houghton Mifflin, 1978).
- *SRA Achievement Series: Work-Study Skills.* Measures ability to read charts and use reference materials. For grades 4-9. (Chicago: Science Research Associates, 1964).
- *Spitzer Study Skills Test.* Measures student's skill in using the dictionary, index, map, graph, and reference materials as well as the student's ability to take notes. For grades 9-13. (New York: Harcourt Brace Jovanovich, 1956).

Diagnosis of the student's weaknesses in the area of reading-study skills is essential so that adequate and specific therapy can be planned. Only those skills that the student needs should be emphasized in remediation.

TABLE 15-1.   Checklist of Reading-Study Skills

Skill	Satisfactory	Unsatisfactory
Understanding specialized vocabulary		
Understanding a textbook chapter		
Concentrating on a reading assignment		
Adjusting rate according to materials and purpose		
Skimming		
Scanning		
Using different parts of a book		
Using a dictionary		
Using a thesaurus		
Using an encyclopedia		
Using an atlas		
Using an almanac		
Using library card catalog		
Using *Readers' Guide to Periodical Literature*		
Outlining		
Notetaking		
Summarizing		
Reading maps		
Reading graphs		
Reading tables		

GUIDELINES FOR HELPING STUDENTS

There are a number of general suggestions which the teacher should consider when helping the student to develop reading-study skills. They are

1. Create an environment and atmosphere that is conducive to learning and achievement.
2. Help the student to set up realistic goals for himself.
3. Help him to become aware of his needs and to see how the development of reading-study skills will help him to achieve his goals.
4. Help him to become determined to overcome his problems.
5. Use materials of interest to him and at an appropriate level of difficulty. Sometimes this suggestion is difficult to follow. When the student is expected to read a selection that is too difficult for him, make it easier by building concepts and developing vocabulary prior to his reading of the material. Encourage the student to set purposes and to read with a questioning attitude. Prepare a study guide for the student to use. Thomas and Robinson (6, pp. 274-280) suggest the use of a Selective Reading Guide-O-Rama for this purpose.
6. Make sure the student has opportunity for reinforcement before proceeding to new skills. Do not proceed too rapidly.

BUILDING A SPECIALIZED VOCABULARY

Many children experience difficulty in reading in the various content fields because of limited technical vocabularies. Suggestions for helping a student build a meaning vocabulary have been made in Chapter 14 and can be used to increase the child's technical vocabularies. In addition, the student should be encouraged to list the words which he finds in his textbooks which are unfamiliar to him. These are the words which he should learn. The student should look in his books for clues to the word's meaning in the context and should refer to the glossary, if there is one, for usable meanings. He or she should examine the prefix, root, and suffix for clues to its meaning and should make use of the dictionary. In addition, the student can build up a reading and spelling vocabulary simultaneously by means of a visual, auditory, kinesthetic, and tactual approach which has been described in Chapter 13. He or she should use the word in a complete sentence so that its full meaning is adequately expressed, and keep a card file of the words studied and review them frequently.

DEVELOPING SKILL IN CHAPTER READING

Many students attempt to read their textbooks in the same manner in which they read story-type materials. Others become lost in a maze of detail and are unable to identify, interpret, and evaluate the main ideas in a chapter. They need a system for study. We recommend a modification of Robinson's SQ3R method (3, pp, 28-33).

1. Preview the chapter by skimming the introduction so as to determine what the writer intends to do. Skim the summary at the end of the chapter if there is one in order to discover what the writer says he has accomplished. Skim the large major headings for the purpose of determining the organization of the chapter.
2. Convert each major heading into a question. Write each question on a 3 x 5 card.
3. Read for the purpose of answering each question.
4. State the answer to each question on the reverse side of the card containing the question. Be sure the student states the answers in his own words.
5. Place the cards in a pile and look at the question on the top card. Recite the answer. Sort the cards into two piles—one for the questions which were answered easily and one for those which caused difficulty. Continue studying in this manner until all the questions can be answered readily.

EXERCISE
15.1. Apply the modification of Robinson's SQ3R method to this chapter.

INCREASING ABILITY TO CONCENTRATE

Concentration is the act of focusing attention upon a subject in order to accomplish a purpose. Many students experience difficulty in concentrating upon a reading activity. Some suggestions that the teacher can use to help them are listed below.

1. Develop the student's interest in the material to be read. Help him to see the relationships between the material he is attempting to read and his own interests, welfare, and ultimate goals.

Encourage him to ask questions such as, "How can this information be of value to me?" "How can I use this material?"
2. Build the child's background for the material to be read. Frequently one's ability to concentrate upon a subject is in proportion to one's knowledge of the subject.
3. Be sure the material is appropriate to the individual's reading level. One's ability to concentrate is somewhat dependent upon the difficulty of the material being read.
4. Help the child to master adequate work-study techniques. Study is an activity that involves more than just looking at a book. It is an active process, and the student should be encouraged to work with pencil, paper, and reference materials.
5. Encourage the student to do his studying in one place and to begin studying the minute he sits down at his desk.
6. Eliminate physical conditions in his or her environment which may adversely affect ability to concentrate.
7. Help the child to develop and maintain good physical and mental health. Fears, worries, and unsolved problems can interfere with the student's ability to concentrate, and in some cases counseling may be necessary. You may be interested in reading Spache's description of several counseling strategies used by psychologists to help individuals experiencing difficulty in reading (5, pp. 280-285).

INCREASING RATE AND FLEXIBILITY

An increase in rate of reading should not be a goal of reading instruction until the student has acquired a mastery of the mechanics of reading. A limited rate of reading is often a symptom of inadequate word identification, an inferior meaning vocabulary, poor comprehension, or difficulties in concentration. When the student shows ability to comprehend the material, then rate of reading can be considered a viable objective. The good reader has many rates of reading. He or she varies reading rate according to the purpose he has in mind when reading and according to the nature and difficulty of the material he is reading.

If the teacher or therapist has decided that increasing rate of reading is a worthwhile objective, the following suggestions may be helpful.

1. Encourage the student to decide what he wants from the material before reading it. If the student understands what his purposes are, he can decide whether to skim the material or to read slowly for detail.
2. Teach the student to study the organization of the material by having him skim introductory statements, the summary, and the major and minor headings.
3. Teach the student to focus his efforts upon trying to find the general ideas he is after. He should be encouraged to let his eyes travel quickly down the page as he looks for key words that relate to his purpose. He should read for ideas expressed by groups of words and should not stop on words or spend too much time on details.
4. Teach the student to look for topic sentences and transition sentences. Frequently the first and last sentences in paragraphs emphasize the topics of paragraphs.
5. Teach the student to be alert to signal words. *Signal words* are words that tell the reader what ideas will follow. Four types of signal words are listed here.
   a. Words that can alert the reader to expect other facts of the same nature are *in addition, further, furthermore, finally, moreover, yet, however, still, on the other hand, next, then, but, first, second, and third, another, also.*
   b. Words that point to the fact that information is to be concluded or summarized are *therefore, thus, hence, for this reason, in brief, consequently, incidentally, to summarize, in conclusion.*
   c. Words that indicate changes in time and space are *later, at last, soon, before, above, following, finally, beneath, preceding, meanwhile, there.*
   d. Words that prepare the reader for specific illustrations or cases are *for example, in particular, especially, for instance.*
6. Help the child to become flexible. The good reader uses many different rates depending upon the difficulty of the material and purpose for reading. He should learn when and how to read rapidly and when and how to read slowly.
7. Eliminate faulty habits such as lip movement and finger pointing. Encourage the student to refrain from looking back over the material he has read and to force himself to read as rapidly as possible without loss of understanding. Encourage him or her to read for ideas and to skip over unimportant words and details.

8. Teach the student how to skim. Skimming is a rapid reading technique to be used when one wants to get a general impression of an entire selection or passage. The teacher may use textbooks or magazine articles for this purpose. Encourage the student to preview the title and to formulate a purpose for reading. Have him read the main headings and the summary.

9. Teach the student how to scan. Scanning is a process of quickly locating a particular word, phrase, sentence, or figure within a selection. Have the student scan a table of contents to find out on what page a chapter begins. Have him scan an index to find out on what pages a certain topic is discussed. Have him scan a selection to find a specific fact. Have him scan a table to find one particular statistic.

10. Encourage wide reading of easy, interesting material.

11. Provide timed practice exercises to increase rate. Have the student keep a record of his or her rate and comprehension on each timed passage. A chart can be devised for this purpose.

12. Use mechanical devices such as tachistoscopes, pacers, and special projectors for motivation. A tachistoscope is an instrument designed to flash a single exposure on a screen at a rapid rate, usually between one second and 1/100th of a second. Pacers are machines that use a shade, metal bar, or light beam that moves down a page to cover successive lines of print. The device should be set at a rate that will push the student to read rapidly. Special projectors are available to use with filmstrips. Caution should be used when working with mechanical devices so that the teacher does not become involved in treating symptoms rather than causes of slow reading.

BASIC LOCATION SKILLS

The following skills are essential if the student is to locate information quickly in textbooks, dictionaries, and other reference materials. Suggestions for developing each skill are provided.

1. Finding quickly a given page in a book.
   a. Give the student practice in finding a given page quickly.
   b. Give the student practice in finding quickly the section of a book in which he or she is likely to find a certain page.

2. Finding words in alphabetical order.

a. Have the student memorize the letters of the alphabet.
b. Ask the student to name or write the letter that immediately precedes or follows a given letter.
c. Have the student arrange letters in alphabetical order.
d. Have the student find all the words in a mixed list that begin, for instance, with *b*, all that begin with *g*, all that begin with *m*.
e. Have the student arrange a series of words in alphabetical order.
3. Deciding on key words.
   a. Have the student find and underline key words in several sentences.
   b. Ask the student to tell under what key word in an index a reference might be found for a question such as "In what year did World War II begin?"
   c. Provide exercises in which the student chooses the one of three words under which a reference is most likely to be made on a stated topic.
   d. Have the student use an index to locate specific information in a book.

EXERCISE
15.2. Develop an exercise in which the student is given practice in deciding on key words.

Learning to Use Different Parts of a Book

The following questions and directions can be used by the teacher and student to develop skill in using the different parts of a book.

1. What does the title tell you about the book?
2. What can you infer from the title page concerning the authors?
3. Is this book likely to contain up-to-date information?
4. What does the preface tell you about the book?
5. Have the student examine the table of contents in order to answer the question, "What is the content and scope of the book?"
6. Ask such questions as, "On what page does the story about the Sioux Indians begin?"
7. Encourage the student to read the introduction and summary and to skim the main headings of a chapter of interest to him. Have him answer the question, "What are the major ideas in the chapter?"

8. Have the student turn to the index of the book and ask him or her to find the page numbers on which discussions of certain topics can be found. Explain that an indication of pages such as 200-203 means that a certain topic begins on page 200 and ends on page 203 whereas 200, 203 means that the topic is discussed on pages 200 and 203.
9. Have the student locate the appendix of the book if there is one. Ask him or her to explain what is in the appendix and why the material is placed in this part of the book.
10. If there is a glossary, ask the student to find the meaning of certain words. Ask him or her to explain the difference between a glossary and a dictionary.
11. If there is a list of maps and illustrations, ask the student to locate it and to find the page on which a certain map or illustration can be found.

Use of the Dictionary

The adult level dictionary is a highly specialized device for investigating the pronunciation and meaning of words. Some suggestions are given for helping a student develop skill in locating information in the dictionary.

1. Show the student how the dictionary is constructed.
   The dictionary is divided into alphabetical sections, each generally marked by a tab. The first section is devoted to an introduction and an explanation of the symbols used to indicate pronunciation, the rules for spelling, and explanatory notes. The next and main part of the dictionary consists of words arranged alphabetically. The student's attention should be directed to the way the pages are planned. The guide words at the top of each page help the reader to find the first, second, third, and fourth letters of the word he is seeking. The student should be shown how the definition of the word is arranged. First the pronunciation is indicated, the word is divided into syllables, and the accent is given. Phonetic symbols are used to indicate the pronunciation. The key to phonetic symbols is usually given at the bottom of each page. The parts of speech of the word are listed next. Then the derivations and origin of the word are explained. Usually the root word is italicized indicating the original language from which the word is derived. The etymology starts with the present form of the word, gives its immediate source, indicates where the source word came

from, and may then go back to earlier origins of the word.

The various meanings of the word are next listed under the headings **1, 2, 3, 4,** or **a, b, c, d.** In some dictionaries, meanings are given in the order of their historical development in our language. The first meaning may or may not be the commonest meaning now. Teach the student what the indications "obsolete," "archaic," and "rare" mean.

The synonyms of the word are listed last.

Call attention to the different kinds of information that can be found in the back of the dictionary. This information varies with different dictionaries, but usually includes a biographical section, a gazetteer, a list of abbreviations, and sometimes a section on foreign words and phrases.

2. Teach the child to follow these steps when using a dictionary.
   a. Find the correct alphabetical section.
   b. Scan the guide words at the top of the page. The guide words indicate the first and last entry words on the page.
   c. Look for the word in the column under the correct page heading.
   d. Learn how to pronounce the word by observing the word in its phonetic form and comparing it with the symbols at the bottom of the page.
   e. Read all the different meanings of the word, checking to see that they are not limited by such phrases as "obsolete" or "colloquial."
   f. Notice the different parts of speech proper to this word and how they affect its meaning.
   g. Always select the meaning that is correct for the student's requirements.
3. Provide practice in using the dictionary by having the student select the meaning of a word that is appropriate in a given context.
4. Provide practice in determining the correct pronunciation of words such as *forehead, coupon, genuine, maraschino, amenable.*
5. Provide practice in using the dictionary to discover the origin of such words as *boycott, sandwich, maverick, quisling.*
6. Provide practice in using the dictionary to determine how many syllables there are in such words as *intolerable, disparity, sesame.*
7. Provide practice in looking up the spelling of a word in the dictionary by helping the student to decide on probable spellings of the word and then looking for these in the dictionary.
8. Have the student use the rhyming section found in many dictionaries to find words that rhyme with a certain word.

9. Have the student use the dictionary to find the sections where answers to the following types of questions can be found.
   a. In what year was the University of Michigan established?
   b. Is Harvard University coeducational?
   c. What does the proofreader's mark ℬ mean?
   d. Should the names of people, races, tribes, and languages be capitalized?
   e. Where is Tobago located?
   f. Who was Montgomery Pike?
   g. What does the astronomical sign ● represent?

Use of the Thesaurus

A thesaurus is a book that contains a collection of words arranged according to the ideas they express. It is not like a dictionary which defines words. Instead the thesaurus begins with a meaning and presents words which represent various aspects of that meaning. Most of the readers of this book are familiar with *Roget's Thesaurus* (4). The following are thesauri for younger children.

Greet, W. Cabell, et al. *In Other Words, A Beginning Thesaurus.* New York: Lothrop, 1969.
Drysdale, Patrick. *Words To Use, A Junior Thesaurus.* New York: William H. Sadlier, 1971.
Greet, W. Cabell, et al. *In Other Words, A Junior Thesaurus.* Chicago: Scott, Foresman, 1977.

The thesaurus is a valuable tool for vocabulary building, and students should be taught how to use it. The following activities are suggestive of many that the creative teacher can develop for helping a student become familiar with the thesaurus.

1. Explain to the student the purpose of the thesaurus, how the information in it is organized, and how to use the index to locate the information wanted.
2. Have the student find as many synonyms as he or she can, by using the thesaurus, for words like *hate, walk, eat, laugh.*
3. Give the student a paragraph in which a word like *nice, get,* or *sad* has been overused. Have him rewrite the paragraph, substituting more expressive synonyms for the overworked words.
4. Encourage the student to write a short selection and to use the thesaurus to find interesting and more precise words to express his or her ideas.

Using Encyclopedias, Atlases, and Almanacs

Encyclopedias, atlases, and almanacs are reference books which students should learn to use. The teacher should explain, show, and demonstrate what is contained in encyclopedias and how the material is organized. She should show the student an atlas, a bound collection of maps, and explain how the maps in an atlas are organized. Many of the skills related to the use of an atlas are included in this chapter in the section concerned with map reading. The teacher should also acquaint the student with almanacs. Almanacs contain a wealth of statistics, tables, charts and information on such topics as sports, current events and personalities, and countries of the world.

Suggested activities for teaching the use of these reference tools are

1. Provide the student with a list of questions about a number of topics. Have him find the key word in the question that will help him in using the encyclopedia.
2. Provide the student with a list of topics. Have him tell in which volume of the encyclopedia he will probably be able to find information about the topic.
3. Have the student answer specific questions about several topics by locating information in the encyclopedia.
4. Have the student practice using the index to the encyclopedia.
5. Have the student answer a list of questions which will require him to use the encyclopedia, an almanac, and atlas.
6. Have the student prepare a chart indicating in what reference books he would have to look in order to locate specific information.

EXERCISE

15.3. Develop three questions you might ask of a student which will require him or her to use reference books. Indicate the reference book needed to answer each question.

Using the Card Catalog

In most libraries nonfiction books are arranged according to subjects and are usually classified according to the Dewey Decimal System or the Library of Congress System. Each nonfiction book has a call number. This number is written or printed inside the cover and on the spine of the book. In cataloging books of fiction, the library classifies each book alphabetically by the author's last name.

Each book in the library has at least two cards which are kept in the card catalog. The card catalog is the index to the library and is comprised of small drawers lettered alphabetically to indicate the coverage of the cards inside. All the cards in the drawers are arranged alphabetically by author's name, by title of the book, and sometimes by subject. In the upper lefthand corner of each card is printed the call number of the book. This shows the location of the book on the shelf. In addition, other information is provided: the title of the book, its author, the place where it was published, the publishing company, the date of publication, and the number of pages in the book itself. The number of illustrations, graphs, and plates is also given.

In teaching the child how to locate a book in the library, the teacher should

1. Take the child to the library and show the card catalog to him. The card catalog should be explained to the student.
2. Have the student use the subject cards in order to find the names of books on different subjects.
3. Have him use the author cards to find books written by various authors.
4. Have him use the title cards to find the name of an author of a certain book.
5. Have the child use the card catalog to find a book he would enjoy reading. Have him fill in a slip of paper on which he records the call number, the title of the book, and the name of the author. Have the student give this slip to the librarian so that she can get the book for him. If the book is in open stacks, let the student select the book directly on the shelves using the book's call number to help him locate it quickly.

Using the Readers' Guide to Periodical Literature

The Readers' Guide to Periodical Literature is the best source for finding magazine articles. It is published in volume form and contains an index to the contents of about 160 popular magazines. It is published twice monthly except during July and August, when it appears monthly. *The Readers' Guide* also appears in annual and two-year volumes that alphabetize all entries for the year or years covered.

Each magazine article is arranged alphabetically under subject and the author's last name. Stories are alphabetized by the first word of the title, except *A* and *The* which are not considered first words. Poems are alphabetized under the section heading *Poems* and under the poet's name.

The following procedure is suggested for teaching students how to use the *Readers' Guide.*

1. Have the student turn to the alphabetical section of the *Readers' Guide* which contains the first letter of either the subject he is interested in, the author's last name, or the first word of the title.
2. Have him scan the columns until he finds the information he is seeking.
3. In many libraries it is necessary to consult a Kardex file in order to determine whether or not the magazine is available in the student's library. Show the student the Kardex file. Explain to him that in the Kardex file a card for each magazine in the library is alphabetically arranged. Have the student look in the file to determine whether or not the library has the magazine he wants.
4. Have the student write the name of the magazine, the volume number, the date of publication, and his name on a call slip. Have him give the slip to the librarian so that the magazine can be brought to him.

ORGANIZATIONAL SKILLS

Notetaking, outlining, and summarizing are organizational skills which students need when they engage in study activities.

Notetaking

The student's notes on a particular chapter or book are a written record of his comprehension. Notetaking requires the ability to discriminate major ideas from minor ones, to determine the relationships between ideas, and to condense information accurately. Notetaking is probably best taught with materials that are well-organized. Some suggestions for helping a student improve his ability to take notes as he reads are given below.

1. Have the student decide on his purpose for notetaking. What use will he make of the information he plans to record? Does he plan to use the information for a paper he is writing? Does he plan to use the notes for review? Knowing the purpose for note-

taking is important because it influences how much detail the student will include in his notes.

2. If the student decides to take notes in the book he is reading, teach him to double underline main ideas and to put a single line under supporting details. Encourage him to write a key word or phrase in the margin to indicate what the paragraph or section is about.

3. If the student prefers to keep notes in a notebook, teach him how to make a summary and how to outline. You may wish to teach him to draw a vertical line down the pages of his notebook. This vertical line would be drawn approximately two inches from the left edge of the paper. The student can use the right side of the paper to record his notes as he reads. After he is through, he can write a summary of the material on the left side of the page.

4. Teach the child to include enough information in his notes so that he will be able to understand them after a period of time has elapsed.

5. If the student plans to quote materials, teach him to copy exactly the material he plans to quote and to document the source of the selection.

6. If the student does not plan to quote materials, teach him how to express the writer's ideas in his own words.

7. Encourage the student to review his notes periodically.

Outlining

An outline involves writing down information from reading material so that the relationships between the main ideas and the supporting details are clearly shown. Two major types of outlines are the topic outline and the sentence outline. In the topic outline, each point is composed of key words or phrases. In a sentence outline, each point is a complete sentence. The most important points are usually indicated by Roman numerals and are placed at the left margin. The next most important points are preceded by capital letters, and the next by Arabic numerals. The further the points are to the right the less important they are. Points of equal importance or rank are placed under each other.

Outlining is difficult for some children to learn. Therefore, it may be necessary to approach this activity gradually by having the student

1. Group words under appropriate headings.
2. Find irrelevant words under a given heading.

3. Classify sentences under appropriate headings.
4. Select sentences that tell about the main idea.
5. Find subtopics in a paragraph and later in longer selections.
6. Select main points to complete a skeleton outline which contains details.
7. Select details to complete a skeleton outline which contains main points.
8. Select main ideas and subheadings for an outline.
9. Outline a chapter.

In teaching the child to outline a chapter, encourage him to

1. Preview the chapter to determine the organization of the chapter and its main ideas.
2. Make a skeleton outline of the main points.
3. Find the supporting detail for each main point and list these beside the capital letter below the main idea they support.
4. If more detail is needed for each of the supporting details, add these in the proper place in the outline.

TABLE 15-2.   Outline Form

Title

   I. Main Idea
        A. Detail supporting Main Idea I
           1. Detail supporting A
           2. Detail supporting A
        B. Detail supporting Main Idea I
        C. Detail supporting Main Idea I

  II. Main Idea
        A. Detail supporting Main Idea II
        B. Detail supporting Main Idea II
           1. Detail supporting B
           2. Detail supporting B
               a. Detail supporting 2
               b. Detail supporting 2
        C. Detail supporting Main Idea II

Summarizing

A summary is a short, informative, and clear statement of what an author has said. The following activities are suggested for helping a student to develop skill in summarizing.

1. Have the student read a newspaper article without a headline. Have him or her write a headline for the article.
2. Have the student read a short paragraph and write a sentence in which he summarizes the main idea of the paragraph.
3. Have the student change a set of directions into a brief summary.
4. Have the child read a long passage and several summaries of the passage. Have him choose the one that is best and explain why it is the best summary.
5. Have the child read a long passage and write his own summary.

READING GRAPHIC MATERIALS

Tables, graphs, and maps are also called charts. They are used to present information for the purpose of comparison. A table is the most compact way to present statistical information. To understand a table, the student must look for two things: the explanatory information given with the title and the various headings distributed along the top and left-hand side of the table.

Any graph can be presented in the form of a table, but a graph portrays the information more vividly. There are various kinds of graphs. Lineal graphs show sequential data; quantitative graphs provide numerical data, spatial graphs show area and location; pictorial graphs represent visual concepts; and hypothetical graphs display an interrelationship of ideas (1).

Getting information from charts requires a specialized kind of reading. The following suggestions may be of value.

1. Have the student read the legend or title to determine what the writer intends to show.
2. Ask him or her to determine what facts are shown vertically and what facts are shown horizontally on the chart.
3. Encourage the student to go from the general to the specific.
4. Have the student record all the facts which he can obtain from the chart and all the inferences which he can make based upon these facts.
5. Have the student read what the author has to say concerning the chart.
6. Have him compare his inferences with those made by the writer.

A map represents statistical information about distances, directions, topography, or any geographical features of an area. The main properties of maps are shape, area, distance, and direction. On most maps the horizontal lines are called parallels and the vertical lines which cross them are known as meridians. These lines are used in determining the latitude or longitude of a certain point. Degrees of latitude are measured as either north or south of the Equator and degrees of longitude are measured as either east or west of the Prime Meridian. Many small maps do not show these lines. All maps are drawn to scale. A map's scale makes it possible to determine the real distance on the earth's surface between any two points shown on that map. Symbols are used in maps to represent such features as rivers, mountains, cities, railroads, highways. An explanation of each symbol is shown in the legend.

In helping a student to read a map more effectively, teach him to

1. Read the title to determine what the map is showing.
2. Study the legend of the map to learn what each of the symbols used in the map represents.
3. Determine the main idea and supporting details revealed in the map.
4. Read what the author has to say about the map.
5. Compare the student's interpretation of the map with the author's.

The following activities may help a student to read graphs, tables, and maps with greater understanding.

1. Have the student make maps depicting some aspect of his or her local community.
2. Have the student answer questions based on information shown in a map, graph, or table.
3. Have the student construct various kinds of graphs based on facts that are important to him. For example, he could make a circle graph to show what percentage of his allowance he spends on clothing, entertainment, food, school materials, etc.
4. Have the student locate designated places on a map.
5. Have the student locate points on a map using latitude and longitude.
6. Teach the student the symbols used for lakes, oceans, continents, railroads, and so forth.
7. Have the student make a bar graph showing the noon temperature for each day during a month.
8. Have the student make a map of current events by placing pictures of recent happenings on a large wall map of the world.

9. Have the student read a bus, train, or airline schedule in order to answer questions asked by the teacher.

READING IN THE CONTENT AREAS

Many students experience difficulty reading in the content areas. The reading teacher or the content area teacher can help by applying the following suggestions.

1. Build the student's mental content so that he has the background of experiences needed to understand the concepts he will be reading about.
2. Develop the meaning of the specialized vocabulary words used in the material.
3. Use a content area textbook that is at the student's instructional level.
4. Introduce the book to the student so that he understands where to locate information in it.
5. Help the student to develop a purpose or purposes for reading.
6. Stimulate the student's interest in the content of the material.
7. Encourage the student to outline, to take notes, or to use the modification of Robinson's SQ3R method described in this chapter.
8. Provide the student with a study guide when needed.

EXERCISE
15.4. Explain why a good reader might have difficulty reading in the content fields.

Literature

Good literature possesses the following qualities: an effective setting, a sound plot, a basic theme, good characterization, a distinctive style of writing, and an attractive and suitable format. The reader of literature should try to see, hear, and feel what the writer is trying to express. The reader should try to see pictures, hear sounds, and reconstruct various sensory experiences as he reads. He should also adjust his rate of reading to the material and purpose of his reading. Sometimes the reader can skim and scan. At other times he or she will want to slow down and savor the ideas, the descriptions, the words used by the writer. In this section we shall suggest ways to help students read and enjoy essays, short stories, novels, plays, poetry, and biographies.

Essays. An essay is an analytic or interpretive literary composition usually written to present a writer's personal point of view. Essays are written for many purposes: to inform, to persuade, to entertain. The student needs to understand the essayist's intent and purpose. In helping a student to read an essay, the teacher can ask such questions as

1. What was the writer's purpose? Was it to inform, to persuade, or to entertain?
2. If the author's purpose was to inform, what was he trying to tell the reader? Was his or her explanation clear? What major ideas did you get from the essay?
3. If the author was trying to persuade, what did the author want you to believe? How did he try to persuade you? Did he use emotional words? If so, what were they? How did these words affect your feeling about what he was saying?
4. If the author was trying to entertain, did he use humor to accomplish his purpose? What parts of the essay did you find amusing? Why did you find these parts humorous?

Short Stories. The reading of short stories and novels is similar in many respects. The reader of both types of literature is concerned with the plot, the setting, character development, and the theme or main idea of the author. Questions such as the following can be asked to help the student understand short stories better.

1. Where did this story take place?
2. When did the story take place?
3. Which character in the story did you like best or least? Why?
4. Were the characters realistic?
5. How did the author build the personalities of the characters?
6. What happened to the main character in the story?
7. Did you like the way the story ended? Why or why not?
8. Did the story have a moral or message? What was it?
9. Did you like the writer's style of writing? If so, what did you like about it?

Novels. The novel is primarily concerned with people, their way of life, their problems, their fears, their anxieties, their successes, and their triumphs. In reading a novel, the reader is primarily interested in the action or plot. He or she is also concerned with the setting and with the portrayal of personalities. The student should be permitted to read the novel for enjoyment. Then discussion based on the following questions should help him to understand and appreciate it.

1. Where did the story take place?
2. When did the story take place?
3. Are you able to "see" the setting? (You may wish to have the student draw a picture representing an important scene or character in the story.)
4. How would you describe the main character?
5. Did any of the characters change in the story? If so, what made them change and how did they change?
6. What was the plot of the novel?
7. Is the story true to the life situations of the time, environment, and circumstances described in the novel?
8. Did the story hold your attention? How?
9. What do you think is the main idea of the novel?
10. Did the novel affect you? In what ways?
11. Do you like the way the author writes? Would you like to read more stories by this author?

Plays. Plays differ from other forms of writing in that the characters of a play are usually listed and the setting is described at the beginning of the play. A few stage directions are provided, and the dialogue is given and labeled according to the character speaking the part. In reading a play the student must visualize the setting, the characters, and the action. He must infer what a character is like by interpreting his words, and he must be able to hear and see the dramatization as though it were taking place on the stage. The reading of plays requires the use of the reader's imagination. He must read through and between the words spoken by the characters and make use of brief stage directions to make the play come alive.

It may help the reader to answer such questions as

1. What is the setting of the play?
2. Who are the characters?
3. What happens to them?
4. What is the purpose of the play?
5. In what way did the plot include the resolution of a conflict?
6. In what way would this play be more or less effective as a novel?

The teacher can also help the student by

1. Developing background for the play.
2. Helping the student to visualize the action in the play.
3. Encouraging the student to visualize the setting of each scene.
4. Having the student read the play aloud. Each character's part should be read to show the meaning and the emotions being expressed.

Poetry. Poetry is the expression, in appropriate language, of personal insight and emotion. It is a form of writing in which the author uses rhythm, repetition, words, allusions, similes, metaphors, and rhyme to create an emotional experience for the reader. The teacher can help the student by

1. Encouraging him or her to read the poem in its entirety silently to obtain the central thought or meaning.
2. Helping the student to understand any figures of speech which may be confusing him.
3. Encouraging him to determine what words help him to experience the mood of the poem.
4. Having the student summarize the thought of the poem in a few sentences.
5. Helping him to understand why the author wrote the poem.
6. Encouraging the student to read the poem aloud in order to express the thought and emotional quality adequately.

Biographies. A biography is a story about a person's life. The following questions can be used to help the student as he or she reads a biography.

1. What aspects of the person's life did you find interesting?
2. Did you like the persons about whom the author has written? Why or why not?
3. Who wrote the biography?
4. Did the author know the subject of the biography personally?
5. How did the author obtain the information presented in the biography?
6. What was his or her purpose in writing the biography?
7. Did the author show evidence of bias toward or against the person he or she was writing about? Why do you think this?

Mathematics

In mathematics the student is chiefly concerned with reasoning and the solving of problems. Effective reading in the field of mathematics requires a different approach from that usually followed in reading other materials. In mathematics facts are presented in condensed form and problems are briefly and concisely worded. Details are often of critical importance. Therefore a high degree of concentration and a slow reading rate are required. Problems should be read in an extremely careful manner several times for the purpose of understanding the significance of each symbol, word, and phrase. The technical meaning of each word and symbol in the problem must be understood.

The teacher or therapist attempting to aid the student who has difficulty reading in the field of mathematics can

1. Help the student to develop an understanding of the technical terms and the specific meanings of common words used in mathematics.
2. Acquaint the student with the symbols and specialized abbreviations used.
3. Aid the student in developing an understanding of mathematical concepts.
4. Stress the importance of slow, accurate, and precise reading.
5. Develop the student's ability to read for detail, to draw inferences, to organize facts, to follow directions, and to discriminate between relevant and irrelevant materials.
6. Develop skill in reading to solve problems by encouraging the student to read for the purpose of answering the following questions and completing the following activities.
   a. What am I asked to find out?
   b. What facts am I given?
   c. What other facts do I need that are not included in the problem?
   d. What procedure must I go through to solve the problem? Sometimes it is helpful for the student to draw a diagram of the process to be followed in solving the problem.
   e. Carry out the computation.
   f. Does the answer seem reasonable?
   g. How can I prove the answer?

EXERCISE

15.5. Apply the steps used in reading to solve problems to the following problem.

Two bicyclists are ten miles apart, each cycling toward the other

at ten miles per hour. A fly starts from one cyclist's nose, flies off at twenty miles per hour to the other cyclist, then back to the first, and so on, back and forth, until the cyclists meet. How far does the fly fly?

Social Studies

Reading in the social studies is primarily concerned with cause-effect relationships and with the prediction of the outcome of given events. The following suggestions may prove helpful in working with a student who has difficulty in reading in social studies.

1. Develop the student's understanding of the key concepts and words which he or she will encounter in the reading assignment.
2. Encourage the student to set a purpose for his reading. Help the student in this endeavor by asking thought-provoking questions. Have the student use his textbook to locate answers to the questions. Encourage him to answer the questions in his own words.
3. Develop the student's skill in chapter reading.
4. Show the student how to locate information by teaching him how to skim a book effectively, how to use the library, and how to read a variety of graphic aids.
5. Teach the student how to read critically.
6. Teach the student how to take notes while reading.
7. Show the student how to organize ideas gained from reading to recognize relationships and sequences of events.

The following study technique may be especially helpful in showing students how to organize information from a variety of sources.

1. Have students look through their notes and decide upon the main topics with which the course has been concerned.
2. Have them make a detailed outline of each of these topics. The outline should include information from textbook, library reading, and class lectures. The task is to assemble everything they know on each topic without reference to the source of their knowledge. They should organize the information into a simple logical outline.
3. Have the students rule lines on a large cardboard as indicated in the diagram.

4. Encourage the students to copy their complete outline on the card as illustrated.

Events	*Causes*	*Consequences*
I.	A. B. C.	1. 2. 3.
II.	A. B.	1. 2.

5. When the summary is complete, have the students study the material by

    a. Reading the outline through from beginning to end in order to get a complete view of the information and to see the relationships between major ideas.

    b. Covering the card and reciting all the related facts they can remember.

    c. Having them read the outline through again attending carefully to the parts they could not remember.

    d. Having them continue to read and recite until they know the outline.

EXERCISE
15.6. Several of your students are experiencing difficulty in reading their social studies textbook. What would you do to help them?

Science

The student who is expecting to read in the field of science should know how to add words to his vocabulary, how to read a chapter effectively, and how to read for detail needed in the solution of a problem. He or she should be able to make inferences from observed facts and to see cause and effect relationships.

The following suggestions are made to help the student who is having difficulty in reading scientific materials.

    1. Help the student to increase his or her knowledge of scientific terms. Since many of the terms in science are formed from Greek and Latin prefixes, roots, and suffixes, structural analysis is recommended.

2. Encourage the student to prepare a card file of the scientific words which he or she needs to learn and to review these words frequently.
3. Teach the student how to use SQ3R as he reads his science textbook.
4. Help the student to develop skill in outlining and notetaking.
5. Encourage the student to relate pictures, tables, graphs, and maps found in science books to verbal descriptions of facts and principles.
6. Provide the student with practice in reading to follow directions.
7. Acquaint the student with the patterns of organization of scientific materials. The content of an article, report, or chapter is organized into units, each containing closely related material which contributes to the development of the general theme. The relationship of these units may be topical, temporal, spatial, or causal.
8. Encourage the student to adjust his rate of reading to the nature of the material and to the purpose for which he is reading. Skimming can be used in making a survey of the material to be read or when attempting to summarize facts for review. Scanning can be used when looking for specific information. In general, however, scientific material should be read slowly and carefully.
9. Demonstrate and explain basic scientific concepts in as concrete a manner as possible.
10. Encourage understanding by asking questions which require interpretation, analysis, synthesis, and evaluation.
11. Stimulate the student to extend his scientific knowledge through wide reading of scientific literature.

SUMMARY

This chapter has been concerned with the development of basic reading skills that are needed by students when they study and read in the content areas. We have recommended that the teacher or therapist locate, primarily through observation and other informal means, the student's areas of difficulty in applying reading to study activities and that the instruction provided the student be based upon his or her needs. The emphasis has been upon remediation rather than the initial teaching of reading-study skills.

REFERENCES

1. Fry, Edward. "Graphical Literacy." *Journal of Reading* 24 (February 1981): 383-389.
2. Otto, Wayne, and Richard A. McMenemy. *Corrective and Remedial Teaching.* Boston: Houghton Mifflin, 1966.
3. Robinson, Francis P. *Effective Study.* New York: Harper & Row, 1946.
4. Roget, Peter. *St. Martin's Edition of the Original Thesaurus.* New York: St. Martin's Press, 1965.
5. Spache, George D. *Diagnosing and Correcting Reading Disabilities.* Boston: Allyn and Bacon, 1976.
6. Thomas, Ellen Lamar, and H. Alan Robinson. *Improving Reading in Every Class* (Abridged Second Edition). Boston: Allyn and Bacon, 1977.

SUGGESTED READING

Alexander, J. Estill (General Editor). *Teaching Reading*. Boston: Little, Brown 1979, Chs. 10 and 11.

Blake, Kathryn A. *College Reading Skills*. Englewood Cliffs, NJ: Prentice-Hall, 1973, Chs. 5, 6, 11, 12, and 14.

Burmeister, Lou E. *Reading Strategies for Middle and Secondary School Teachers* (Second Edition). Reading, MA: Addison-Wesley, 1978, Chs. 5, 6, 7, 8, 9, and 10.

Burns, Paul C., and Betty D. Roe. *Teaching Reading in Today's Elementary Schools* (Second Edition). Chicago: Rand McNally College Publishing Co., 1980, Chs. 6 and 7.

Heilman, Arthur W. *Principles and Practices of Teaching Reading.* (Third Edition). Columbus, OH: Charles E. Merrill, 1972, Ch. 14.

Ransom, Grayce A. *Preparing to Teach Reading.* Boston: Little, Brown, 1978, Chs. 12 and 13.

Smith, Richard J., and Dale D. Johnson. *Teaching Children to Read* (Second Edition). Reading, MA: Addison-Wesley, 1980, Chs. 14 and 15.

Zintz, Miles V. *The Reading Process* (Third Edition). Dubuque, IA: Wm. C. Brown Company Publishers, 1980, Chs. 11 and 15.

16

Dealing with
Special Problems

OBJECTIVES

This chapter will help the classroom teacher or tutor teach reading to people who are

1. Culturally different.
2. Intellectually gifted.
3. Mainstreamed into the regular classroom.
4. Candidates for special approaches.

In this chapter the nonspecialist teacher or tutor is given suggestions on ways to help people with special problems. Chapters 9, 10, and 11 dealt with assessing these students and presented ways to work with the less seriously handicapped.

Some of the students with special problems spend all of their time in regular classrooms. People speaking Black dialect, or some language other than English, are more often than not the responsibility of the regular teacher. The intellectually gifted, too, are seldom segregated. Some school systems, when they can afford it and have the professional staff, do give these individuals the special help they need, but usually the emphasis is placed on making the classroom teacher more adept at teaching them.

On the other hand, the special education students have a well-established history of segregation into rooms of their own and, for the last two decades, of spending part of their time in the mainstream of the school.

In any case, the nonspecialist teacher is faced with the need to understand and help the special problem students.

THE CULTURALLY DIFFERENT STUDENT

We are in a state of flux in this country in our attitude toward teaching the culturally different child. Our courts have handed down decisions which mandate special assistance for both the speaker of Black English and the non-English-speaking individual. Sometimes, and in some places, there are programs for these people, but usually little or no money is provided, which makes it next to impossible for most school systems to carry out the mandates. There are also many people who believe that both groups of students need no special help at all. Until there is a resolution to these problems the classroom teacher will undoubtedly be carrying the responsibility for their reading education.

Multicultural Students

There are an estimated 3.6 million students in the United States who need some form of special English language help to enable them to cope with the regular school curriculum. The greatest proportion of these are Hispanic-Americans but there are seventy-three other linguistic minorities that have been identified by the federal government as being large enough to constitute separate groups (10, pp. 4-5).

Instruction in two languages was practiced in many areas of the United States during the nineteenth century and up to World War I. At that time it began to be considered disloyal to use any language but English in the schools. This attitude prevailed until the 1960s when the Bilingual Education Act (Title VII of the Elementary and Secondary Education Act, 1965) went into effect. Subsequent actions by the courts and the government have bounced back and forth on the issue of requiring federally aided schools to provide special assistance to these students.

No matter what the status is of bilingual education at any particular time, the classroom teacher will need to know something about helping those students. The following suggestions might be useful.

1. Maintain, throughout their education, acknowledgement of the worth of their country of origin. If the teacher acquaints herself with the history of the country and shows appreciation for its accomplishments, she probably will be giving the student a better self-concept.
2. Begin by teaching spoken English before teaching reading. Use all of the labeling devices typically found in kindergartens and first grades. Speak clearly, but maintain natural speaking patterns.
3. Listening and read-along activities help solidify the cadence of our language which, in turn, can enhance reading ability.
4. Teach idiomatic expressions, with emphasis on Americanisms.
5. The language experience approach has obvious advantages. Use intensive emphasis on oral language development.
6. Whenever possible, keep children in a group with English-speaking children, so they are learning the language of their peers.
7. Emphasize the phonic principles of English. The sound-symbol relationships of different languages are not the same and need special instruction.
8. Give extensive practice in using contextual clues, both orally and in reading.
9. Do not embarrass the children by making them read aloud in front of the other children.
10. Make sure that, in every instance, the students are understanding what they read rather than simply translating.
11. Have them read complimentary articles and stories about their native country, but written in English.

Speakers of Black English

Students who speak Black dialect are at a greater disadvantage in some ways than people whose primary language is quite different. The patterns of standard English and Black English are too close for comfort. Many Black children seeing the sentence, "He goes to school," find it most irrestible to say, "He go to school." The primary differences in the two dialects aside from slang expressions, are in word endings. The Black dialect seldom includes endings that indicate plurality, tense, or possession and a final *th* is usually pronounced as *f*. The use of the double negative and redundant pronouns are other facets of Black speech.

Black students need to learn standard English in order to succeed in our educational system. Many prominent Blacks stress the urgency of this need, not only for success in education but also in their eventual field of endeavor. They also stress, as with the multicultural student, their need to have pride in their own heritage.

The attitude of the teacher is of primary importance. Children who learn Black vernacular at home only to have it frowned upon in school can lose their sense of identity and begin to hate school. The teacher can explain that we all talk in different ways in different situations. The child's home language is good for home and the neighborhood, and he or she should learn the school language for other times.

The teaching of standard English should begin immediately. Almost all Black children have been exposed to it all their lives through radio, TV, and movies. They have a receptive set for the American dialect which should be built upon from the very first day at school.

Other ways the classroom teacher can help are listed here.

1. Teach them to listen and imitate. Rules of syntax are less important than the appropriate speech itself.
2. Teach the correct forms of the mispronounced words and reinforce them, even to the point of having them memorized. Internalization of a language pattern requires overlearning. Also, endless oral repetition provides the student with multiple exposure to auditory and motor memory (the physical act of speaking).
3. Have the children learn plays, poetry, and songs that use standard English.
4. Modify the language experience approach by writing mispronounced words correctly.
5. Teach word families (see Chapter 13) but always include sample sentence practice.

6. Use VAKT to give a multisensory approach to the whole word.
7. Do not slight the comprehension building activities in the effort to improve the pronunciation of words and the syntax of the sentences.
8. Have the student read about Black heroes.

EXERCISE
16.1. Some people think language experience stories should be written exactly as the child tells them. Other people think that the stories should be edited slightly. If a child said "mouf," would you change it to "mouth" in the written version? Defend your answer.

It is apparent that most of these suggestions are geared toward improving oral language rather than reading. Most linguists insist that since reading is the process of getting meaning there is no need to treat Black students as different in any way from the other children (5, p. 600). The teacher or the school system must decide if it is the prerogative of the teacher of reading to match the students' oral speech patterns with the material that they are reading.

THE INTELLECTUALLY GIFTED

Mike, a nine-year-old boy, was brought to the authors' university reading clinic because both the school personnel and the parents had run out of ideas on how to challenge him academically. He was a pleasant, ordinary-looking boy who wore glasses. He appeared timid but warmed up quickly when conversing with the staff. His mother said that he was hopelessly addicted to jokes, puns, and all forms of comedy. He read college texts on his favorite subjects, which were math, physics, and chemistry. His father had helped him build a chemistry lab in the basement. Mike was liked by his classmates but often preferred to spend free time alone.

The Stanford-Binet Intelligence test results indicated that he had a mental age of 17 years and 6 months, and his IQ was 186. The word "genius" is no longer used professionally, so this score places him at the extreme top of the very superior range. As for the academic tests administered to him, all of his scores ranged at the college level except spelling, which measured at ninth grade.

Mike had spent only six weeks in the third grade before he was moved on to fourth grade. The trouble was, he was no more suited to fourth grade work than third. He needed dedicated teachers who not only would challenge and excite him but who would open up new vistas for him to explore. But, he also needed exposure to nine-year-old people and activities. His physical and social development were at that level.

He was lucky in that his teacher was willing to keep him going at a higher level than the other children in his room, but she did not have the resources to give him what he needed.

EXERCISE
16.2. What grade placement would you suggest for Mike? Defend your answer.

The intellectually gifted child can be recognized by certain characteristics. He or she usually has superior verbal ability, is curious about all aspects of the environment, has a lengthy attention span, and is adept at solving problems. The child might also be a perfectionist and expect perfectionism in others. Such children often hide their talents in order to be more socially acceptable. They usually have a keen sense of humor and an ability to manipulate ideas.

Most authorities believe that gifted children need help in school if they are to develop their extraordinary abilities to the fullest. Some gifted children drop out of school or become troublemakers, apparently because they are bored by the unchallenging atmosphere. Even those who get along reasonably well often function far below their presumed capability.

There are various types of programs offered in the United States, such as enrichment centers, special classes, summer programs, and "mentorships". This last is where children are given the opportunity to work in professional fields under the guidance of experts. Besides utilizing such resources that the school can provide, the teacher can also follow some of these suggestions.

1. Call on the special talents of other teachers for instruction in areas of interest to these children.
2. Provide cross-grade or even inter-school mobility.
3. Promote apprenticeships in the business or political community.
4. Give them help in interpersonal relationships. Help them accept themselves and be accepted by others.
5. Cater to their inventiveness by having them choose novel ways to present material they have learned.
6. Emphasize *why* and *how* questions rather than *who, what, where,* and *when.*
7. Avoid assigning busy work. We all know the teachers who have

a supply of extra work pages for those who complete assignments well ahead of other children.

8. See that they receive a balanced program, including the arts, sciences, mathematics, physical education, and foreign languages.
9. Teach them speed reading techniques.
10. Teach them to use reference materials and to become familiar with the library's offerings.
11. Have them research in depth what the regular class is studying more superficially.
12. Teach them outlining, synthesizing, and abstracting.
13. Find ways to have them learn computer language.
14. See that they learn to type.
15. Permit them to skip drill exercises that they do not need.
16. Provide word games, puzzles, chess boards.
17. Give them a chance to teach someone who needs the help.
18. See to it that the school lauds intellectual excellence as much as athletic prowess.

MAINSTREAMING

Public Law 94-142 requires that all individuals from ages three to twenty-one who have not graduated from high school be provided with the most appropriate education in the least restrictive environment. Thus, children who are certified as eligible for special education are mainstreamed into the regular classroom as often during the week as is beneficial to them. This, in turn, means that the classroom teacher must become proficient in providing for their special needs.

The children who are identified as eligible for special services include those with such physical difficulties as poor vision or hearing, spasticity, loss of use of limbs, and so on. They also include the mental retardate, emotionally impaired, the hyperactive child, and the learning disabled.

The suggestions offered here for dealing with these students are not intended to supplant the instruction that the experts supply in most school districts but are designed to give some direction to the nonspecialist teacher or tutor.

The Visually Handicapped

Children with low vision or who are legally blind can be found in the regular classroom. Usually there will be support personnel who give suggestions to the teacher but the major responsibility remains in her hands.

1. Reading materials should have large type on nonglossy paper, short lines of print, and large spaces between the lines.
2. Lighting should be strong but nonglaring, and should not shine in the child's eyes.
3. Magnifiers help most of these students.
4. Word or phrase cards for sight word practice should have large, distinct letters.
5. Although most of the word attack skills are appropriate for these students, the use of contextual clues should be stressed. The principle of identifying a word or phrase from minimal cues is especially important for people with vision problems.
6. Comprehension building activities should be stressed, as they are for normally sighted children.

For the blind child the resource teacher will probably teach him braille and possibly to use special machines that convert print to speech. Phonics is seldom taught to the blind child because braille uses many abbreviations for common words. An important consideration for the classroom teacher to remember is the limited experiential background of these children. New concepts must be explained to them in ways they can understand. It is suggested, for instance, that texture, size, shape and smell be used for identifying objects (13, pp. 434-444).

The Hearing Impaired

The severely hard-of-hearing or the deaf child is seldom taught reading in the regular classroom unless he or she is functioning very well academically. The specialists have found that one of the most important things to do with these children is to use oral speech when teaching reading. Teachers should not only use full sentences but should include complicated ones when appropriate. The children need extensive practice with the language patterning in order to become successful readers.

Since they will be depending heavily or entirely on lip reading, the teacher should be sure she has their attention and that the light is on her face. She should restate sentences in other words if her meaning was not clear the first time. She should stand still when talking.

The hearing impaired child can be taught reading by an integrated program of sight word instruction and modification of the visual-visual-auditory and the language experience approaches.

Other suggestions for teaching the hard-of-hearing student are as follows.

1. Teaching sight words must begin with those words that can be pictured or demonstrated. Labels should be used in abundance. Phrase cards should be included as soon as possible.
2. The visual-visual-auditory method, where a clear plastic overlay is placed on a picture, can be used in the regular way, including the auditory stimulus. For these children, lessons in writing the words themselves should begin almost immediately. This provides the combination of the visual, kinesthetic, and tactile stimuli for them.
3. The above procedure can lead to the language experience story. The extent of its use is limited only by the amount of language the child can produce. In any case, the teacher should include marker words such as *the, a,* and *of* that many deaf children omit when speaking.
4. After the child has begun to read, his or her instruction can be much like the other students except that phonics will not be helpful.

The Mental Retardate or Slow Learner

Chapter 10 contains extensive suggestions for working with these children. Here are a few other ideas for teaching them reading. The goal is to help them develop conceptual rather than rote competency.

1. Teach them the sight words that are vital to their well-being, such as *stop, railroad crossing, danger,* and *poison.* Other words can be taught after the survival words.
2. Use the multisensory approach whenever possible.
3. Teach them to recognize, trace, and form the letters of the alphabet.
4. Use the language experience approach at the very beginning, but give substantial help with inducing ideas. Their own stories written down should be read and reread by them in order to foster the notion that the symbols stand for words and sentences.
5. Teach very few rules. Generalizing is difficult for them.
6. Teach word families, but include them often in simple sentences.

7. Help them transfer all skill development to the actual reading activity.
8. Use concrete experiences rather than abstract ones.
9. Build assured success into the program.
10. Give them a chance to make decisions occasionally. They often are programmed to wait to be told what to do.
11. Give precise knowledge of their successes rather than a blanket statement such as, "That's good." They need to learn to judge the worth of their endeavors. Say, for instance, "You read that with good expression. Your only mistake was in this word: *morning.* You said *meaning.* Let's read that sentence again."

Although it is stressed that teachers should not expect too much of retarded children, it is also cautioned that they should expect enough. Too often an overprotective attitude keeps teachers from challenging the children within their capabilities. A carefully nurtured drive to succeed can make them learn more than would seem possible.

EXERCISE

16.3. Liza was a large, clumsy fifteen-year-old who had the good fortune to be born to parents who loved her dearly and gave her the desire to learn. They brought her to the clinic because they wondered if a reading tutor should be hired for her.

Her IQ on an individual intelligence test measured at 53, which indicates a mental age of approximately eight years. The pattern of subtest scores was typical of the brain injured individual. For instance, on a subtest where variously colored blocks are to be arranged in specific designs she apparently had no concept whatsoever of either the color patterns or the shapes. In spite of her handicap she knew such things as who wrote *Romeo and Juliet* and where Chile was located. Her vocabulary, also, was better than her overall intelligence. She worked willingly and appeared to be doing her very best.

On an informal reading inventory she had the following scores:

	Oral	Silent	
Independent	P	PP	
Instructional	1.5	P	
Frustration	2.0	1	
Listening Capacity			3

Would you suggest a reading tutor? Why, or why not?

The Emotionally Impaired

One description of an emotionally disturbed child is "one whose behavior consistently arouses negative feelings toward himself from those upon whom he is emotionally or physically dependent" (1, p. 230).

The children typically have the following characteristics.

1. They have no positive relationship to children or adults.
2. They have not achieved academically to their presumed ability.
3. They exhibit inappropriate behavior, such as unwarranted anger or depression and withdrawal.
4. Very often they are hyperactive.

The nonspecialist teacher or tutor ordinarily will be called on to work with only those children who have at least a tenuous hold on their emotions. Reading instruction for the minimally emotionally impaired is essentially the same as for the other children, but there are some suggestions which may be helpful.

1. Rather than telling the student to stop what he is doing, tell him *to* do something that you want him to do, that he can do, and that he wants to do. This leads eventually to a certain control over his behavior.
2. Use reassuring physical contact, such as a warm pat on the shoulder, if he or she can tolerate it.
3. Have his desk away from any "don't touch" articles.
4. Break tasks up into small segments, so each is capable of being achieved.
5. Give him permission to walk around the room, or even out into the hall, when he feels an urgency to get away.
6. Keep the routine predictable.
7. Be strong, objective, but reassuring.

The Hyperactive Child

Arnie was a "difficult baby" from the day he came home from the hospital. He could not be put on a regular schedule for eating or sleeping. He was irritable, colicky, and demanding. As he grew older, he was a head-banger and a tantrum-thrower and became so aggressive that the neighbors would not allow him in their homes.

Hyperactivity, or hyperkinesis, is an impairment which can be found in some emotionally disturbed children and many of the learning disabled. Robin and Bosco (12), in a recent study, found that there is an estimated three percent of the population who are hyperkinetic; that there are more boys than girls, and more first-borns than later siblings; and that socioeconomic status is not a factor.

There are many theories advanced for ways to mitigate the problem. One of the more popular, unproven, treatments is the additive-free diet. Others include massive doses of vitamins, fluorescent lighting, coffee drinking, and the elimination of sugar in the diet. The most often-used remedy is stimulant drugs which, paradoxically, have a calming effect on hyperactive children, enabling them to focus their attention for longer periods of time. All of the suggested remedies have apparently been used successfully on some children and have been unsuccessful on others.

Until such time as research will lead us down the right path, the teacher, whether in the regular or special classroom, is going to have to cope with this type of child.

1. Teach relaxation techniques and give practice sessions in them daily.
2. Teach impulse control by having such exercises as "How slowly can you stand up?" "—raise your hand?" "—draw a line from here to there?" "—write your name?"
3. Give the child approval for good behavior.
4. Give him an acceptable outlet for his need to move, such as a lump of molding clay to squeeze.
5. Have the child read all the way through a selection using materials of interest to him. For instance, he might read a simple joke or puzzle in order to tell it to a friend. He needs practice in prolonging activities to their solution. Give him the feeling that he can accomplish an entire assignment.
6. The very appearance of a lengthy task might well trigger avoidance. One way to mitigate this in a reading assignment is to cut a slit down the spine of a manila folder, and put only the pages to be read through the slit. Thus, the size of the whole book does not overwhelm him.

According to Cratty (2), what is critical to the learning of these children is self-control and the achievement of an optimal arousal level.

The Learning Disabled

How the brain interprets the information the senses deliver to it is perception. People with a dysfunction in this central processing are called learning disabled (see Chapters 9 and 10). The dysfunction can occur in receiving, processing, storing, retrieving, and expressing information. The learning disabled individual is diagnosed as having poor visual, auditory, and/or motor processing ability.

The term *dyslexia* has been used to designate those individuals whose learning disability exemplifies itself in reading problems. Many efforts have been made to ascertain the cause but they have been unsuccessful. It was assumed that dyslexic individuals were victims of brain damage that was so slight that it would not reveal itself on an electroencephalogram. Other theories have been proposed from time to time, but have never been proven. One of these theories has been investigated by Levinson (8). After an unsubstantiated study of 115 reading disabled children, he came to the conclusion that dyslexia is caused by cerebellar-vestibular difficulties. He said, "Early childhood otitis media and labyrinthitis may create or complicate the dyslexic disorder" (8, p. 88). He reports that treating these children with various brands of anti-motion sickness medicine has mitigated their dyslexic symptoms.

In the last section of this chapter various specialized reading programs for learning disabled students are described, but some general suggestions are offered here.

1. Avoid overdrilling on words out of context. When a child has a precarious hold on one or more of his sense modalities, he cannot assume the added burden of learning something that is meaningless to him.
2. Give listening, read-along activities to associate the various modalities. The teacher can even give permission to dance while he sings and listens to songs, or to beat time to simple poems.
3. Always see to it that the child knows why he is learning something. If he sees the logic of it he can more easily fit it into his store of previous knowledge.
4. Make sure that any perceptual training is related to the reading act since there is no evidence that automatic transfer occurs (see Chapter 10).
5. Have the student use clay to form the letters in words. Have him trace words written out of sandpaper or velvet. Have him then use the words in a sentence.
6. Have the child use the visual-visual-auditory method of learning new words and as a basis for language experience stories.

Learning disabled children as a group have poorer short-memory skills than nondisabled children with comparable intelligence. Researchers (11) have found that this is due primarily to the fact that they do not use skills they actually possess of association or categorizing in order to remember. When they are instructed in the use of these skills with the memory task they are asked to complete, their scores improve appreciably. This should be done in the following manner.

1. Present the material to be learned with accompanying directions to associate the items or to categorize them.
2. Provide developmental activities of categorizing which are directly related to the presentation.
3. Give sufficient practice through highly motivational activities to attain mastery.
4. Review the material to assure retention.

SPECIALIZED READING PROGRAMS

There are some specialized reading systems that have been devised which utilize sensory modality training in the learning process. Some of the more well-known systems are described briefly here. Their presentation does not necessarily imply an endorsement by the authors of this book. As Cratty (2, p. v) says, "Most of the activities described are based on unsubstantiated hypotheses rather than upon results of completed research."

Gillingham-Stillman Method

This method is primarily for people with visual processing difficulties. It is a highly structured, systematic technique aimed at the individual who tends to reverse letters and words. On the theory that one must teach to strength, the auditory-phonic approach is used. First the letter names are taught, then the sound equivalents for the letters and, third, the sounds are blended into words. The kinesthetic sense is utilized by having the student trace the blended words. Students using this method are not allowed even to be in the same room when other reading or spelling systems are being taught in order to avoid confusion. The steps of the procedure must be followed rigidly because they are a "series of logical sequences, the omission of any one of which will jeopardize the complete success of the procedure" (4, p. 42). The steps are as follows.

1. Translate visual letters into the name of the letter.
2. Associate the *sound* of the letter with the visual symbol and its letter name.
3. Translate the auditory symbol into muscle response for speech and writing. The child traces, copies, and writes the symbol as he says it.
4. After the child is taught two vowels and eight consonants, teach him to blend the letters into one-syllable words.
5. See that the child learns to spell each of the words by repeating it, naming the letters, writing it as he or she says the letters, then reads the word.
6. Teach the child more letters, using white cards for consonants and salmon cards for vowels.
7. Introduce spelling rules as needed.
8. Have the child combine words into sentences and stories. The story's purpose is not to entertain or enlighten but to develop the ability to recognize the words. At no time is the child permitted to guess at a word from the context.

EXERCISE
16.4. What do you see as the positive and the negative aspects of this program?

Hegge-Kirk-Kirk Method

This system was first presented in 1936, and in 1970 a slightly altered version called *Remedial Reading Drills* (7) became available. It is a systematic, synthetic phonic system presented by carefully programmed instruction. The learning is accomplished by small steps, repetition, review, and feedback. The authors base the program on certain psychological principles. First, the principle of reproductive (or retroactive) inhibition, means in this instance, that only one sound of a letter should be taught because too many associations will cause the student to forget them all. Second, the principle that numerous exposures lead to learning has grapheme-phoneme associations presented through numerous drills and repetitions. Third, the principle that motivation accelerates learning, is provided through a system of small, easily successful steps. And, fourth, the principle that articulation is an aid to learning is followed by having the child execute all of the drills orally. It is also assumed to aid retention of the learned material (9, p. 274).

1. The child is introduced to the program by learning the "short" sound of *a* and the regular speech sounds of consonants.

2. He is taught to blend the sounds through exhaustive practice. No one is permitted to skip any of the drills since it is considered reinforcing to have continued success.
3. More short vowel sounds are taught and the oral blending into words continues. The teacher is to keep distortion of consonant sounds to a minimum so that the child does not hear *puh-a-tuh* when the word is *pat*. (This is impossible to do completely since she must say each sound in isolation.)
4. The emphasis is on the child's accuracy of blending rather than on rate.
5. There are fifty-five drill exercises which deal with common vowel sounds, consonant sounds, combination sounds and advanced sounds.
6. There are thirty-seven supplementary exercises for irregularly pronounced combinations, such as *-alk* or *-ought*.
7. Sentences, such as "The cat sat on a fat rat," are incorporated into drills as soon as possible.
8. Story reading begins late in the program and must be phonically oriented with no picture clues.

Fernald Technique

This method, developed by Grace Fernald in 1929, (3, Ch. 5) is the original form of VAKT which has been incorporated into many subsequent reading programs. It is a multisensory approach to learning word forms, and the means by which this is accomplished are quite different from the two methods described previously. Both Gillingham-Stillman and Hegge-Kirk-Kirk concentrate on breaking a word down into its individual parts and then synthesizing the parts into a whole word. Fernald, on the other hand, makes no effort to teach the child to break a word into its component parts.

Fernald developed her technique for use by two different groups; those with a partial disability, and those with total or extreme disability. The stages of the program are the same, but the students progress at different rates.

Stage One. The child selects a word he wants to learn, regardless of its length or complexity. The teacher writes the word with crayon in large print or script. The child traces the word with his finger as he says it in syllables. He repeats this until he can write the word without looking at the copy. First he writes it on a scrap of paper, and then he incorporates it into a story. The teacher types his story and the child reads it to her. Sometimes in the beginning he may have to learn-by-tracing every word in his story. He keeps an alphabetized file box of words he has learned, for review, and for the incidental learning of the alphabet.

Since this is the "whole word" method, if the child makes an error when he writes the word, his paper is removed from view and the tracing part of the procedure is reinstituted. He may not erase or cross out mistakes because that would emphasize individual elements of the word. This tracing stage takes from two to eight months.

Stage Two. Now, tracing is no longer necessary. The child looks at the word and vocalizes it to establish the connection between the sound of the word and its form. Thus, visual stimulation evokes the vocal recall. The child may occasionally need to revert to the tracing period for a short while.

Stage Three. The student learns directly from the written word without tracing or copying it. He also begins to read from books and is taught to figure unknown words by using contextual clues. If that still does not help, he is told the word he does not know.

Stage Four. The student generalizes sufficiently to recognize new words by their similarities to words he already knows.

During this program the student can go back to a previous stage as is necessary if his retention rate decreases.

The Fernald method is essentially an analytic, as opposed to a synthetic, phonic program in that the child is expected to internalize typical sound-spelling relationships rather than learning them by rote.

EXERCISE
16.5. Indicate the essential differences in the Gillingham-Stillman, the Hegge-Kirk-Kirk, and the Fernald methods by describing the initial step of each.

The Neurological-Impress Method (6, pp. 277-282)

This method is also called "echo reading" or the "impress method." The intent, as conceived by Heckelman in 1969, is to expose children only to accurate, fluid reading patterns rather than to their own mistake-ridden, halting reading. It is a visual-aural-oral approach to learning to read. It is to be used fifteen minutes a day in consecutive daily sessions for a total of no more than twelve hours.

The teacher selects material at the child's independent reading level. Newspapers, magazines, or books may be used, and it is suggested that they be of interest to the student. The child is told to do as well as he can in just saying the words along with the teacher. She sits next to, and slightly behind the student and talks into his ear. She reads with expression as her finger follows along the line of print. In the beginning she reads slightly louder and faster than the student, but as soon as possible she attempts to have him lead the reading. If he falters, she takes over the lead again by raising her voice. Eventually the student takes over the finger gliding too, with the teacher guiding his finger in a smooth, continuous motion until the pattern is established. The finger movement must be synchronized with the visual, oral, and aural senses to tie them in with the tactile sensation.

Neither word recognition nor comprehension is of concern with this method; the psychomotor skills involved in reading are the ones being taught. It is assumed that by exposing the student only to accurate, fluid reading patterns they would become deeply imprinted and thereby supplant the earlier, incorrect patterns.

EXERCISE
16.6. Contrast the tactile elements of the Fernald Technique and the Neurological-Impress Method.

The utility of any of these methods or one of the many other published programs is predicated on the careful matching of the student with the technique. The child's modality strengths and weaknesses and his or her motivation and interests must all be taken into account.

SUMMARY

This chapter has dealt with helping students with special problems. Some bilingual and Black-English-speaking individuals need help in coping with standard English. The intellectually gifted are in need of accelerated programs. People with such problems as poor vision or hearing or an emotional impairment demand special attention, as do the mentally impaired and the learning disabled. The hyperactive child, who may be emotionally or learning disabled, also must be given special handling.

Finally, four approaches to reading that utilize sensory modality training and are geared to children with special problems are presented.

REFERENCES

1. Bower, Eli M. *Early Identification of Emotionally Handicapped Children in School* (Second Edition). Springfield, IL: Charles C. Thomas, 1969.
2. Cratty, Bryant J. *Movement, Perception and Thought.* Palo Alto, CA: Peek Publications, 1969.
3. Fernald, Grace. *Remedial Techniques in Basic School Subjects.* New York: McGraw-Hill, 1943.
4. Gillingham, A., and B. Stillman. *Remedial Work for Reading, Spelling, and Penmanship.* New York: Hackett and Wilhelms, 1936.
5. Goodman, Kenneth S. "Dialect Rejection and Reading: A Response." *Reading Research Quarterly* 5 (Summer 1970): 600-603.
6. Heckelman, R. G. "A Neurological-Impress Method of Remedial-Reading Instruction." *Academic Therapy* 4 (April 1969): 277-282.
7. Hegg, T. G., S. A. Kirk, and W. D. Kirk. *Remedial Reading Drills.* Ann Arbor, MI: George Wahr, 1970.
8. Levinson, Harold N. *A Solution to the Riddle Dyslexia.* NY: Springer-Verlag, 1980.
9. Myers, Patricia I., and Donald D. Hammill. *Methods For Learning Disorders* (Second Edition). New York: John Wiley, 1976, 274.
10. Pifer, Alan. "Bilingual Education and the Hispanic Challenge." *Annual Report.* New York: Carnegie Corporation of New York, 1979.
11. _____. *Report from Research Instruction for the Study of Learning Disabilities.* New York: Teachers College, Columbia University, 1980.
12. Robin, Stanley S., and James J. Bosco. *Parent, Teacher and Physican in the Life of the Hyperactive Child.* Springfield, IL: Charles C. Thomas Publishing Co., 1981.
13. Ward, Marjorie, and Sandra McCormick. "Reading Instruction for Blind and Low Vision Children in the Regular Classroom." *The Reading Teacher* 34 (January 1981): 434-444.

SUGGESTED READING

Aukerman, R. C. *Approaches to Beginning Reading.* New York: John Wiley, 1975.
Bader, Lois A. *Reading Diagnosis and Remediation in Classroom and Clinic.* New York: Macmillan, 1980, Ch. 6.
Cheek, Martha Collins, and Earl H. Cheek, Jr. *Diagnostic-Prescriptive Reading Instruction.* Dubuque, IA: Wm. C. Brown, 1980.
Gilliland, Hap. *A Practical Guide to Remedial Reading* (Second Edition). Columbus, OH: Charles E. Merrill, 1978: 282-283.

Johnson, Kenneth R. *Teaching the Culturally Disadvantaged. A Rational Approach*. Palo Alto, CA: Science Research Associates, 1970, Chs. 6 and 7.

Larson, Alfred D., and June B. Miller. "The Hearing Impaired." *Exceptional Children and Youth: An Introduction*. Denver: Love Publishing, 1978: 463-465.

Myers, Patricia I., and Donald D. Hammill. *Methods for Learning Disorders* (Second Edition). New York: John Wiley, 1976.

Reed, James C., Edward F. Rabe, and Margaret Mankinen. "Teaching Reading to Brain Damaged Children: A Review." *Reading Research Quarterly*. Newark. DE: International Reading Association 5 (Spring 1970): 379-401.

Renzulli, Joseph S. *New Directions in Creativity*. New York: Harper & Row, 1976.

Rupley, William H., and Timothy R. Blair. "Mainstreaming and Reading Instruction." *The Reading Teacher* 32 (March 1979): 762-65.

Stauffer, Russell G., Jules C. Abrams, and John J. Pikulski. *Diagnosis, Correction, and Prevention of Reading Disabilities*. New York: Harper & Row, 1978, Chs. 11 and 13.

Tierney, Robert J., John E. Readence, and Ernest K. Dishner. *Reading Strategies and Practices: A Guide for Improving Instruction*. Boston: Allyn and Bacon, 1980, Units 5 and 7.

Van Spanckerin, W. "The Emotionally Disturbed Child." in John A. R. Wilson, ed. *Diagnosis of Learning Disabilities*. New York: McGraw-Hill, 1971, Ch. 10.

Vellutino, Frank R. "Alternative Conceptualizations of Dyslexia: Evidence in Support of a Verbal-Deficit Hypothesis." in Mariane Wolf, et al., eds. *Thought and Language/Language and Reading*. Cambridge, MA: Harvard Educational Review, 1980: 567-87.

17

Appraising the Results of Remediation

OBJECTIVES

This chapter will help you to

1. Appraise the results of remediation.
2. Understand some basic principles of evaluation.
3. Become aware of some of the problems encountered in evaluating remedial gains.
4. Examine and evaluate several methods of appraisal.
5. Appraise your own professional skills.

Every professional worker who provides remedial instruction in reading should be concerned with evaluating the effectiveness of remediation. This chapter provides guidance in answering two important questions: (1) How much improvement has an individual student made as the result of the remediation provided? (2) How effective am I as a professional worker in diagnosing and treating reading problems?

APPRAISING THE RESULTS OF REMEDIATION

The following questions can serve as a general guide to the evaluation of a remedial program.

1. Has performance in reading improved?
2. To what extent has performance improved, particularly in those areas stressed in the remedial program?
3. Does the student do more reading at home and at school?
4. Does the student use the library more frequently?
5. Is the student doing better work in the classroom?
6. Do the parents report that improvement has been made?
7. What evidence of improvement does the teacher report?
8. What evidence of improvement does the student report?
9. Is the student's attitude toward reading better?
10. Has the student's attitude toward himself or herself as a person and as a reader improved?
11. Has there been an elimination or mitigation of the factors that were inhibiting the student's reading growth?

BASIC PRINCIPLES OF EVALUATION

The following points of view concerning evaluation are important in appraising the effectiveness of remediation.

Evaluation Should Be Comprehensive

Throughout this book we have emphasized the fact that reading is a function of the whole individual and is more than an accumulation of specific reading skills. We have emphasized the need to study the individual as a whole and to identify those factors that inhibit growth in reading. Treatment consists of changing or mitigating inhibiting factors so that growth in reading can occur. This does not mean that specific reading skills are unimportant, but it does imply that evaluation of remediation should involve more than comparison of pre- and posttests of specific reading skills. It is equally important to evaluate the effect of therapy on such factors as self-concept, attitudes, interests, personal adjustment, social adjustment and total classroom performance.

Evaluation Should Be in Terms of Established Goals

How do you know you have arrived at your destination if you don't know where you are going? Specifically, how do you know whether or not a student has progressed in his reading achievement if the goals of instruction are unknown? The development of goals for reading instruction is a crucial aspect of evaluation. Evaluation consists of assessing the student's progress toward achievement of those goals. Have the goals been attained? If not, why not? Was it because the diagnostician used inappropriate diagnostic techniques to assess initial student behavior? Was it because instructional objectives were poorly defined? Was it because the remedial program was poorly designed to affect student progress? To what extent have instructional goals been attained?

Evaluation Should Be Objective

In any evaluation it is important to control bias. One of the ways to do this is to use evaluation techniques that are objective. The use of pre- and poststandardized tests provides an objective way to evaluate change in reading performance. However, an increment in an individual's test score after several months of remediation may or may not indicate a real gain in achievement. The amount of change may be within the standard error of measurement of the test, and change may be due to chance. Another objective way to evaluate improvement is through the use of performance objectives (see Chapter 12). A well-stated performance objective is a statement about observable behavior. It includes the precise conditions under which the learner's behavior will be demonstrated and evaluated, and it includes the standards for the specific behavior expected. For example, let us assume that prior to instruction you have set the following performance objective for a child. When presented the Dolch list of 220 words one at a time on a flashcard, the child will pronounce each one correctly within two seconds. He will do this with 100 per cent accuracy by the end of six months of therapy. You now have a standard by which to evaluate or judge objectively the effectiveness of remediation in this specific area of reading instruction.

Evaluation Can Also Be Subjective

Tape recordings of oral reading and the use of informal reading inventories made at the beginning and end of remediation programs provide information for informally assessing change in reading performance. Observations of reading behavior can be used to infer changes in attitudes toward reading and toward self. Observations of the kind and amount of reading the child does now in comparison to the kind and amount of reading he did at the beginning of remediation often yield information which is of greater value to the teacher and therapist than the results of grade scores obtained from the administration of standardized tests. The student's evaluation of remedial progress also provides information which, although subjective, can give the teacher insights as to the value of the remediation program.

Results of Evaluation Must Be Interpreted

Data resulting from an evaluation of remediation should be carefully interpreted. What do the test scores really mean? Do they suggest a significant change in reading performance? Are the gains the result of remediation or are other factors involved? Has growth in reading been due to instructional procedures, to the enthusiasm of the teacher, or to favorable attention focused on the child? How honest has the child been in his or her self-evaluation? Has he really expressed his opinions or is he telling us what he thinks we want to hear? Do the parents believe that the child has made progress? What is the opinion of the teacher concerning the child's progress? To what extent has emotional bias affected the evaluation process? These are all questions that should be carefully answered when evaluating the results of remediation.

Evaluation Should Be Continuous

Evaluation is not the final act in helping the disabled reader. Evaluation is an ongoing process. Throughout the remedial program, achievement and attitudes should be continuously evaluated. If insignificant changes are being made, the teacher or therapist will want to know why and will want to make modifications or changes in therapeutic procedures so that growth in reading can occur.

Throughout therapy the teacher should constantly be alert to a need to alter aims, materials, and procedures if circumstances indicate that a change is essential. Evaluation is similar to diagnosis in that it provides an opportunity to identify again the needs of the individual which will serve as the basis for planning future instruction and therapy.

EVALUATION BASED ON STANDARDIZED TESTS

Standardized tests can be used in a variety of ways to appraise the results of remediation. Bliesmer (1) suggests three evaluation techniques. These will be discussed, along with some advantages and disadvantages of standardized tests as an evaluation tool.

Comparison of Pre- and Posttest Scores

One of the most popular ways of appraising progress in reading is through the use of pre- and posttest scores. Norm-referenced standardized tests are usually used for this purpose. They are chosen because of their apparent objectivity, reliability, and validity, and because some standardized tests provide equivalent forms. Equivalent forms of the same test permit repeated testing with a reasonable amount of assurance that the same aspects of reading are being measured. When using standardized tests one must be sure that the pre- and posttests are equivalent. Do they measure the same aspects of reading? Are they of comparable difficulty?

EXERCISE

17.1. Immediately prior to Sandra's entrance into a remedial reading program, she was given Form 1 of a well-known standardized reading test. Her performance was equivalent to a grade level score of 2.1. At the end of six months of remediation, Form 2 of the same test was given. Her performance on this test was equivalent to a grade level score of 2.9. What critical questions concerning the use of pre- and posttests would you ask as you attempt to evaluate Sandra's apparent gain of 8 months in reading ability?

Comparison with Past Performance

Another method of appraising growth in reading is to compare gains in reading made during the remedial program with average yearly gains in reading made before the remedial program. For example, prior to entering a remediation program, Mary Fran had received four years of reading instruction. She had achieved a reading level of 3.0. Her average rate of growth each year was .5. This is found by subtracting 1.0 from her reading level (3.0) and dividing by the number of years of reading instruction (4). 1.0 must be subtracted from the reading level because it is assumed that children entering first grade have not yet received instruction in reading and consequently are starting with a reading level of 1.0. During six months of remediation, she gained 12 months in reading. Her rate of growth during this time was 2.0 (12 months divided by 6 = 2.0). Her rate of growth is greater than it has been in the past, suggesting that she is profiting from the remedial program. This method is based on the assumption that growth in reading is steady and evenly distributed. It does not take into account that there are natural spurts and lags in growth of any kind.

Comparison with Reading Potential

Another popular method is to find the differences between reading potential and reading achievement levels at the beginning and end of a remedial program. (See Chapter 3 for a review of ways to determine reading potential.) For example, prior to remediation Karen's estimated potential for learning to read was 6.0. Her reading achievement level was 4.0. The difference between potential and achievement is 2.0. At the end of the remedial program her potential was 6.8, and her reading achievement level was 5.6, the discrepancy between the two being 1.2. Obviously, there is a decrease of .8 in the gap between Karen's potential and her reading achievement (2.0 − 1.2 = .8). Therefore, it can be postulated that improvement has been made.

EXERCISE
17.2. Can you identify a major problem encountered in using potential as a standard? If so, what is it?

Caution: Advantages and Disadvantages of Standardized Tests

One of the major advantages of using standardized tests is the objectivity which they provide, thus reducing the influence of the evaluator's bias or prejudice. Another advantage is the care with which the authors have constructed and selected test items and the fact that these items have been tried out on many more students than possible for the classroom teacher with the items she develops for her tests. On the other hand, standardized tests have certain characteristics which limit their usefulness as an evaluation tool (1, 2, and 4, Chapter 12). These characteristics are

1. Grade level scores on tests are not equal units for measuring gains.
2. Standardized tests contain errors in their measurement. The amount of error makes score changes possible by chance.
3. It is an established fact that when the same test is readministered or when an alternate form of a test is administered to a group, those who made low scores on the first administration of the test tend to make scores which are higher and therefore closer to the mean on the second administration. Those who made initially high scores tend to make scores which are lower and therefore closer to the mean on the second administration. This movement of scores toward the mean is known as the regression effect.

EXERCISE
17.3. In view of the limitations of standardized tests as a means of appraising growth in reading, would you use them? Defend your answer.

INFORMAL METHODS OF EVALUATION

Evaluation of change in reading behavior can be made informally by the use of criterion-referenced tests, informal reading inventories, tape recordings of oral reading, interviews, and the student's appraisal of his or her own achievement.

Criterion-Referenced Tests

Many reading teachers and reading therapists use criterion-referenced tests to appraise reading growth. Criterion-referenced tests have an advantage over norm-referenced tests in that they evaluate the student's degree of mastery in performing specific skills. Furthermore, they can be teacher-made measures designed to assess the student's ability to perform in the areas in which instruction has actually been given.

EXERCISE

17.4. Mr. Thomas has administered a pre- and postcriterion-referenced test in structural analysis to Cheryl. Her performance, in terms of per cent of mastery, on the pre- and posttests is shown below.

	Pretest	Posttest
Inflectional endings	50%	70%
Compound words	70%	100%
Contractions	0%	50%

In what areas of structural analysis has Cheryl made progress? In what areas does she need additional instruction?

Just as there are limitations to standardized tests, so are there limitations inherent in criterion-referenced tests (3). Some of these are

1. Criterion-referenced tests may be based on poor objectives.
2. Objectives involving the transfer and retention of reading skills are often neglected.
3. Objectives involving attitudes and appreciation are often ignored.

Informal Reading Inventories

The teacher or therapist can use pre- and postinformal reading inventories and evaluate both the qualitative and quantitative changes in reading behavior. Two sets of similar inventories should be used, one at the beginning of the program and the other at the end. They should be administered by the same person and the type of miscues and comprehension errors on each set compared. In addition, comparison of the initial and final independent, instructional, frustration, and listening levels should be made. As suggested in Chapter 6, an audio recording should be made of the oral section of the Informal Reading Inventory to facilitate accuracy of noting reading behavior.

Tape Recordings of Oral Reading

Two recordings of the same selection or of different selections of equal difficulty read aloud by the child can be compared in terms of several factors.

1. What changes were observed in the fluency of reading that may suggest increased comprehension and improved skill in word identification?
2. What changes were observed in the effectiveness of expressing ideas?
3. What changes were observed in the application of word identification skills?
4. What changes were observed in the quantity and quality of mispronunciations? repetitions? substitutions?

Interviews

An estimate of the student's progress in reading can be achieved through interviews with the parents and his or her teacher. Open-ended questions should be used for this purpose and the need for complete honesty and objectivity from parents and teacher should be stressed. The following questions are suggestive of ones that might be asked.

1. What changes, if any, have you observed in the child's reading performance?
2. What changes, if any, have you observed in the child's ability to do his or her school work?
3. What changes in attitude toward reading have you observed?
4. What changes in the amount of reading done by the child have you observed?
5. What changes, if any, in self-confidence have you observed?

Self-Appraisal

One of the best sources of information regarding the effectiveness of the remedial program is the student. He should be encouraged to make judgments concerning his own performance in reading, the changes which may have occurred as a result of remediation, and the effectiveness of the remedial program itself. In order to secure an accurate account of his or her feelings and attitudes the student must feel free to make both a positive and negative appraisal. Some areas to be considered when asking a student to evaluate his or her own progress and the program are listed next. Obviously, the essence of each question should be expressed in language appropriate to the student.

1. What portions of the remedial program did you enjoy the most? the least?
2. Which materials did you enjoy the most? the least?
3. Which activities did you enjoy the most? the least?
4. Do you think you have improved? In what ways?
5. What reading skills do you feel you now possess?
6. What reading skills do you think you need to acquire?
7. Have your attitudes toward reading changed as a result of the remediation? If so, what are the changes?
8. How would you describe yourself now—as a good, poor, or excellent reader?

Caution: Advantages and Disadvantages of Informal Methods

Informal methods of evaluation have advantages and disadvantages. Some of the advantages are

1. They provide an opportunity to measure change in terms of the objectives of instruction.
2. They provide an opportunity to investigate such factors as attitudes and interests which is almost impossible with more formal instruments.

Some of the limitations of criterion-referenced tests have already been delineated. Some of the disadvantages of the other informal methods of appraisal are

1. Prejudice and bias are difficult to control. There is a tendency to find change and improvement if that is what we are looking for.
2. Reports by parents and students can be influenced by their desire to please the evaluator. Frequently, their reports over-emphasize certain aspects of behavior and neglect other equally important factors.
3. Two sets of informal reading inventories are seldom equivalent, thus making valid comparisons difficult.
4. The significance of the difference in performances on pre- and postinformal reading inventories is difficult to ascertain. For example, does a reduction of the number of oral reading miscues indicate improvement in reading? Are the inventories so designed that an increase of one comprehension question results in the appearance of a large gain?

EXERCISE
17.5. In view of the limitations of informal methods of appraisal, would you use them? Defend your answer.

APPRAISAL OF PROFESSIONAL SKILLS

The professional teacher, reading clinician, and therapist should be concerned with evaluating their skills in the area of diagnosis and treatment. This is not an easy task, but it is an important one if professional growth and development are to continue.

We suggest that the following combined questionnaire-checklist be used in evaluating professional skills.

TABLE 17-1. Questionnaire-Checklist for Evaluating Professional Skills

Question	Response		This Is an Area That	
	Yes	No	Is Satisfactory	Needs Improvement
Diagnosis				
1. Was the diagnostic process complete enough to investigate all areas of the student's skill development?				
2. Were the reading strengths and needs of the student adequately appraised?				
3. Were the interests of the student investigated?				
4. Were the attitudes of the student explored?				
5. Were physical factors adequately investigated?				
6. Were cognitive factors studied?				
7. Were environmental factors considered?				
8. Were emotional factors investigated?				
9. Were standardized tests accurately administered, scored, and interpreted?				
10. Were interviewing procedures well performed?				
11. Were informal inventories adequately administered and interpreted?				
12. Were observations keenly made and interpreted accurately?				
13. Were data resulting from the diagnostic process accurately analyzed and synthesized?				
14. Was the accuracy of the initial diagnosis substantiated by later evidence?				

Instruction and Therapy

1. Was the remedial process based on the diagnosis?
2. Were the teaching procedures adapted to the learning style of the learner?
3. Were the materials appropriate to the reading level, interests, needs, and goals of the student?
4. Were the instructional procedures selected to accomplish specific objectives?
5. Was the instruction directed toward helping the student overcome specific weaknesses?
6. Was the remedial instruction meaningful to the student?
7. Was adequate and meaningful practice provided so that reading skills were mastered?
8. Were a variety of activities provided in each instructional period?
9. Were physical, cognitive, environmental, and emotional factors which were found to be inhibiting the student's progress eliminated or mitigated?
10. Were appropriate techniques for demonstrating progress used throughout the remedial program?
11. Was the student given ongoing evidence of growth?
12. Was an enthusiastic environment created for reading?
13. Was adequate attention paid to helping the child increase his or her feelings of worth?
14. Was the cooperation of the parents secured?
15. Was each remedial session well planned?
16. Were conferences with parents tactfully and effectively conducted?

TABLE 17-1. continued

Question	Response		This Is an Area That	
	Yes	*No*	*Is Satisfactory*	*Needs Improvement*
17. Was the student provided with honest praise and commendation?				
18. Were materials produced by the teacher to assist in providing instruction for the specific needs of the student?				
19. Were records kept of the student's reading behavior in order to plan and implement instruction?				
20. Was there close cooperation between the reading therapist and the regular classroom teacher?				
21. Was diagnosis an ongoing part of the remedial instruction?				

Outline below your plans for improving your professional skills.

ADDITIONAL EXERCISE
17.6. If you have been engaged in the diagnosis and treatment of a disabled reader during your study of this book, evaluate your skills, using the combined questionnaire-checklist and outline your plans for improving your professional skills.

SUMMARY

Evaluation is an integral part of remediation and should be carefully planned and executed. Appraisal of the students' growth in a remedial program involves more than an assessment of reading skills. It also includes an evaluation of self-concept, attitudes, interests, personal and social adjustment, and total classroom performance. Teachers should evaluate their own effectiveness in the area of diagnosis and treatment in order to assure their own professional growth and the best possible help for the student.

REFERENCES

1. Bliesmer, Emery P. "Evaluating Progress in Remedial Reading Programs." *The Reading Teacher* 15 (March 1962): 344-350.
2. Maginnis, George H. "Evaluating Remedial Reading Gains." *Journal of Reading* 13 (April 1970): 523-528.
3. Otto, Wayne. "Evaluating Instruments for Assessing Needs and Growth in Reading." in Walter H. MacGinitie, ed. *Assessment Problems in Reading*. Newark, DE: International Reading Association, 1973, 18.
4. Spache, George D. *Diagnosing and Correcting Reading Disabilities*. Boston: Allyn and Bacon, 1976.

SUGGESTED READING

Austin, Mary C., Clifford L. Bush, and Mildred H. Huebner. *Reading Evaluation*. New York: The Ronald Press, 1961.
Ekwall, Eldon E. *Diagnosis and Remediation of the Disabled Reader*. Boston: Allyn and Bacon, 1976, Ch. 13.
Shreiner, Robert, ed. *Reading Tests and Teachers: A Practical Guide*. Newark, DE: International Reading Association, 1979.

Spache, George D. *Investigating the Issues of Reading Disabilities.* Boston: Allyn and Bacon, 1976, Ch. 19.

Wilson, Robert M. *Diagnostic and Remedial Reading for Classroom and Clinic* (Third Edition). Columbus, OH: Charles E. Merrill, 1977, Ch. 10.

18

Reporting the Findings

OBJECTIVES

This chapter will help you to

1. Write a diagnostic report.
2. Write a therapy report.
3. Present an oral report to the client, his or her parents, teacher, or to an interested agency.

Both the results of diagnostic procedures and of therapy should be reported to the client and his agents. The reporting should be done in writing and also by face-to-face communication. This chapter presents suggested outlines to use in written reports and ways to conduct a successful conference on the results of diagnosis or therapy.

THE DIAGNOSTIC REPORT

These reports are written for school files, for parents, for the clients themselves, and for various interested agencies. All but the ones written for the school files should follow the traditional psychological report format. Even informal reports, for private or school file use, will be more helpful if they conform to an outline.

After a report is written, the diagnostician should make an appointment with the client and his representatives to discuss the results in person.

Writing Formal Diagnostic Reports

The content should be directed toward the problem as stated. If the reason for conducting the diagnostic procedure is kept in mind, the report can be addressed exactly to that problem. It is vital that the information included be truthful and yet tactfully stated. There often is a desire to soften unpalatable facts, or even to eliminate them, but that can defeat the purpose of the examination. Being tactful, on the other hand, can make it more possible for the parents or client to accept the diagnosis and recommendations.

The language of the report should be clear, concise, and pleasantly formal. Statements should be unequivocal and without pedantic jargon. Redundancy should be used only for emphasis. Abbreviations and contractions should never be used in formal reports.

Although there is no one single best format to be used, all formal reports will include the same types of information. A typical format is presented on page 329.

The first several items are self-explanatory, but a caution must be made about the birthdate. Slashes to indicate month, day, and year should not be used because many countries reverse our order of the first two numbers. Thus, if a report read 1/12/82, there would be no way of knowing whether it was the twelfth day of January or the first day of December. Also, for age and grade, the precise years and

TABLE 18-1.   Reading Diagnostic Report

Examination Date _____

Examiner _____

Name:

Address:

Parents' Names:

Birthdate:

Age:

Grade:

Referred by:

Reason for Referral:

Background Information

Test Results

Interpretation of Causal Factors

Recommendations to the Home

Recommendations to the School

A concluding sentence such as: If you have any questions, or wish to discuss

these findings further, please contact me at _____ .

---

months should be noted. For instance, an eight-year-old child, six months in the third grade would have these notations: Age: 8-0, Grade: 3.6.

The *Reason for Referral* may be stated in a sentence or two and should give the exact reason that the referral was made.

The *Background Information* section is usually done in essay form. As concisely as possible, state the developmental history, making sure to include physical, cognitive, environmental, and emotional considerations. This information will come from the case history data blanks, school reports, observation, and interviews.

For *Test Results*, every test name should be written out in full, and the form or level should be included when applicable. All of the information for each test, such as raw scores, standard scores, age or grade level equivalents should be listed. Next, there should be an explanation of the meaning of the scores since nonprofessionals may not understand. For example:

Gates Association Test

Subtest	Trial 1	Trial 2	Trial 3
Visual-Auditory	50%	80%	100%
Visual-Visual	20%	30%	30%

In order for that to mean anything to the lay reader, an explanatory sentence should be added: "The results of this test indicate that X learns better by hearing information than he does by seeing it."

The writing of the diagnosis or *Interpretation of Causal Factors* was presented in Chapter 12. It is a formal statement of the factors which caused or contributed to the problem.

EXERCISE
18.1. Below is information gathered by a clinical team about a boy with a reading problem. Construct a formal report about Randy, including a formal interpretation of causal factors. The *Test Results* section is done for you, and you need not write the recommendations to home and school at this time.

Randy B., who was born on March 28, 1983, was brought to the reading clinic on March 11, 1996. The reading teacher, Jean Burnette, referred him because she was worried that his poor reading and emotional problems were causing him to slip farther and farther behind in all academic subjects.

Life patterns

1. Randy's birth was normal although he was "very dark blue" in color, according to the mother.
2. He is the second oldest of six children.
3. Family is undemonstrative but supportive of each other.
4. Randy does cause friction among the children when he gets depressed.
5. He was hyperactive in kindergarten. Teacher asked that he be examined by a neurologist. Diagnosis was minimal brain damage. Ritalin was prescribed and has been continued to the present.
6. He spent two years in first grade and has been getting remedial reading help since then. Teachers report that he varies from being hyperactive to depressed. He has a short attention span, but a good sense of humor.
7. They also say he hates being in the remedial reading class, and he seems to feel inferior to the other children.
8. He is in a Scott Foresman third-fourth grade reader in his regular sixth-grade classroom.
9. In the remedial reading class the Neurological Impress method is being used; the teacher and Randy read the material aloud in concert. No comprehension checks are made (see Chapter 16).

10. Natural science interests him. He hates math and spelling. The teacher says he is the best artist in the school.
11. Randy takes care of the family's three dogs but he has no other household duties.
12. He has several friends and loves the outdoors.

TEST RESULTS
Informal Reading Inventory

	Oral	Silent	
Independent	2.5	3.0	
Instructional	4.0	4.0	
Frustration	4.5	5.0	
Listening Capacity			6.0

He can read independently material written at third-grade level of difficulty, instruction should be at fourth grade, and he becomes frustrated with material above that level. When material is read to him he can understand up to sixth-grade level of difficulty.

The only word attack skill that Randy used consistently was contextual clues. He would either guess at a word or he would skip it entirely. He did well with factual questions but he seldom answered inferential questions.

Peabody Individual Achievement Test (2)
(Only three of the five subtests were administered.)

	Raw Score	Grade Equiv.	%ile
Reading Recognition	35	3.8	8
Reading Comprehension	35	3.7	10
Spelling	34	3.4	4

His word recognition, reading comprehension and spelling measure at about mid-third-grade level.

Wechsler Intelligence Scale for Children, Revised (8)
According to the test, Randy is functioning in the average range of intelligence, with better manipulative skills than verbal. There were large peaks and valleys in the subtest score profile, indicating both great excellences and serious deficiencies. His lowest two scores were in number oriented tests where he functioned no better than an average seven year old.

On the other hand, he is operating as well as a fifteen or sixteen year old in attention to detail and organizational ability. His meaning vocabulary is adequate. There does seem to be much anxiety present in Randy.

Keystone Visual Survey Test (3)
The results indicate that Randy's vision is adequate both at near and far point.

Pupil Rating Scale. Screening for Learning Disabilities (6)
There appears to be a minor visual perception problem. His auditory perception and memory are good.

Informal Personality Inventory
Randy apparently is excitable, distractible, and prone to jealousy. He feels frustrated and is sensitively aware of being criticized for untidiness and lack of good grades.

The next part of the formal report is the *Recommendations to the Home.* Almost invariably this section of the report requires persuasive techniques. Since the client is referred because of a problem there must be suggestions to solve it. Once in a great while the family is already doing all of the right things, but that is not ordinarily the case. In the recommendations, make the implicit assumption that the parents are worthwhile, capable people and that they are eager to help.

Also, it is wise to remember their ego involvement. People tend to view their children as extensions of themselves, so they will not take kindly to the assertion that their offspring is incapable, obnoxious, or uncaring. Rather than saying, "Your child must be cured of his lazy habits," a better way to put it would be, "In order to increase his motivation to improve his reading, ... "

The actual format of this section of the report should be in numbered items rather than essay. That way the suggestions are easier to remember and easier to read. As MacLuhan says, the medium is the message, and a large bloc of material is remembered only in its high spots, where as with individual units each can have its own importance.

The kinds of suggestions to consider making might include the following.

1. Build mental content and experiential background. Have discussions, take trips (be specific with proposed places), listen to the child and answer his questions or help him find the answers.
2. Build a good self-concept. For example, "Since each person

has his own unique pattern of strengths and weaknesses, it is suggested that Bob's parents emphasize his superiority in physical and manipulative activities and minimize those areas in which he does not excel."

3. Set a good example. For instance, "Since Jeff and his father have such a close relationship, the two of them could read farm magazines and catalogs together. This also might give Jeff the idea that reading is a skill worth being mastered."

4. Give him a purpose for reading. In the above example the father and son could be reading the catalog in order to decide on the best tractor to buy. Other possibilities are reading a recipe to make a favorite cake or having a treasure hunt to get a prize.

5. Go to the library with him regularly.

6. Promote responsibility and independence.

7. Do not compare siblings.

8. Help with reading only if asked by the child. Parents are the first, and often the best, teachers of their children, but giving reading lessons at home usually results in tears and recriminations.

9. Treat him in a manner commensurate with his age. Some parents expect too much of a child and others expect too little. One mother we counseled was driving her thirteen-year-old daughter the four blocks to school every day, handed her her lunch money as she got out of the car, made her bed, chose her clothes, and never asked her to take any responsibility. Thus, learning to read was too arduous a task for the child.

10. Have many interesting looking books in the home.

11. Urge cooperation with the school.

Finally, if at all possible, praise the parents for the positive influence they have on their child. For example, "The parents are to be commended for providing a loving, nurturing home life."

EXERCISE
18.2. Write a set of recommendations to Randy's parents (see Exercise 18.1).

The *Recommendations to the School* have a somewhat different slant. The ego involvement is not so much with the child as with the teaching being done in the classroom. Care must be taken not to imply that poor teaching is the cause of the difficulty. Most teachers, however, are eager for suggestions that will help the student learn to read. The suggestions should include the reading difficulty level of the books the child should read, the specific areas of inadequacy, the individual's optimal learning method, his or her interests and any cautions that might be helpful to the teacher. The objectives, methods, and procedures to use should also be listed. Below are the recommendations prepared for a boy in sixth grade. They might serve as examples.

1. Mark's instructional level is second grade. High interest, low vocabulary books, perhaps on sports subjects, would be good for him.
2. When Mark comes to a word he does not know, he should attempt to figure out its meaning for a few minutes before anyone helps him.
3. In regard to Mark's occasional reversals, such as "b" for "d", he should be taught one of the letters, perhaps "b", and the other should be disregarded until the first letter has been overlearned. Confusion often results when minimal-difference pairs are taught together.
4. He needs work on syllabication. Using VAKT may help him recognize these word elements.
5. Mark needs to learn how to make inferences, see cause and effect relationships, and predict outcomes. Ask "why" questions for reading assignments, and also ask him to guess how he thinks a story will end.
6. Mark has a pleasant speaking voice. Have him read to the kindergarteners and first-graders. Make sure, however, that they do not have higher reading skills than he does.
7. Before Mark reads give him a purpose for reading by posing questions such as "Read to find out why the boy acted as he did."
8. A heavy phonics program is no longer necessary for Mark. He is ready to learn structural analysis and the use of contextual clues. A modified cloze technique could be useful for the latter skill.
9. It should be helpful to the teachers and to Mark if, together, they keep a record of his specific progress. Some kind of ladder or chart with reasonably small steps, and spaces for successful completion, can give him a feeling that he *is* learning.
10. It is recommended that the teacher and the parents maintain contact all during the year so that their efforts on Mark's behalf are coordinated.

EXERCISE
18.3. Write a set of recommendations to Randy's teacher or tutor (see Exercise 18.1).

Writing Informal Diagnostic Reports

Very often informal reports are written for one's own files, the student's cumulative folder, or for some in-school agency. All of the information that goes into a formal report might be included, but the language need not be so specialized.

All of the pertinent identifying data should be listed, such as name, age, birthdate, grade, date of testing, and examiner. In Chapters 4 and 12 analysis sheets were presented which could be used as the method for reporting test results and the student's specific needs. Also, if at all possible the teacher or tutor should decide what were the causal factors of the child's difficulty. Adding this to an informal report can guide any remediation that follows. Attitudes, interests, and motivational factors should also be included.

In spite of the fact that most of the information will be listed by check marks on the analysis sheet, it is a good idea to spell out the most important areas to cover in therapy. For instance, the recommendations to the school listed for Mark, might look like this in an informal report.

1. Use second-grade books for instruction.
2. Make him figure out words for himself.
3. Teach *b*, then discrimination of *b* and *n*, before teaching *d*.
4. Use VAKT to teach new words.
5. Teach inference, cause and effect, and predictions.
6. Send him to the kindergarten room to read to the children.
7. Use directed reading techniques.
8. Teach structural analysis and contextual clues. Forget phonics.
9. Together with him, keep a chart of his progress.
10. Confer with his mother regularly.

THE DIAGNOSTIC CONFERENCE

After the diagnostic report has been written, the teacher or diagnostician should arrange to have a conference with the people most intimately involved. These will include the parents and the student and may include a teacher, reading teacher, or agency representative.

Parent Conferences

The parent conference is an essential one, even if someone else made the initial referral for testing. Parents have the right to know whatever a school or other agency knows about the abilities, the performance, and the problems of their offspring.

If at all possible, both parents should attend the conference together. Having both of them hear what is said will eliminate some misunderstandings or confusion. Also, this helps to make them both feel responsible for carrying out the recommendations.

The conference should be held in a private spot to ensure that there will be no interruptions. It also tends to reassure the parents that all private information is kept confidential.

These conferences should be a skillful amalgam of directive and nondirective counseling techniques. The diagnostician or teacher imparts all the findings, gives the diagnosis and recommendations, and suggests ways to carry them out. She also listens to what the parents say and imply and tries to explore with them any problems that may arise.

She must be sure she is giving real information that the parents can absorb and use, not simply being pleasant and encouraging. She should also allow the parents to clarify their own feelings and then help them work out solutions within those boundaries. For instance, if one parent hates to read aloud and the other parent is seldom home, another family member might be enlisted to read to the client. Or the parents could provide read-along books and tapes.

Client Conferences

Client conferences, obviously, are also vital. The student himself is the person who is going to have to put forth the effort to improve. He or she should be given the results of the testing and an explanation of the suggested course of treatment. Also, any motivational inducements should be explored.

Joey, an eight-year-old client the authors tested recently, was in the very superior range of intelligence but was reading just barely at third-grade level. He also exhibited some aggressive tendencies. He apparently had a doting father who never denied Joey anything. At the client conference he was told, "Joey, the tests we gave you show that you are really bright. You can figure things out for yourself. You know a lot about arithmetic and how to put puzzles together. And, you are very good in geography.

"We found out, too, that you aren't reading as well as you could.

The reading test we gave you shows that you take wild guesses at words instead of figuring them out. Another thing, you apparently finish your workbook pages long before anyone else does, and then you look around for some trouble to get into. Would you agree with that?

"You told us the other day that you want to become an astronomer when you grow up. Is that right? That's fine, and you have the ability to do it, but you are going to have to do a lot of careful reading if you want to succeed. We think you need to learn some better ways to figure out words you don't know. For instance, a new word in astronomy has been made up, *exobiology*. If you learned how to figure out new words by *meaning units,* you could tell what that word meant. *Exo-* means outside, the outer universe, *bio-* means life, and *-ology* means the knowledge or study of. So you could decide, all by yourself, that *exobiology* means "the study of life outside of our own planet or creatures from outer space."

"Your teacher says she can let the aide work with you to learn meaning units of words whenever you *correctly* finish your work pages ahead of the other children. This could mean that you will be getting a head start on becoming an astronomer. What do you think of that? Are you willing to try it for a while?"

Teacher Conferences

Conferences with teachers or other agency representatives must be sanctioned by the parents or guardians. Almost invariably permission will be given to discuss the recommendations to the school but the parents will not always agree that personal family matters should be divulged. The diagnostician must honor their wishes in this regard.

The tone of this type of conference should be one of mutual exploration into the best ways to help the client. The limits set by time factors in the classroom and the materials available need to be taken into account. Also, care must be taken not to violate the philosophy of reading instruction in that classroom.

The Last Step

After the conferences have been held, the report should be altered as needed. Anything that came to light during the talks which affects the recommendations should be incorporated into either the formal or informal report.

Helping an individual learn to read better must be a cooperative venture. The client, parents, teacher, and tutor should all be aiming for the same goals, and by the same paths. It is up to the diagnostician to try to achieve this unanimity.

THE THERAPY REPORT

Coordination of the reading program and cooperation among the people working with a student are the primary reasons for writing a therapy report. Of course, it is also a way of substantiating the time and effort expended by the client and therapist. Another reason for writing a report is that it requires the therapist to assess the degree of success that has been achieved.

The statement of the problem, the semester goals, the materials and procedures, and the evidence of growth must all be scrutinized before an adequate therapy report can be devised.

Therapy reports, as is true for diagnostic ones, can be done formally or informally. They should be written reports, but usually should also be presented orally to the interested parties.

Writing Formal Therapy Reports

Before writing a formal report the writer should ask herself or himself (5, pp. 5-6)

1. Do I have all the data at hand?
2. Do I know the format I should use?
3. Who will my readers be?
4. How can I write a report that will be functional to parents and future therapists or teachers?
5. Can all ambiguous terms be defined and clarified?
6. Can I write it so that its meaning is clear, coherent, logical, and easily comprehended?
7. Can I make predictions and recommendations that are sound, wise, and feasible?

A suggested format for formal therapy reports is presented in Table 18-2.

The identifying data should be included in its entirety even if there is a formal diagnostic report on the student. The information is needed in order to read the report with understanding, and it can be irritating to have to shuffle between two reports.

The *Background Information* need not be so extensive for a therapy report, but it should include data that is pertinent to past and future reading instruction for that individual.

Tests Administered usually includes only those given by the therapist at the beginning and ending of therapy. Any vital information which came from testing by other people can be summarized in the *Interpretation of Tests* section. This interpretation should discuss all of the relevant test results and their meanings. The original findings which were used to identify the long-range goals and the comparison of pre- and posttest scores should be summarized.

TABLE 18-2.   Reading Therapy Report

Dates _____ to _____

Therapist _____

Supervisor _____

Name:

Address:

Parents' Names:

Birthdate:

Age:

Grade:

Referred by:

Reason for Referral:

Background Information

Tests Administered

Pretests _____   Posttests _____
             date   date

Interpretation of Tests

Goals

Materials and Procedures

Progress

Recommendations to the Home

Recommendations to the School

An example of *interpretation of tests* taken from a third-grader's report is as follows.

At the beginning of therapy James was able to identify just over 50% of the Primer level words on the Basic Dolch Word List (1). The Kottmeyer Spelling (4) pretest indicated that James needed intensive phonic instruction, especially long vowels and vowel digraphs. His comprehension of first-grade books was adequate. Posttest results indicate that he spelled correctly many more of the words on the Kottmeyer list. His comprehension scores now place him at second-grade level of competency.

The *Goals* portion of the report contains the long-range goals which were formulated at the beginning of therapy (see Chapter 12). They should be directed to the problems identified through analysis of test results, background information, and observation. Since diagnosis is an ongoing process, long-range goals often need to be modified or changed as the sessions continue. For example, the original long-range goals for a twelve-year-old girl were aimed at improving her comprehension skills and her self-confidence. During the third week of therapy it was learned that she did not know how to skim. The final portion of the *Goals* section said,

> An additional goal was added in October, based on her own felt need:
> To develop skimming ability.

Materials and Procedures should include only the primary instruments and procedures. For example, the following was part of the materials and procedures section of the report on the twelve-year-old girl mentioned above.

> Comprehension development was approached in two ways. She worked on specific skills at the literal level by playing board games. These skills primarily involved finding the main idea, recalling details, and identifying cause and effect statements. The method used to develop her interpretive reading skills was to ask her to make inferences after reading selections from the *Scholastic Sprint Series* (7) written at the fifth-grade level of difficulty.

The *Progress* section of the report can be written in essay style. It should take into account the long-range goals, and it should address itself to any attitudinal changes the student might have experienced. It should be as positive as possible without distorting the truth. The therapist should remember that scores on tests will seldom show appreciable improvement over only a few months' time. For one thing, the band of expected error on standardized tests is usually at least several months, and for another, people who are therapy candidates tend to have slower growth rates than the average student. A statement like this might be made: "While his performance did not bring him up to grade level, it is a noteworthy gain over his previous abilities in this skill."

Areas that showed very little growth or even a decline should also be mentioned. One of the goals for Edward, a therapy student, was to improve his vocabulary. The progress report for that goal said "An attempt was made to increase Edward's vocabulary. It is evident that he has learned the meaning of about fifteen new words but this area still represents a weakness. Further efforts to enhance his vocabulary are needed."

Recommendations to the home and to the school are essentially the same as they are for the diagnostic report. The suggestions to the school, however, can be more specific. The actual book the child has been reading and the particular games that were successful with him can be mentioned. It is also helpful if the recommendations include notice of any materials or procedures that were found to be inappropriate for that particular student. Ancillary considerations that affected progress can be mentioned, too. For instance, some students accomplish the most if activities are changed frequently, and others become immersed in a certain part of the lesson and are reluctant to leave it for something new.

EXERCISE

18.4. How would you phrase a suggestion to the classroom teacher that she discontinue holding a particular retarded reader up to ridicule?

Parents who take the trouble to get extra help for their child will want to feel that the effort was worth it. The positive gains the child has made should be clearly presented. It is necessary, too, to tell them what still needs to be done. There should be recommendations that will involve the parents in the further progress of the child's reading ability. Four important points to remember are

1. Parents can stimulate mental growth.
2. Parents can encourage emotional maturity.
3. Parents can encourage emotional stability.
4. Parents can stimulate a desire to read.

EXERCISE

18.5. Devise a specific recommendation for each of the items above.

Another area that should be covered in the recommendations is whether or not the student should continue with further therapy. This is not merely a consideration of his need for more help but should take into account the possibility that the child needs a rest from extra work, or that his parents plan an extended vacation, or indeed, that it is vital to continue the sessions since real progress is being made.

Writing Informal Therapy Reports

It is seldom wise to write a sketchy, informal report of therapy. Even if the therapist plans to continue on with the same student, an interim report should be written. Semester breaks are times to take stock of what has gone before and what should be accomplished in the future. This is more easily done if the actual words are set down on paper, and the formal report outline provides the impetus for thinking through all of the ramifications of the therapy.

THE THERAPY CONFERENCE

After the therapy report has been written, whether formally or informally, the interested parties should be invited to come to a conference.

Parent Conferences

Conferences with the parents should be held several times during the semester. They can be encouraging talks which keep the parents abreast of the progress being made. Suggestions can be made as the need arises, and any minor problems can be cleared up as they appear.

During the final conference the recommendations to the home can be fully explored. It is during this final session that the therapist must try to lay a foundation for the child's lifelong growth in reading ability. The written recommendations can provide the springboard for suggesting many specific ways parents can promote reading activities. Some possibilities might be to have the child

1. Read a recipe that interests him or her.
2. Make out the grocery list.
3. Help locate the products at the grocery store.
4. Read contents of packages to compare ingredients.
5. Follow the recipe to make something for the family meal.
6. Check the TV schedule for a program the child wants to watch.
7. Find information from newspaper advertisements for something the child wants to buy.
8. Read instruction sheets for something the child wants to make.
9. Look up names and numbers of his or her friends in the phone book.
10. Write notes and phone messages as needed.
11. Read road signs when out driving.
12. Read maps when traveling.
13. Look up words in the dictionary that the child does not understand.

Client Conferences

Conferences with the client should be on a daily basis. During every session the student should be aware of his triumphs and his continued needs. The final conference should be positive and encouraging and should acknowledge all the effort he has expended in trying to improve. Suggestions can be given to him about certain books that he might enjoy reading on his own and about how he can maintain the growth he has already achieved. If some kind of chart or record has been kept of his successes, this is the time to present it to him with appropriate ceremony. If the therapist can leave the student with an enthusiasm to continue to grow in reading ability, she will have given him a bridge into the regular classroom.

Teacher Conferences

It is an unfortunate fact that tutors and reading teachers seldom have the opportunity to sit down with the classroom teacher and explain the therapy procedures that were used with a child. Whenever it is possible to talk with her, the basis of the conference should be one of mutual sharing by experts. The therapist should describe what went on during the sessions and should offer the recommendations in a more tentative manner than that used with the parents. Therapist and teacher together can reformulate the recommendations to fit them into the reality of that particular classroom.

CONCLUSION

The basic reason for reporting the results of diagnosis or therapy is communication. The job of the reporter is to collect all of the factual data and the subjective information, arrange it into a coherent whole, and then produce an orderly, relevant report. It should encompass the past, present, and future. It should be a useful instrument for the client, parents, teachers, and any interested outside agency. It is a difficult task, but its successful completion can be a source of satisfaction to reader and writer alike.

REFERENCES

1. Dolch, Edward W. "A Basic Sight Vocabulary." *The Elementary School Journal* 36 (February 1936): 456-460.
2. Dunn, Lloyd M., and Frederick C. Markwardt, Jr. *Peabody Individual Achievement Test.* Circle Pines, MN: American Guidance Service, 1970.
3. *Keystone Visual Survey Test.* Meadville, PA: Keystone View Co., 1972.
4. Kottmeyer, William. *Basic Goals in Spelling, Grades 1 through 8* (6th Edition). New York: Webster Division, McGraw-Hill, 1980.
5. Martin, William T. *Guidelines for Psychological Reports.* Jacksonville, IL: Psychological and Educators Press, 1970.
6. Myklebust, Helmer R. *The Pupil Rating Scale. Screening for Learning Disabilities.* New York: Grune and Stratton, 1971.
7. *Sprint Books.* New York: Scholastic Book Services, 1980.
8. Wechsler, David. *Wechsler Intelligence Scale for Children, Revised.* New York: The Psychological Corporation, 1974.

SUGGESTED READING

Artley, A. S. "Good Teachers of Reading—Who Are They?" *The Reading Teacher* 29 (August 1975): 26-31.

Carter, Homer L. J., and Dorothy J. McGinnis. *Diagnosis and Treatment of the Disabled Reader.* New York: Macmillan, 1970, Ch. 15.

Cheek, Martha Collins, and Earl H. Cheek, Jr. *Diagnostic-Prescriptive Reading Instruction.* Dubuque, IA: Wm. C. Brown, 1980, Ch. 6.

Ekwall, Eldon. *Locating and Correcting Reading Difficulties.* Columbus, OH: Charles E. Merrill, 1970, Ch. 14.

Kavale, Kenneth. "Teachers, Parents, and Reading Instruction. A Learning Alliance," in Kenneth VanderMeulen, ed. *Reading Horizons: Selected Readings.* Kalamazoo, MI: Western Michigan University Press, 1979: 44-49.

Glossary

Accommodation. The act of adjusting the lens of the eye to keep a sharply focused image on the retina.

Acronym. Word formed from the first letters of several words.

Acuity. Sharpness or keenness.

Affix. Prefix or suffix. A meaning unit attached either to the beginning or ending of a root word in order to change the root in some way.

Amblyopia. An unexplained reduction of central visual sharpness generally affecting only one eye.

Analogy. A form of inference in which it is assumed that if two things agree with one another in one or more respects they will agree in yet other respects.

Analysis questions. Questions which require the student to separate the whole of what has been read into its parts.

Analytic phonics. Learning the sounds of words rather than the isolated sounds of letters. Sample words are used to represent letter sounds.

Analytical observation. Observation for the purpose of identifying and interpreting specific aspects of behavior in order to evaluate causal factors contributing to an effect.

Analytical test. A test designed to measure some aspect of behavior into smaller elements.

Aniseikonia. A condition in which there is a difference in the size and/or shape of the image of each eye.

Antonym. A word that is the opposite of another in meaning.

Aphasia. A total or partial loss of the power to use or understand words, believed to be due to brain damage.

Application questions. Questions that require using information gained from reading in problem-solving situations.

Articulation disorder. Difficulty in uttering speech sounds.

Assessment. The act of determining the rate or amount.

Astigmatism. A condition of the eye in which the rays of light are not all focused on the retina resulting in a distorted focus rather than a sharp point focus.

Attention. The active selection of, and emphasis on, one component of a complex experience, and the narrowing of the range of objects to which the individual is responding.

Attitude. An enduring, learned predisposition to behave in a consistent way.

Audiogram. A record of a test of an individual's hearing.

Audiologist. An individual trained in the measurement of auditory acuity.

Audiometer. Instrument for measuring acuteness of hearing.

Auditory acuity. Keenness of hearing.

Auditory discrimination. Ability to discriminate between sounds.

Auditory memory. Memory for what is heard.

Auditory perception. Mental awareness and integration of auditory sensations.

Auditory-vocal association. The ability to say a word that one hears.

Bandwagon. A propaganda technique. Claim is made that "everyone is doing it."

Basal reader approach. A developmental approach to the teaching of reading by means of special textbooks.

Basal series placement tests. Informal tests designed by the publishers of basal reader series. Yield information to guide the teacher in placing the child in a book that is appropriate for him and information regarding his specific reading skills.

Behavioral objective. The exact kind and degree of improvement the learner should display within a stated time period.

Bilingual education. Basics are taught in the student's native language. Later the change is made to a second language.

Binocular coordination. Coordinated action of the two eyes.

Binocular difficulties. Difficulty in using both eyes simultaneously and equally.

Black English. Vocabulary, syntax, and pronunciation of English that are characteristic of Black Americans.

Bound morpheme. A meaning unit of a word that does not constitute a word by itself (Ex. the *ed* at the end of want: wanted).

Brain-damage. Any structural injury or insult to the brain, whether by surgery, disease, or accident.

Card catalog. An index to the books and other material in the library.

Card stacking. A propaganda technique which presents only facts that support one side.

Causal factors. Physical, cognitive, environmental-emotional factors which precipitate reading difficulties.

Central processing dysfunction. Impaired processing of incoming information received from one or a combination of the auditory, visual, or haptic sensory channels.

Cerebral dominance. Assumption that one cerebral hemisphere generally leads the other in functional control. In most individuals, the left side of the brain controls language and is considered the dominant hemisphere.

Chronological age. The number of years a person has lived.

Cloze procedure. A technique for the purpose of measuring comprehension and readability of reading materials. Cloze tests are constructed by deleting words in a passage and substituting spaces that are to be filled in with appropriate words. Can also be used for instructional purposes.

Cognition. The mental process or faculty by which knowledge is acquired.

Cognitive ability. Ability to become aware of objects of thought or perception. Includes understanding and reasoning.

Cognitive style. A person's characteristic approach to problem solving.

Compound word. A word consisting of components that are words.

Concentration. The act of focusing attention upon a subject in order to accomplish a purpose.

Concurrent validity. A measure of how well a test agrees with other tests measuring the same thing.

Connotation. Meaning suggested by a word apart from its explicit and recognized meaning.

Consonant. A voiced or voiceless speech sound which is impeded, diverted, or stopped by the lips, tongue, or throat.

Consonant blend. A combination of two or more consonants in which the regular sound of each can be distinguished.

Consonant cluster. Two or more consonants occurring together in a syllable.

Consonant digraph. Two-letter combinations that represent a single sound.

Construct validity. Determines the adequacy of the administration, scoring, and interpretation of the results of a test.

Content validity. The similarity of the contents of a test to actual behavior.

Contextual analysis. A means of identifying a new reading word by anticipating the meaning through the words and ideas adjacent to the new word.

Contraction. Word that has been shortened by omitting one or more letters within the word or between words.

Convergence. The act or power of turning the eyes inward from their normal position of rest so that the image of a near object will fall on corresponding parts of the retina in each eye.

Criterion referenced test. Test designed to measure specified behaviors performed by an individual toward mastery of a specific skill.

Cross dominance. Control that is right-handed and left-eyed or left-handed and right-eyed.

Culturally different child. An individual whose cultural background and speech patterns differ from those characteristic of the predominant culture.

Decibel. A measure of sound intensity.

Decoding. Converting a message from its printed symbols into ordinary language.

Deductive method. Method of teaching where the rule or principle is described and then the student finds examples of the rule.

Deep structure. The basic meaning of the sentence. Deep structure takes into account the relationships among the elements of the sentence, some of which are unstated and must be understood by the reader's use of his own mental content.

Denotation. Specific meaning as distinct from connotation.

Derived score. Adjustment of a raw score to facilitate comparison with other scores.

Deviation score. The difference between a raw score and the mean.

Diagnosis. Identification of abnormality from symptoms presented and from a study of its origin. Any classification of an individual on the basis of observed characteristics. An explanation of difficulty.

Dialect miscues. Deviations from the text when reading orally which are due to regional or ethnic variations of spoken language.

Digraph. A two-letter combination that represents a single sound.

Diphthong. The smooth joining together of two adjacent vowel sounds in the same syllable.

Directed reading approach. An approach to the teaching of reading consisting of five stages: (1) readiness, (2) directed silent reading, (3) discussion, (4) oral rereading, and (5) follow-up activities.

Directed reading-thinking approach. An approach to the teaching of reading whereby the teacher encourages the child to preview the material, to identify purposes for reading, and to make predictions concerning the material he is about to read.

Directive counseling. Guidance dominated by the therapist.

Disabled reader. An individual whose reading is significantly below expectancy when such factors as age, intelligence, and cultural, linguistic and educational experiences are considered.

Distributed practice. An arrangement whereby the periods of practice are spaced out as widely as the total available time permits.

Dyslexia. Broadly defined, reading disability. The National Advisory Committee on Dyslexia and Related Reading Disorders concluded in 1969 that dyslexia is not a useful term.

Ego involvement. Absorption with self.

Emotional maturity. Extent to which an individual is able to control impulses and emotions.

Emotional stability. A characteristic of a person not given to swings in mood or marked changes in emotional attitude.

Encoding. Transforming a message into oral or graphic language.

Evaluation questions. Questions that require the student to make judgments about the material.

Experiential background. Information gained through living.

Expressive vocabulary. Words used in speaking or writing.

Eye movement. Change in position of the eyeball.

False positive. Cases where a test gives an erroneous positive indication of disease.

Far point acuity. The clearness of the visual image at a distance of 20 feet or farther.

Figurative language. Language that conveys a meaning different from the literal meaning of the words.

Fixation. The turning or holding of the eyeball in such a position that an object or fixation point lies along the fixation line, which is the line drawn from the fovea through the pupil.

Free morpheme. A meaning unit of a word that is a word by itself.

Frequency. The number of cycles per second of a sound wave.

Frustration level. The level at which the individual is thwarted or baffled by the difficulty of the reading material.

Functional illiteracy. Inability to read or write well enough to function in one's environment.

Fusion. The blending of the right and left eye images into one composite image.

General vocabulary. Words used in everyday conversation and correspondence.

Gestalt. A unified physical, psychological or symbolic configuration that should be viewed only as a whole.

Glittering generalities. A propaganda technique in which use is made of vague phrases that promise much.

Grade placement. Grade in which child is actually placed.

Grade score. Average achievement for a given grade level. For example, a grade score of 6.1 means that the performance level of an individual is one month in the sixth grade.

Graphic writing. The meaning of a word is indicated by the way it is written. For example, *Shaky*.

Grapho-phonic clues. A strategy for decoding printed words to oral words using the letter-sound correspondences of language.

Gustatory. Pertaining to the sense of taste.

Haptic stimuli. Information received through touch or tactual and kinesthetic awareness.

High frequency words. Very familiar and often-used words in the language.

Homograph. A word identical with another in spelling, but differing from it in origin and meaning and sometimes in pronunciation.

Homonym. Homophones and homographs.

Homophone. A word identical with another in pronunciation but differing from it in origin, spelling, and meaning.

Hyperactivity. Excessive mobility or motor restlessness.

Hyperbole. An exaggeration or overstatement.

Hyperkinesis. See hyperactivity.

Hyperopia. Farsightedness. Objects at a distance are seen more plainly than those near at hand.

Idiom. An expression that has come to have a figurative meaning from common usage.

Incomplete dominance. Lack of consistent preference for one eye, hand, or foot.

Independent level. The highest level at which the individual can read with full understanding and freedom from mechanical difficulties.

Inductive method. A method of teaching where the student is supplied with many examples of a rule or principle and then he is asked to discover what the rule or principle is.

Inflectional ending. A morpheme at the end of a word indicating plurality, comparison, or possession. This type of word ending does not change the part of speech of the root or base word.

Informal reading inventory. A series of graded passages used to identify independent, instructional, and frustration reading levels and listening level.

Instructional level. The highest reading level at which systematic instruction can be initiated.

Intelligence quotient. Mental age in years and fractions of years divided by chronological age.

Intensity. Loudness or softness of a sound.

Interpretation of causal factors. A formal statement of the factors that caused or contributed to the problem.

Interpretive questions. Questions that require the reader to draw inferences concerning information that is implied but not stated explicitly in the material.

Interpretive reading. Involves drawing inferences from implicitly stated material

Intonation. The significant speech pattern or patterns resulting from pitch sequences and pauses.

Irony. An expression used in a humorous or sarcastic way to mean exactly the opposite of what it says.

ita. An initial teaching alphabet.

Kinesthetic perception. Awareness of muscular motion, position, or weight.

Language experience approach. Approach to the teaching of reading that is built on the individual's experiences. The child dictates his experiences and the teacher writes them. The written account of the story is the basis for reading instruction.

Lateral dominance. The preferred use of one side of the body.

Lateral imbalance. A tendency of one or both eyes to deviate inward or outward from their normal position.

Learning disability. Delayed development in one or more of the processes of speech, language, reading, writing, and arithmetic believed to be caused by possible cerebral dysfunction and/or emotional disturbance. It is not a result of mental retardation, sensory deprivation, or cultural or instructional factors. (Kirk and Bateman)

Learning modality. The pathways through which an individual receives and learns information.

Linguist. A specialist in languages.

Listening level. The highest level at which the student can comprehend what is read to him.

Literal understanding. Recognizing and recalling what the author has explicitly stated.

Mainstreaming. Placing handicapped children in regular classes and integrating them into the regular school program while receiving support from special resource teachers.

Maladjustment. State in which a person falls short of being able to do what is expected of him by others or by himself.

Marker words. The little function words such as *the, a,* and *and* which are necessary for connected discourse but are difficult to picture.

Maze technique. A modification of the cloze procedure. Maze tests are constructed by deleting words in a passage and providing three words from which the individual is to select the one that best fits the context.

Memory questions. Questions that require the reader to recognize and recall facts and ideas explicitly stated in the material.

Mental age. Level of development in intelligence expressed in terms of the age at which the average child attains that level.

Mental content. Total awareness at any given moment.

Mental retardate. A person whose mental growth has been slowed down or delayed.

Mental set. An attitude.

Mentorship. State of serving as a tutor or counselor.

Metaphor. A comparison between two unlike things or actions without the words *like* or *as.*

Minimal-difference pairs. Two stimulus objects that differ from each other only slightly.

Miscue. An actual rendition in oral reading that deviates from the text.

Miscue analysis. Examination of a reader's oral reading miscue to understand his use of graphic, phonological, syntactic, and semantic information. (K. Goodman)

Morpheme. Smallest unit of meaning in a word. For example, the word *dogs* has two morphemes: *dog* and *s.*

Morphemic analysis. Studying the meaning of a word by examining its separate morphemes.

Motivation. The act of providing an incentive.

Myopia. Nearsightedness.

Neurology. The science of the nerves and the nervous system, especially the diseases affecting them.

Non-directive counseling. Guidance by a therapist. The counselor accepts, recognizes, clarifies, and objectifies the feelings of the client and aids him in developing insight concerning the nature of his problem.

Normal curve. A bell-shaped curve representing the distribution of a series of values of a variable.

Norm-referenced test. A measurement that has been given to a representative group of individuals for the purpose of establishing the average scores made by the groups of individuals at various age and/or grade levels.

Observer errors. Faulty observations made by the observer that are usually made because of inexperience, bias, prejudice, and preconceived ideas.

Olfactory. Pertaining to the sense of smell.

Onomatopoeia. Using words with sounds that suggest their meaning.

Open-ended questions. Questions that allow an unrestricted response.

Ophthalmograph. A camera for filming eye movement.

Ophthalmologist. A physician who diagnoses and treats eye diseases and disorders.

Ophthalmology. The science that treats the structure, functions, and diseases of the eye.

Orthography. The act of writing words with the proper letters according to accepted usage.

Otologist. A physician who diagnoses and treats disorders and diseases of the ear.

Otology. The sum of what is known concerning the ear.

Pacer. A machine that uses a shade, metal bar, or light beam that moves down a page to cover successive lines of print.

Pediatrics. The science dealing with the medical and hygenic care and diseases of children.

Percentile. A derived score that indicates the percentage of scores at or below a given raw score.

Perception. The awareness, or the process of becoming aware, by means of sensory processes.

Perceptually handicapped. A perceptual handicap may be receptive, expressive, or associative. It can affect the auditory, visual, or tactile modalities of learning, or motor response.

Performance objective. A statement of the precise conditions under which the learner's behavior will be demonstrated and evaluated. Includes the standards for the specific behavior.

Perseveration. Continuing to behave or respond in a certain way when it is no longer appropriate. For example, repeating the same word over and over.

Personification. The characteristics of a human being are given to something nonhuman.

Phoneme. A minimal speech sound unit.

Phoneme-grapheme association. Sound/symbol relationship.

Phonetics. The branch of linguistics dealing with the study of sounds.

Phonics. The science of speech sounds as applied to reading.

Pictorial clues. An element in a picture that provides meaning.

Pitch. High and low sounds.

Plain folks.   A propaganda technique. Appeals are made to the common man suggesting that an important person is ordinary like the rest of us and therefore can be trusted.

Possessive forms.   Words that denote ownership.

Posttest.   A test administered at the end of an instructional period.

Prefix.   Meaningful element attached to the beginning of a root word.

Pretest.   Test administered at the beginning of an instructional period.

Probable error.   A measure of the variability of a measure; the extent to which the obtained values deviate from the measure in question.

Projective technique.   A method of analyzing a subject's responses to somewhat unstructured stimuli for determining personality characteristics.

Proprioceptive.   Pertaining to the response of body tissues such as muscles, tendons or joints to the nerve impulses that they initiate or to stimulus elsewhere in the body.

Psycholinguistics.   The field of study encompassing all areas in which psychology (mind) and linguistics (language) overlap.

Psychology.   Science of human behavior.

Rapport.   Unconstrained, intimate, and friendly relationship between two persons.

Raw score.   The number of points received on a test when the test has been scored according to directions.

R-controlled vowel.   When a vowel is followed by an *r* in a syllable the vowel is given an irregular pronunciation.

Readability.   The sum total of all the factors that make a written selection comprehensible.

Readability formula.   A prescribed method for determining the difficulty level of a selection.

Reading clinician.   A reading specialist primarily concerned with diagnosis and treatment of reading disabilities.

Reading consultant.   A reading specialist with training in education with emphasis upon supervision of teaching methods.

Reading coordinator.   Another term for reading consultant.

Reading diagnostician.   Another term for reading clinician.

Reading disability.   Condition in which there is a significant discrepancy between a person's reading potential and actual performance.

Reading expectancy age.   Optimum reading age of a student.

Reading expectancy quotient.   A quotient that expresses how a child's present general level of reading ability compares with his expected reading level.

Reading miscue inventory. An inventory designed to analyze the oral reading of an individual for the purpose of gaining insights into his reading strengths and weaknesses.

Reading potential. Optimum reading expectancy for a student.

Reading quotient. Reading age, multiplied by one hundred to remove the decimal point, divided by chronological age. A means of comparing the individual's present level of reading with that of others of his chronological age.

Reading specialist. A teacher trained to teach reading to individuals who experience severe reading problems.

Reading therapist. A reading specialist who provides disabled readers with remediation.

Receptive vocabulary. Words understood through reading and listening.

Recognition span. What the eye sees and the brain recognizes during one fixation.

Recreational reading. Reading for enjoyment and entertainment.

Refractive dysfunction. Malfunction of the eyes so that a clear image does not form upon the retina.

Refractive errors. Imperfect vision resulting from structural deficiencies of the eye.

Regression. Right-to-left return of one or both eyes during reading.

Reliability. Extent to which a measurement is uninfluenced by variable factors.

Remediation. The act of providing both diagnosis and treatment.

Return sweep. Movement of the eyes from the end of one line to the beginning of the next.

Reversal. An interchange or reversal of form. For example, *was* for *saw* or *big* for *dig.*

Root. An original word form from which words have been developed by addition of prefixes, suffixes, or inflectional endings.

Sampling errors. Mistakes made because not enough observations of the individual's total behavior have been made.

Scanning. A rapid reading technique for locating specific information.

Self concept. An individual's beliefs about himself.

Semantic clues. Clues provided by the meaningful relations among words.

Sensation. Impression received by the sense organs.

Sibling. One of two or more persons having one common parent.

Sight vocabulary. Words that a reader recognizes instantly and has meaning for.

Sight word. Any word that is immediately identified by the reader.

Signal words. Words that alert the reader to what is coming in the written material.

Simile. A comparison between two unlike things or actions is made using *like* or *as*.

Skimming. A rapid reading technique for getting a general impression.

Snellen chart. A screening device for testing vision.

Sociology. Science of the origin and evolution of society.

Spasticity. Exaggerated tendon reflexes and muscular spasms.

Standard deviation. A statistic used as a measure of dispersion in a distribution.

Standard English. Language patterns typical of the dominant American culture.

Standard error of measurement. The band of probable error surrounding a score, within which the true score would be found.

Standard score. A derived score that transforms a raw score in such a way that the set of scores will always have the same mean and same standard deviation.

Standardized tests. Tests that have been given to a large and representative sampling of the population. They are characterized by norms that permit comparisons.

Stanine. A unit consisting of 1/9 of the total range of the standard scores of a normal distribution. The mean falls at 5 and the standard deviation at ±2.

Stem. A word form from which words have been developed by the addition of prefixes, suffixes, or inflectional endings.

Sten. A standard score band that divides a distribution into ten parts.

Stereopsis. Depth perception. The ability to judge distances in space is determined in part by maturational factors.

Strabismus. Inability of one eye to attain binocular vision with the other eye because of imbalance of the muscles of the eyeballs.

Structural analysis. The process of studying an unknown word by identifying its meaningful units.

Suffix. Meaningful element attached to the end of a root word.

Suppression. Psychological blocking of vision in one eye. Involuntary exclusion of anything from awareness.

Surface structure. The words and the order of the words in a sentence.

Survey test. Test designed to give comprehensive coverage of an area.

Syllabic consonant. A syllable made up of such sounds as *m, n, l,* or *ng,* as in the word *little.*

Syllabication. A word attack skill consisting of breaking a word down into its appropriate syllables.

Syllable. A unit of pronunciation that always includes either a single vowel sound, a diphthong or a syllabic consonant. It also may include one or more consonants.

Synecdoche. An expression in which the name of a part is used to mean the whole or the whole is used to mean the part.

Synonym. A word having the same or almost the same meaning as another word.

Syntactic clues. Signals provided by word endings, function words, and word order. Grammatical clues.

Synthesis questions. Questions that require the reader to put the parts together to create a new whole.

Synthetic phonics. Learning regular letter sounds before learning to blend them into words.

Tachistoscope. An instrument designed to flash a single exposure on a screen at a rapid rate, usually between one second and 1/100th of a second.

Tactile. Pertaining to the sense of touch.

Technical vocabulary. Words having special meaning in particular subject matter areas.

Testimonials. A propaganda technique. Some prominent person endorses an idea or product.

Therapy. Treatment intended to cure or alleviate a disordered condition.

Thesaurus. A book that contains a collection of words arranged according to the ideas they express.

Transfer. A propaganda technique. The attraction of a respected organization or symbol is associated with a particular person, product, or idea, thus transferring the respect of the symbol to a new product or person.

Transfer of learning. A term for alterations in behavior brought about by having performed behavior relevant or related to it.

Translation questions. Questions that require the reader to put explicitly stated material into another form.

Typographic clues. Clues provided by the style and arrangement of printed matter.

VAKT. A visual, auditory, kinesthetic, tactual method of word study.

Validity. The degree to which test results serve the uses for which they are intended.

Vertical imbalance. A tendency of one eye to deviate upward.

Visual acuity. Keenness of vision.

Visual memory. Ability to reproduce visual items from memory.

Visual-motor coordination. Ability to coordinate vision with movements of the body or with movement of a part or parts of the body.

Visual-motor processes. Skills normally accomplished through visual perception and an integrated motor response.

Visual-motor sequencing ability. Ability to reproduce sequences of visual items from memory.

Visual perception. The identification, organization, and integration of sensory data received by the individual through the eyes.

Vowel. A voiced speech sound that is not impeded, diverted or stopped by the tongue or lips.

Vowel digraph. Two vowels occurring together that represent a single sound.

Vowel diphthong. A blend of two vowels that do not lose the identity of each vowel.

Word analysis. Figuring out an unknown word by syllables and phonic elements for the purpose of pronouncing the word and possibly recognizing its meaning.

Word identification. The act of pronouncing and decoding the meaning of a printed word.

Word recognition inventory. An informal measure for assessing a student's sight vocabulary and word analysis skills.

Appendix A

Extensive background information on an individual who will be examined by a reading diagnostic team is necessary. Clinical history and school data blanks can be useful tools for this purpose. The two forms offered in Appendix A should be regarded as suggestive of the many facts to be obtained in the study of a person's behavior.

The rights of privacy of each individual involved in the study should be respected. *All data are confidential.*

CLINICAL HISTORY

Please attach recent picture

All information furnished will be considered confidential and will not be made available to unauthorized persons. The completed form should be returned directly to the Reading Center and Clinic.

Name _____

Age _____ Birthdate _____ Sex _____
     yrs. — mos.

Grade _____ School _____

Parents _____   _____
       mother   social security number

       _____   _____
       father   social security number

Address _____
                                     _____
                                     phone

       _____
                           zip code

Problem _____

_____

Referred by _____

Person completing this form _____ Date _____
                                                  Day   Mo.   Yr.

FAMILY HISTORY

Include children in order of birth. Give some account of anyone else living with the family.

Name	Age	Occupation	Education	Living with Family	Remarks
Mother					
Father					

360

DEVELOPMENTAL HISTORY

Age of mother _____ and father _____ when child was born.

Weight of baby at birth _____ lbs. _____ ozs.

Mother's health during pregnancy _____

Any shocks or accidents during pregnancy _____

Was baby delivered feet first, head first, breech, Caesarean? _____

Were any instruments used? _____

Any injuries, marks, malformations _____

Any convulsions or bleeding _____

Any difficulty in starting breathing _____

Was baby breast or bottle fed? _____ Nurse easily _____

Give age in months at which following took place:

First tooth _____   Walking alone _____

Full set of second teeth _____   Feeding self _____

Creeping on all fours _____   Said single words _____

Sitting alone _____   Got voluntary control of urination _____

Have there been any serious diseases, accidents, convulsions or operations (include

dates)? _____

Are there any physical deformities? _____

He/she is very _____ fairly _____ not very _____ energetic

Is he/she well coordinated in activities or are there some in which awkwardness is

displayed? _____

Is he/she right- or left-handed? ____ Any attempt to change the handedness ____

Has there been any writing backwards? _____

Are there any activities that can be done better with the usually nonpreferred

hand? _____

Is there any left-handedness in the family? _____

PERSONAL HABITS

Eating (control, fastidiousness)

Dressing (fussy, neat)

Cleanliness (washing, things out of mouth)

Sleep (quickly, soundly, dreams)

Toilet (regularity, soil or wet bed)

Speech (articulation, stuttering)

Sense of responsibility and to what extent

SOCIAL BEHAVIOR

Likes to play (hard, alone, with others, age)

Likes pets

Favorite pastime

Sociable with other children

Get along (quarrelsome)

Affectionate and sociable with parents

Sociable with strangers

Adjusts well outside of home (party, picnic, doctors, Sunday School, etc.)

Obedient

Obstinate

Deceptive

Sensitive

Jealous

Nervous

Needs special discipline (what)

Sensible, reasonable about things (sense of value)

Sense of humor

Cry easily

Tantrums

Moody

Babyish.

Timidity or fears

INDEPENDENCE AND SELF-RELIANCE

Plays contentedly alone and how long

Leads other children

Stands up for rights, for possessions

Takes responsibilities at home

Errands

Money

Selfish or self-centered

Lacks self-confidence

Suggestible

Shows initiative, originality, imagination, concentration

SPECIAL TRAITS

Note any special achievements, excellences, distinctive characteristics. Also any peculiarities, habits or weaknesses that need guidance or correction.

SPECIAL NEEDS

Has he/she ever gone to a clinic, counselor, rehabilitation center, special hospital? Where, when and what were the results?

HOME CONDITIONS

Neighborhood, home itself, home atmosphere, religion, income, thrift and culture levels, care and control of children, attitude of parents to children and each other, attitude of child to other children in the home and to parents. Dominant member of household? Family friction? Language spoken in home?

GENERAL SCHOOL HISTORY

Grade	School Attended	Age at Entering (In Yrs. and Mos.)	No. of Yrs. in Grade	Quality of Work
K				
1st				
2nd				
3rd				
4th				
5th				
6th				
7th				
8th				
9th				
10th				
11th				
12th				

Average mark received during the past year in each subject

Subject	Grade	Subject	Grade
Reading		Mathematics	
Spelling		Music	
Language		Physical Education	
Writing		Art	
Social Sciences			

Grade now in _____

Grade or grades "skipped" and why

Grade or grades repeated and why

Is slow progress in any subject due to difficulties in reading (comment in detail)

Attendance regular or irregular (cause and amount)

Attitude toward teachers

Attitude toward school

Is library used and how much

Favorite subjects and school activities

Remarks

REPORT OF MEDICAL EXAMINER

The Reading Center and Clinic cannot accept a client without the concurrence or recommendation of the family physician.

Client's name _____ Age _____

Address _____

Parents _____

Examination made by _____ M.D., on _____

Address _____

Vision _____ _____ Hearing _____ _____
     right   left   right   left

General Condition (Physical growth and development, nutrition, nervous stability, teeth, nasopharynx, heart, lungs, glands, spine, etc.)

Abnormalities (of growth, development, function, gait, posture, speech, etc.)

Findings other than negative

General Impressions

Recommendations

Reported by _____ Date _____
           physician's signature

Additional Remarks

We are willing to allow advanced students to participate in the study of our child on the day that he/she is tested at the Reading Center.

Mother's signature

Father's signature

SCHOOL DATA

All information furnished will be considered confidential and will not be made available to unauthorized persons. The completed form should be returned directly to the Reading Center and Clinic.

Student's name _____

Your name _____

Your professional position _____

School _____

Address _____ Phone _____

_____
                                 zip code

Date _____
        Day   Month   Year

1. In what capacity have you known this individual and is he/she your student now?

2. As you see it, is this student maladjusted? If so, is the maladjustment of a social, emotional, or scholastic nature, or is it a combination of two or more of these factors?

3. How long has this student had difficulty in reading?

4. Is this student aware of a reading problem? If so, do you think there is a desire to improve in reading and is there willingness to put forth effort to do so?

5. What is this student's attitude toward reading?

6. What reading program has this student experienced in the past?

7. What kind of a reading program is he/she having now? Basal series? Which one? Which level book is he in?

368

8. Has this student ever been given special attention in relation to his/her reading difficulty? What was the nature of the attention given?

9. Did this student seem to realize that he/she needed help and did he/she cooperate in the efforts to remedy the difficulty?

10. Do you think that you have gained this student's confidence? If so, what problems are discussed with you?

11. How well adjusted is this student in the classroom?

12. Does he/she get along well with other children? Have one particular friend? Does he show or provoke any animosity?

13. What kind of remarks are made about this student by his/her peers?

14. What is your personal reaction to this student? Like or dislike and why.

15. What is this student's attitude toward you? Seems to like you, wants to please you, or tends to be defiant, disobedient, or passive?

16. What has this student been successful in doing?

17. What are his/her extra-curricular activities?

18. Member of Boy Scouts, Girl Scouts, Four-H Club, or other organizations?

19. How regular is school attendance?

20. Is this student shy, quiet, self-conscious, introverted, easily offended?

21. Impulsive, hot-tempered, irritable, excitable, nervous, overactive?

22. Cheerful, humorous, distractible, depressed, indifferent, cooperative?

23. Shows self-confidence?

24. Are there any antisocial attempts made to gain recognition such as trying to be funny or babyish?

25. Are any special disciplinary measures required? If so, please describe.

26. Has any unusual aptitude or interest in any one subject ever been shown? If so, has there been a tendency to neglect other subjects in the interest of this particular one?

27. Does this student ever say that he/she hates this or that subject?

28. As far as you know, does the home provide a climate which would stimulate an interest in reading?

29. Does this student appear to have good relationships with his/her parents?

30. In your judgment, what are the parents' expectations of their child?

31. Have the parents ever come to you to discuss their child's problems? To what extent do they seem concerned?

32. Would you say the parents are either strict or overprotective?

33. Do you think this student is expected to accept responsibility at home?

34. In the classroom, is this student able to keep at a task until finished or is he/she easily distracted?

35. Can this student follow directions, work independently, and assume responsibility or is individual help required?

36. How would you describe the quality of work he/she is presently doing in school?

37. Do you consider the presence of this student in the school a deterrent to the healthful, normal development of others?

38. Do you think there is anything in the home or community environment which might be upsetting to this student?

39. Do you think that some of the trouble is the unfortunate result of conditions over which he/she has no control and that an alteration of such conditions would markedly improve behavior?

40. Do you think that this student is mentally incapable of doing the work, is lazy, is distracted by outside interests, or is suffering from some emotional trouble?

41. As far as you know, is this student suffering from any physical disorder or abnormality of any kind? If so, state what it is.

42. What do you think is the probable cause of this student's difficulty?

TEST DATA

Intelligence Tests

Name	Score	Date
1.		
2.		
3.		
4.		

Reading Tests

Name	Score	Date
1.		
2.		
3.		
4.		

Other Tests

Has this student ever been referred to the school diagnostician for a psychological evaluation or to the visiting teacher for study? If so, please summarize briefly the results of findings and indicate the date these services were rendered.

Additional Remarks

Appendix B:
A List of Published Informal Reading Inventories

Analytical Reading Inventory. Second Edition (Mary Lynn Woods, and Alden J. Moe). Columbus, OH: Charles E. Merrill, 1981.

Basic Reading Inventory. Second Edition (Jerry L. Johns). Dubuque, IA: Kendall/Hunt Publishing Company, 1981.

Classroom Reading Inventory. Third Edition (Nicholas J. Silvaroli). Dubuque, IA: Wm. C. Brown Company, 1976.

Content Inventories–English, Social Studies, Science. (Lana McWilliams, and Thomas A. Rakes). Dubuque, IA: Kendall/Hunt Publishing Company, 1979.

Diagnostic Reading Inventory. (H. Donald Jacobs, and Lyndon W. Searfoss). Dubuque, IA: Kendall/Hunt Publishing Company, 1979.

Ekwall Reading Inventory. (Eldon E. Ekwall). Boston: Allyn and Bacon, 1979.

Informal Reading Assessment. (Paul C. Burns, and Betty D. Roe). Chicago: Rand McNally College Publishing Company, 1980.

Mann-Suiter Developmental Reading Inventories in *Handbook in Diagnostic Teaching: A Learning Disabilities Approach*. (Philip H. Mann, and Patricia Suiter). Boston: Allyn and Bacon, 1974.

The Contemporary Classroom Reading Inventory. (Lee Ann Rinsky, and Esta de Fossard). Dubuque, IA: Gorsuch Scarisbrick, Publishers, 1980.

Author Index

Author Index

Subject Index

Subject Index

physical factors, 119-135
picture clues, 210
Picture Story Language Test, 128, 129, 135
placement tests, 41
plays, suggestions for reading, 284-285
plural endings, 218
Plus Ten Vocabulary Booster Program, 242
poetry, suggestions for reading, 285
predicting outcomes, 256
prefixes, 216, 219
principles,
    of diagnosis and treatment, 3-11
    of remediation, 193
Podunk and Such Places, 243
professional skills, appraisal of, 321-324
projective techniques, 171-173
Public Law 94-142, 106, 297
Pupil Rating Scale, 133, 136, 332, 344

questions, to develop comprehension,
    246-247

rate of reading, 268-270
raw score, 85
    conversion of, 100
Raygor Readability Formula, 198-199
r-controlled vowel sounds, 224, 229
readability formulas, 196-200
Readers' Guide to Periodical Literature,
    276-277
reading
    affective aspects of, 17-18
    definition of, 14-19
reading clinician, 52-53
reading comprehension, 16
    cause-effect relationships, 255
    detecting propaganda, 258-259
    distinguishing facts and opinions, 258
    distinguishing reality from fantasy, 258
    following directions, 255
    for details, 254
    for main ideas, 254
    identifying character traits, 255
    judging adequacy, worth, and accept-
        ability, 259
    making comparisons, 255
    predicting outcomes, 256
    sequence, 254-255
    understanding figurative language, 256-
        257
reading consultant, 52
reading coordinator, 52
reading diagnostician, 52-53
reading disability
    categories of, 24-26
    consequences of, 2-3
    identification of, 26-28, 31-35

incidence of, 3
reading graphic materials, 280-282
Reading Homonyms, 243
reading in the content areas, 282-289
reading literature, 282-285
reading mathematics, 285-287
Reading Miscue Inventory, 76-77, 81
reading potential, methods for determining,
    29-31
reading retardation related to limited learn-
    ing ability, 26, 28
reading skills, taxonomy of, 14-18
reading specialist, role of, 52-61
reading-study skills, 16-17, 264-282
reading tests
    analytical, 92-94
    criteria for selecting, 89-90
    survey tests, 90-92
reading therapist, 52
reliability, 87
remediation
    appraisal of, 312-325
    guidelines for, 200-201
    principles of, 3-11, 193
reports
    diagnostic, 328-335
    therapy, 337-342
Riley Articulation and Language Test,
    Revised, 128, 136
roots, 218
Rorschach Technique, 172, 180

science, developing reading skills in, 288-
    289
Scope-Visuals, 243
self-appraisal, 319-320
self-concept, 162-163
self-confidence, 5-6
semantic clues, 208-210
Sentence Completion Test, 172
sentence reading, 248-250
severe reading disability, 24-25, 27
short stories, suggestions for reading, 283
Short Form Test of Academic Aptitude,
    145, 157
short vowels, 223, 228
sight vocabulary, 205-208
silent letters, 223
Skeffington String Test, 123
Slingerland Test, 133, 136
Slosson Intelligence Test, 29, 36, 142, 157
slow learner, 299-300
social studies, developing reading skills in,
    287-288
Snellen Chart, 122-123
Spache Binocular Reading Cards, 123, 136
specialized reading programs, 304-308